# ZEW Economic Studies

Publication Series of the Centre for
European Economic Research (ZEW),
Mannheim, Germany

# ZEW Economic Studies

**Vol. 1:** O. Hohmeyer, K. Rennings (Eds.)
**Man-Made Climate Change**
Economic Aspects and Policy Options
1999. VIII, 401 pp. ISBN 3-7908-1146-7

**Vol. 2:** Th. Büttner
**Agglomeration, Growth, and Adjustment**
A Theoretical and Empirical Study
of Regional Labor Markets in Germany
1999. XI, 206 pp. ISBN 3-7908-1160-2

**Vol. 3:** P. Capros et al.
**Climate Technology Strategies 1**
Controlling Greenhouse Gases.
Policy and Technology Options
1999. XVIII, 365 pp. ISBN 3-7908-1229-3

**Vol. 4:** P. Capros et al.
**Climate Technology Strategies 2**
The Macro-Economic Cost and Benefit
of Reducing Greenhouse Gas Emissions
in the European Union
1999. XIII, 224 pp. ISBN 3-7908-1230-7

Patrick A. Puhani

# Evaluating Active Labour Market Policies

## Empirical Evidence for Poland During Transition

With 24 Figures
and 41 Tables

Springer-Verlag
Berlin Heidelberg GmbH

ZEW
Zentrum für Europäische
Wirtschaftsforschung GmbH
Centre for European
Economic Research

**Series Editor**
Prof. Dr. Wolfgang Franz

**Author**
Dr. Patrick A. Puhani
Centre for European
Economic Research (ZEW)
L 7,1
68161 Mannheim
Germany

ISBN 978-3-7908-1234-3

Cataloging-in-Publication Data applied for
Die Deutsche Bibliothek – CIP-Einheitsaufnahme
Puhani, Patrick A.: Evaluating active labour market policies: empirical evidence for Poland during transition; with 41 tables / Patrick A. Puhani, ZEW, Centre for European Economic Research. – Heidelberg; New York: Physica-Verl., 1999
(ZEW economic studies; Vol. 5)
Zugl.: München Univ., Diss., 1998/D 19
ISBN 978-3-7908-1234-3 ISBN 978-3-642-58685-9 (eBook)
DOI 10.1007/978-3-642-58685-9



Originally published by Physica-Verlag Heidelberg New York in 1999



Cover design: Erich Dichiser, ZEW, Mannheim

SPIN 10734740 88/2202-5 4 3 2 1 0 – Printed on acid-free paper

To My Parents

# Foreword

Most west European countries and the transition economies spend significant shares of their public budget for active labour market programmes to fight the ever-rising unemployment rates. The declared objective of these programmes is to increase the re-employment chances of the unemployed. Hence, a new research area in economics investigates the performance of these government programmes. Another recently evolving promising field is the study of the emerging labour markets in eastern Europe.

The book by Patrick Puhani combines these developments in an innovative way. The study investigates which active labour market programmes in Poland are valuable and which are not by applying modern statistical methods to both macro and micro data. The book finds that training programmes increase the re-employment chances of the unemployment. However, job subsidies and public works decrease the re-employment opportunities of the unemployed. This result adds to a more pessimistic view in international research that these programmes are not generally effective.

In 1998, the book has been accepted as a dissertation by the Faculty of Economics at the University of Munich.

IZA, Bonn and University of Bonn
July 1999

Prof. Dr. Klaus F. Zimmermann
Ph. D. supervisor

# Foreword

The objective of Puhani's dissertation is to give a scientific evaluation of Poland's experience with active labour market policies in the nineties.

Regarding the situation in most transition economies, any effort to contribute to our understanding of labour market programmes deserves the attention of interested economists as well as policy makers.

Puhani's text, clearly, is addressed to the professional economist. Moreover, a sound background in econometric theory and practice is helpful, since – as almost always in empirical research – the tremendous quantity of Puhani's statistical results are open to interpretation and speculation.

To be sure, the statistical problems to find unambiguous answers in real world data to Puhani's central question, i.e. in how far does a certain policy lead to a persistent reintegration of unemployed into the regular labour market, are manifold.

Due to Puhani's very detailed and transparent discussion of methodological issues, as a very important and – at least in my judgement – reasonably robust result emerges the conclusion that in the context of a transition economy in the nineties education and professional training are far more promising than government run employment programmes or wage subsidies.

I hope that Puhani's micro-based analysis and his detailed empirical material will find its way to the professional public.

Dresden, July, 1999

Prof. Dr. A. Karmann
Referee of the Herbert Quandt-Stiftung

# Acknowledgement

This research was undertaken with support from the European Commission's Phare ACE Programme 1995 under the project 'Labour Market Policies, Income Support, and Work Incentives in Transition Economies.'

I am grateful to Prof. Dr. Klaus F. Zimmermann, Seminar for Labor and Population Economics (SELAPO), University of Munich, for many helpful suggestions and discussions and for supervising me on my Ph.D. thesis.

I would also like to express my thanks to Dr. Viktor Steiner, Centre for European Economic Research (ZEW), Mannheim, for arousing my interest on the subject and for many helpful comments and discussions.

Without the co-operation of the University of Lodz and the Polish Central Statistical Office (GUS) this research would not have been possible. I thank Prof. Dr. Eugeniusz Kwiatkowski and Leszek Kucharski, University of Lodz, as well as Prof. Dr. Janusz Witkowski, GUS and Warsaw School of Economics, for their co-operation and helpful comments.

My discussions with Prof. Dr. Michael Lechner, University of St. Gallen, and my colleague Florian Kraus have influenced this study, too.

Conversations and seminars with my colleagues at the ZEW have also inspired my work. I thank Doris Blechinger, Joachim Brade, Hermann Buslei, Dr. Herbert Buscher, Martin Falk, Prof. Dr. Wolfgang Franz, Klaus Göggelmann, Dr. Norbert Janz, Dr. Bertrand Koebel, Thomas Kohl, Florian Kraus, Prof. Dr. François Laisney, Detlev Le Juge, Dr. Friedhelm Pfeiffer, Frank Reize, Hannes Spengler, Kersten Wagner, Dr. Johannes Velling, Elke Wolf, and Volker Zimmermann. Robert Bräutigam, Manfred Kark, and Andreas Michelfeit from the ZEW computing department made sure I stayed on friendly terms with my computer. I received excellent research assistance from Tobias Berger, Eva Sandner, and Anja Triebe.

I had stimulating conversations with my fellows from SELAPO, University of Munich, in various seminars, as well as with the participants of the Economic Faculty Seminar at the Center for Economic Studies (CES), University of Munich.

This dissertation was written whilst I was employed at the ZEW, Mannheim. I would like to express my thanks to the ZEW for actively supporting my dissertation project.

Furthermore, I am grateful to the Maximilianeum Foundation for facilitating my stay in Munich.

Patrick A. Puhani

# Contents

# 1 Introduction

> *'Well-designed labour market policies often have the advantage of achieving efficiency and equity objectives simultaneously. While the main policy emphasis will be on the supply side, special demand-side measures for the disadvantaged continue to play a role, in line with the social objectives of labour market policy, as a step towards regular employment.' OECD (1990, p.7)*

Active Labour Market Policies (ALMPs) have a long history in today's OECD countries. Already in the 1930s, these programmes were proposed by John Maynard Keynes to combat unemployment. In their election pamphlet 'Can Lloyd George Do It?' Keynes and Henderson (1929, p.107) write on public works schemes

> *'One of the commonest objections brought against the policy of development is that the majority of the unemployed are not fitted for the kind of work which would be offered. This objection is only plausible if the whole factor of indirect employment is ignored. To argue as though it were proposed to put the great mass of the unemployed on outdoor work like road construction is a mere caricature of the Liberal scheme.'*

In Keynes's view, ALMPs were therefore mainly to be used as a tool for macroeconomic demand management. Indeed, Keynes stresses that the main purpose of ALMPs is to induce multiplier effects ('*indirect employment*') by increasing aggregate demand. Keynes perhaps acknowledged - as his critics seem to have claimed - that many ALMP participants are not the right match for the jobs they are doing during the programme. However, these microeconomic issues only played a secondary role for Keynes.

In the immediate post-WWII period, ALMPs were widely used in Sweden, but not as a means to decrease unemployment, which was virtually absent at the time. Instead, labour supply adjustment through ALMPs was seen as a tool to contain wage push inflation in segments of the economy with labour supply bottlenecks. Thus, labour market programmes became an alternative to incomes policies and price restraints in the fight against inflation under a policy aiming at full employment by way of Keynesian demand management (OECD, 1990). At the same time in the United States, so-called manpower policies were developed to help disadvantaged groups reintegrate into the labour market. In addition to that, the OECD in the 1960s even saw a role for ALMPs to promote economic growth by investment in human capital (OECD, 1990).

In the face of the rising and persistently high levels of unemployment, especially in the European OECD countries, the fight against unemployment has become again the focus of active labour market policies since the late 1970s. Apart from training programmes and direct job creation schemes, job subsidies enjoy an increasing popularity amongst policy makers. Today's view of the purpose of ALMPs concentrates almost exclusively on the microeconomic level. Active labour market policies are supposed to either preserve the human capital of participants who are in danger of becoming long-term unemployed, or help the long-term unemployed find their way back into the labour market by placing them into an employment relationship. Alongside with the general tendency to deregulate markets and to promote work incentives, ALMPs have also come to be a means of welfare policy. Instead of simply handing out benefits as in the traditional welfare system, some, especially Anglo-Saxon, policy makers favour the idea of tying the right to welfare to the duty of work. Welfare then becomes workfare. As the OECD (1990) argued in its report 'Labour Market Policies for the 1990s', active labour market policies can also be used to fight poverty by equipping the poor with the necessary human capital they need to compete in a free market world.

It was in the same year when the OECD (1990) published this illustrative document of policy guidance, when the former command economies of eastern Europe officially abandoned their communist economic doctrines and introduced market reforms. It was clear to the reformers in eastern Europe that not only systemic adjustments, such as new institutional arrangements, were in need. The new economic system also required the people of Eastern Europe to adopt to the radically different demands of a market economy. The opening of the borders and the availability of western capital and technology changed the skill requirements of the eastern labour force radically and almost instantaneously. Hence, it was apparent that one of the features of the new economic system would be hitherto unknown open unemployment. Given the ideologically driven industrial policies with a bias against services under the communist regime and the largely obsolescent production methods, mass redundancies and mass unemployment were to be expected.

Right at the start of the transition process the transition countries including Poland therefore implemented a network of public employment service (PES) agencies, whose purpose is to register unemployed people and vacancies and arrange matches between them. The PES agencies are also responsible for handing out unemployment benefits and giving job search advice to the unemployed. Moreover, a variety of active labour market programmes has been introduced. These ALMP programmes are designed similarly to the ones in the west and carry the spirit of the 1990 OECD report. The most popular types of programmes implemented today are training for the unemployed, job subsidies, direct job creation, loans and subsidies for the unemployed to become self-employed, youth measures such as apprenticeship schemes or subsidised jobs for young people, and measures for the disabled (Scarpetta and Reutersward, 1994). The selection of participants for the various programmes is generally carried out by PES officials. Whereas measures like subsidised jobs or direct job creation are mainly targeted at the long-term unemployed, training programmes and support for business creation focus on the unemployed with better job prospects and skills.

Clearly, there is a strong equity argument in favour of supporting the long-term unemployed. This is especially valid in the transition context, when many people are irritated by the new challenges facing them. However, there are also efficiency arguments in favour of active labour market programmes. Capital market imperfections are generally used as the main argument in favour of publicly supporting training or business expansion schemes (Chapman, 1993). Job subsidies and direct job creation programmes can solve asymmetric information problems between the unemployed job applicant and the employer. As employers cannot observe the motivation and productivity of job applicants, they may use the previous unemployment history as a screening device to make inferences about the suitability of an applicant. Many employers may therefore unjustifiably exclude the long-term unemployed from effective competition for employment by not inviting them for a job interview.

However, critics of active labour markets programmes may argue that participation in ALMP programmes may also be used as a screening device against ALMP participants. Furthermore, job subsidies may promote the employment opportunities of the supported persons, but harm those who do not receive any subsidies, because they become more costly to employ. There are significant doubts whether ALMPs fulfil their prescribed role even for the participants, though. As the institutional structure of the public employment service had to be newly established in the transition economies, it seems only natural that PES officials at first face difficulties providing an efficient service to the labour market. Not only do the labour offices have to accomplish completely new tasks, they are also understaffed compared to their western counterparts (World Bank, 1993). Unsurprisingly, much of the job broking in Poland is therefore carried out privately or through the well-established institutions of the main trade unions. A different factor which makes ALMPs attract critique is the interplay between active and passive labour market policies. The initial generosity of the passive support system, which mainly consists of unemployment benefits, has been curtailed in the transition countries relatively soon. In Poland, the eligibility period for the receipt of unemployment benefits was unlimited up to 1992, when the period was generally restricted to 12 months. It has been alleged that labour office officials therefore use active labour market policies to prolong the period of benefit receipt for some people after the passive support has run out (Schwanse,

1996). Although this might happen in good faith in the social needs of the persons concerned, such policies on the side of the labour office officials are certainly not conducive to the reintegration of the ALMP participants into the world of work. On the other hand, labour office officials may have incentives to choose those unemployed people for the ALMP programmes who have the best *a priori* chances of finding a new job. Such cream-skimming behaviour mostly results from programme evaluation methods which use simplistic indicators, such as the share of people employed after the ALMP programme, as measures of ALMP and labour office success.

In fact, an empirical programme evaluation is not an easy matter. Except in the case of randomised social experiments, where programme participants are chosen by a random number generator, one has strong reasons to believe that the average programme member is different from the average unemployed person in more respects than just the participation in a programme. This so-called selection problem has to be carefully addressed when carrying out a programme evaluation. In the recent microeconometric literature, two main strands of approaches have emerged to tackle the issue of sample selection. This first is the classical regression-type approach, the other the statistical matching approach based on what is known as the Rubin causal model (Rubin, 1974). The regression approach controls for the potential heterogeneity between programme participants and non-participants by controlling for a set of observed, and possibly unobserved, characteristics in a pre-specified statistical model of the outcome variable of interest, which can be the wage or the duration in unemployment. By contrast, the statistical matching approach, which was formulated in the statistical literature and only recently applied to economic problems, does not require an econometric model of the outcome variable. Instead, it focuses directly on the issue of selection by attempting to find - amongst the people who have not participated in the programme - those who are in terms of observed characteristics most equal to the ones who did participate. Having found the best matches according to this criterion, one can estimate causal effects of the programme by simple mean comparisons of the outcome variable.

Whilst the traditional evaluation literature works with individual data, there is a growing empirical literature on programme evaluation using the so-called augmented matching function approach on macroeconomic data. Ordinary matching functions model outflows from unemployment to employment (matches) as a 'product' produced with a stock of unemployed persons and a stock of vacancies. This framework has been extended in the augmented matching function approach to incorporate resources devoted to active labour market policies as factors increasing the matching efficiency and thus raising the number of outflows to jobs given a fixed stock of unemployed persons and vacancies. Whereas the advantage of analyses working with microeconomic data is that they can explicitly model the effects of ALMPs on individual labour market histories, macroeconomic data have the capacity to capture possible external effects of ALMP programmes.

These external effects may, for example, arise when ALMPs, rather than increasing the total number of people who become re-employed, merely favour the employment of the subsidised people at the expense of the non-subsidised people. Although microeconomic studies in such a case would suggest that there are positive effects of the programme in question, the macroeconomic data would exhibit much smaller or even no effects. Micro- and macroeconometric approaches should therefore be seen as complements rather than substitutes for the evaluation of ALMPs. Both approaches will therefore be used in our analysis.

This study is structured as follows. Chapter 2 gives a short overview of the Polish economy in transition with a special focus on the labour market. The potential of active labour market policies cannot be judged in an isolated way, as it depends on the general economic and institutional conditions. Therefore, we also give an outline of the regional impact of the transition process and present classifications of the 49 Polish voivodships (administrative units) into modern, industrialised, agricultural and high, medium, and low unemployment ones, respectively. These classifications are used especially in the macroeconometric analysis. Following the description of the Polish economy and labour market in general, Chapter 2 also discusses the types of active labour market policies that are implemented in Poland. Polish ALMPs are set into an international perspective and the incentive mechanisms provided by the institutional regulations that govern active and passive labour market policies are discussed.

Chapter 3 carries out a macroeconometric evaluation of the Polish ALMP programmes. We both analyse the effects on outflows from unemployment and the effects on outflows from employment. In the first case, we apply the augmented matching function approach. Both time-series evidence for the whole of Poland and panel data evidence at the voivodship level are presented. Unfortunately, the way the macroeconomic data is structured, one can only estimate the effects of training programmes with this method. In the second part of our macroeconometric analysis, we estimate the effects of all ALMP programmes on the outflows from employment to unemployment on the voivodship level. The purpose of this latter part is to investigate whether any of the programmes either prevent subsidised workers from being sacked or whether they cause job losses of non-subsidised workers who are displaced by unemployed subsidised workers.

Chapters 4 and 5 are the microeconometric parts of this study. Chapter 4 discusses methodological issues in microeconometric evaluations and surveys previous work in the field on transition economies. In particular, we formally present the sample selection problem and the two approaches we use to address it: the recently introduced statistical matching method as well as the more traditional regression-type approach in the form of duration models. To avoid confusion of terms, we would like to stress that the statistical matching method is in no way related to the macroeconomic concept of the augmented matching function, although it also carries the word 'matching' in it.

In Chapter 5, we present the empirical results of the microeconometric analysis. Although individual data on ALMPs have been available for Poland since August 1994, this data has not been conducive to microeconometric evaluation analysis. Knowing that another survey on ALMPs was to be carried out in August 1996, we made some suggestions to the Polish Central Statistical Office how scientific analysis could be facilitated by an alternative design (Steiner, Puhani, and Kwiatkowski, 1995). Our main proposal was to collect retrospective calendar information on the labour force state, participation in ALMP programmes, as well as the receipt of unemployment benefits. Such information has been collected in the Supplement to the Polish Labour Force Survey of August 1996. As far as we know, our study presents the first microeconometric evaluation of the re-employment effects of Polish ALMPs on this data. We analyse training, subsidised jobs (called *intervention works* in Poland), and public works programmes. Whilst the North American literature mostly estimates wage effects of labour market programmes, the Polish context of high unemployment (*cf.* Chapter 2) warrants an analysis focused on job opportunities. Therefore, our evaluation based on the statistical matching approach compares the unemployment rates of participants and non-participants after the ALMP programme. Similarly, we use duration models in the regression-type evaluation to estimate the effects of ALMPs on unemployment duration.

Chapter 6 finally provides a summary of our results and draws policy conclusions that follow from the empirical work presented here.

# 2 The Polish Labour Market in Transition

The Polish transition process officially started with the introduction of the Economic Transformation Programme on January, 1st 1990. The programme is also known as the Balcerowicz plan, Balcerowicz having been the first non-communist Polish finance minister under a Solidarity-led government. The main developments in the macroeconomy that occurred after the implementation of the reform programme are briefly described in Section 2.1. A more specific view on the Polish labour market during transition is provided in Section 2.2, yet we devote an extra section (2.3) to the regional dimension of the unemployment problem. Section 2.4 then describes the active labour market policies that have been established in Poland since 1990.

## 2.1 General Macroeconomic Developments

The main changes implemented with the Economic Transformation Programme of 1990 were free convertibility of the Zloty, price liberalisation, the opening of the Polish economy in terms of free trade and investment, as well as a tight monetary and fiscal regime. In addition, the privatisation programme started with the privatisation of many small firms. Furthermore, there were institutional changes such as the creation of a proper central bank, legislation on private financial institutions and anti-trust legislation. The main pillars of the transition were therefore macroeconomic stabilisation, liberalisation, and institutional reform (Balcerowicz, 1994). The profoundness of the implemented reforms made Poland one of the countries which adopted the shock therapy approach to the transformation of the economic system.

Despite of several critical voices from the political establishment in Poland, the stabilisation course initiated by Balcerowicz has not been repealed. Even when the Solidarity-led government was voted out of office in September 1993 and the post-communist left took over, the reform policies went on steadily, although the left had first promised to slow the transition down. It may seem rather surprising that economic reforms go on although the main political parties, the post-communist SLD and the conservative anti-communist AWS do not explicitly endorse economic liberalisation. But 'Poland's economy is said to be above politics.' (The Economist, 20th September 1997). Although, there have been delays concerning privatisation and the reform of the pension system (OECD, 1996, Chapters 2 and 3), macroeconomic stabilisation has been a success as we will see below.

The tight monetary and fiscal regime imposed by the Balcerowicz plan was a reaction to the macroeconomic situation just before the transition. In 1989, Poland's rate of inflation was at 300 percent. By 1992, it was reduced to under 40 percent (Table 1). Nowadays, Poland fulfils the Maastricht criteria for joining the European Monetary Union as far as government debt and the budget deficit are concerned (OECD, 1996, Chapter 1). As early as 1992 real GDP growth started picking up again, and since 1994 the growth rate has exceeded 5 percent every year at acceptable current account deficits. Also since 1994, the current account deficit as a percentage of GDP remained below the real growth rate (Table 1). Nevertheless, the sudden tightening of the policy stance in 1990 had a price to be paid for in terms of falls in employment.

**Table 1:** Macroeconomic Indicators 1989-1996

| | 1989 | 1990 | 1991 | 1992 | 1993 | 1994 | 1995 | 1996 |
|---|---|---|---|---|---|---|---|---|
| Rate of inflation | 300.0 | 481.4 | 55.3 | 38.5 | 30.5 | 28.4 | 28.3 | 18.3 |
| Real GDP growth | 0.6 | -11.6 | -7.0 | 2.6 | 3.8 | 5.2 | 7.0 | 6.0 |
| Current account (% of GDP) | -1.7 | 5.2 | -2.8 | -3.7 | -6.7 | -2.8 | -3.6 | -3.0 |
| Unemployment rate | '0.0' | 6.3 | 11.8 | 13.6 | 16.4 | 16.0 | 14.9 | 13.6 |
| Real wage growth | 11.6 | -27.4 | 0.2 | -2.9 | -3.0 | 2.9 | 3.8 | 6.5 |

*Note*: inflation is measured by the GDP deflator.

Sources: *Datastream; except real wages: 1989-1994: European Commission (1995), 1995-1996: GUS (1997).*

As can be seen from Table 1, the peak in unemployment occurred in 1993, three years after the big slump in output of 1990. The lag in the fall of employment with respect to output can be explained by the fact that employers first reacted to the fall in demand by reducing hours worked (Franz, 1995). Also, the fall in real wages by nearly 30 percent in 1990 may have had a significant influence to protract the fall in employment. However, real wage figures in times of high inflation have to remain very rough. Table 1 shows that the real wage adjustment has not been sufficient to prevent employment losses. However, many workers would have been redundant even if wages had sunk extremely low, because the capital of many plants has been unproductive even with zero labour costs.

On the other hand, it is not just the average real average wage in the economy which is decisive for the demand for labour, but also the wage structure. Although the wage structure in Poland today looks similar to the ones of western countries (Rutkowski, 1996a; 1996b), there are wage rigidities in certain sectors of the economy. In an analysis of the Polish wage and unemployment structure between 1992 and 1995, Puhani (1997a) shows that *ceteris paribus* the relative wages of blue-collar workers as well as workers in the mining, manufacturing, and construction industries have shown no relative downward response despite of the negative unemployment record of these groups over the observation period.

It was not only the mere squeeze in output which shocked the Polish labour market, but also the need for restructuring that came with it. Before the transition, state-governed price structures led to significant shortages in the goods markets and misallocations of production. Furthermore, it was declared government policy to favour heavy industry against the development of the service sector. International trade was regulated and highly geared towards the communist countries of the Council for Mutual Economic Assistance (CMEA[1]). Much of Eastern European trade involved imports of raw materials from the Soviet Union, which were processed in large state-owned enterprises to be re-exported into the Soviet Union. These large state-owned enterprises were characterised by a high degree of vertical and horizontal integration. As a consequence, there were hardly any small to medium-sized firms. Whereas the average number of employees per industrial plant was 378 in Poland in 1990, the corresponding figure was around 80 employees in western economies (Lipton and Sachs, 1990). The resulting lack of both internal and external competition gave no incentives for technical progress. As a consequence, methods of production became obsolete by modern international standards, and in many fields production was too labour intensive.

## 2.2 Employment and Unemployment Developments

By abruptly exposing the Polish economy to the competitive forces of modern market economies, the transition programme had to trigger resource reallocations on a massive scale. The costs of this process were mostly to be borne by the labour market (Franz, 1995). Whereas total employment in Poland in 1989 amounted to just under 18 million people, it had fallen to just under 16 million people in 1996 (Kalaska and Witkowski, 1997).

Table 2 shows that the fall in employment occurred mainly in the public sector, which accounted for 54 percent of total employment at the beginning of transition. Although the private sector was a net job creator even during the economic crisis in the first phase of transition (1990-1993), it could only absorb about half of the job losses in the public sector between 1990 and 1996. Kwiatkowski and Kucharski (1995) show that the most dynamic trades in the private sector have been construction and trade, which they attribute to the low set-up costs and skill requirements in these industries. The labour market revival since 1994 is a sign for optimism, as since then private-sector job creation was more than twice as much as public-sector job destruction (Table 2). Nevertheless, because of the slow pace of privatisation, the public sector in 1996 still accounted for 36 percent of total employment, which is way above western levels of around 10 percent.

---

[1] Also abbreviated COMECON.

**Table 2:** Employment Changes 1989-1996

| | Sector of ownership | | Economic sector | | | Total |
|---|---|---|---|---|---|---|
| | Public | Private | Agric. | Industry | Services | |
| Employment share (%) 89 | 54.3 | 45.7 | 28.0 | 34.9 | 37.1 | 100 |
| Employment share (%) 96 | 36.4 | 63.6 | 27.6 | 29.2 | 43.2 | 100 |
| Abs. change in empl. (thous.) 90-93 | -3,216 | 588 | -1,032 | -1,679 | 83 | -2,628 |
| Abs. change in empl. (thous.) 94-96 | -650 | 1,374 | 434 | 104 | 186 | 724 |
| Abs. change in empl. (thous.) 90-96 | -3,866 | 1,962 | -598 | -1,575 | 269 | -1,904 |

*Notes*: Agric.: Agriculture; Abs.: Absolute; empl.: employment; thous.: in thousands.
Source: *Kalaska and Witkowski (1997).*

Also, the distribution of employment across economic sectors suggests that the restructuring process in Poland was far from complete in 1996. Although there has been a slight shift away from industrial towards more service sector employment, the share of employees in the service industry is at 43 percent still way below the OECD average of around 65 percent. Most of the increase in service employment has occurred in trade and financial intermediation (OECD, 1996, Chapter 2). Poland may have a comparative advantage in agriculture, but its share of agricultural employment is more than twice as large as the one of OECD countries with large agricultural sectors like Portugal, Ireland, and New Zealand. However, the share of agriculture in total output is at around 8 percent in Poland about the same as the one of Portugal, Ireland or New Zealand (OECD, 1996, Chapter 2). Thus labour productivity in Polish agriculture is very low by western standards. The reason is probably a large pool of surplus labour, who often work as part-timers. This may explain that agriculture even saw the largest increase in employment of all sectors between 1994 and 1996 (Table 2).

The overall fall in employment which occurred between 1990 and 1993 is mirrored in the high unemployment rate. Since 1994, unemployment has started to fall as private sector job creation accelerated. Table 3 shows that there is a divergence in the measured unemployment rates of the labour office registers on the one hand, and the Polish Labour Force Survey (PLFS) on the other. The reason for this divergence lies in the different definitions of unemployment. Whereas in the PLFS, the unemployed have to fulfil the three International Labour Office (ILO) criteria of being out of work, looking for a job, and being ready to take a job within the following two weeks, registered unemployment counts everybody as unemployed who is registered as such with a labour office. Hence, persons who are registered in order to draw unemployment benefits, but who do not actively look for a job are not counted as unemployed in the PLFS. The advantage of the register data on the other hand, is that it is more accurate as it covers the whole population. The PLFS only samples around 50,000 people from the Polish population. The small sample size can become important when one looks at regional unemployment data, which we will do in Chapter 3 below.

As can be seen from Table 3, the unemployment rate of women has been higher than the one for men in both 1992 and 1996. What is more, the gap between men and women even increased while the unemployment rate for the whole population sunk. In principle, the communist regime was very supportive of female employment, which was reflected in generous maternity and child-care benefits. In addition, subsidised child-care facilities were provided by large enterprises and the state. Kotowska (1992), however, argues that 'females were perceived as the additional labour force' and that the traditional understanding of the woman as a wife and mother had not changed during the communist period. Subsequently, the breakdown of the communist regime saw the abolition of many public child-care facilities, as enterprises could not longer fulfil many social tasks a the market economy. Women in transition economies are now more likely to take leave when they become mothers, because they cannot afford to pay for private child-care facilities (*cf.* Zimmermann, 1993, on eastern Germany). Hence it has become more costly and risky for employers to employ women. According to a study by Coopers & Lybrand (1991), the monthly cost of private child care can vary from 2 to 20 percent of the average monthly wage in Poland. Women's opportunity costs of employment as well as the costs to employers to employ women have thus risen under the new regime. Coopers & Lybrand (1991) report that in 1991, only 23 percent of job offers were for women, whereas 77 percent were for men. For married women between 21 and 25 years of age, the unemployment rate according to the PLFS of February 1993 therefore even reached 50 percent (Puhani, 1995).

Youth unemployment is an important problem in Poland. As the econometric evidence of Boeri and Steiner (1997) and Puhani (1996) shows, young age is in general an advantage when looking for a job in Poland. The high rate of youth unemployment results instead from the limited labour market opportunities of young people with no previous labour market experience. One cause of the youth unemployment problem were redundancy regulations which made it comparatively expensive for firms to sack older workers. Instead, few new entrants to the labour market were employed. Normally, one would also expect a high unemployment incidence amongst older workers. But the unemployment rates for people over 45 years of age have remained comparatively low (Table 3). Yet it is the early retirement schemes with generous pensions rather than job opportunities which makes the picture look relatively bright for this age group.

**Table 3:** The Structure of Unemployment 1992 and 1996

| | 1992 | 1996 |
|---|---|---|
| Unemployment rate (registered) | 13.6 | 13.6 |
| Unemployment rate (PLFS) | 13.7 | 11.5 |
| *Unemployment by gender (PLFS)* | | |
| Men | 12.4 | 9.9 |
| Women | 15.2 | 13.4 |
| *Unemployment by age (PLFS)* | | |
| Youth (15-24) | 29 | 26.2 |
| Over 45 years old | 7.8 | 6.5 |
| *Unemployment by education (PLFS)* | | |
| Higher | 5.3 | 2.9 |
| Basic vocational | 16.9 | 14.1 |
| Share of long-term unemployed (PLFS) | 36.9 | 40.3 |

*Notes*: the long-term unemployed are defined as having been unemployed for more than 12 months; PLFS: Polish Labour Force Survey.

Sources: *OECD (1996); Kalaska and Witkowski (1997); Datastream.*

A sharp divergence in unemployment incidence also emerges for people with different educational attainments. In both 1992 and 1996, the unemployment rates for university graduates were at a level that roughly corresponds to the natural rate (Table 3). On the other hand, the unemployment incidence was high amongst persons who only completed a basic vocational education. The excellent labour market opportunities for workers with a higher education becomes evident when one compares their population share in Poland with that in western market economies. In Poland in 1989, only 20 percent of the population aged between 20 and 24 years of age were enrolled in higher education. The corresponding figure for market economies like western Germany or Spain was around 30 percent, though (OECD, 1993a). The neglect of tertiary education under the communist regime has led to a severe scarcity of highly qualified labour which is also reflected in high wage differentials for this group (Rutkowski, 1996a; 1996b; Puhani, 1997a). On the other side of the coin, there are - just as in western economies - too many low-skilled workers who have difficulties finding employment. Nevertheless, the low-skilled have also benefited from the improved situation on the Polish labour market in 1996, as can be seen from Table 3.

However, the recovery on the Polish labour market has not reduced long-term unemployment. The share of the long-term unemployed in total unemployment has even increased from 37 to about 40 percent between 1992 and 1996. Compared to most western countries, this share is very high (*cf.* western Germany with 34 percent, the Unites States with 12 percent in 1993). However, Italy has an even higher long-term unemployment share of 58 percent (Franz, 1995). Poland's build-up of unemployment has its roots not in high inflows into unemployment, but rather in the very low outflows. In 1992, the average monthly outflow rate from unemployment was 4.3 percent in Poland, 6.5 percent in Hungary, 10.2 percent in Slovakia, 25.1 percent in the Czech Republic, and 16.9 percent in western Germany (Franz, 1995). Poland thus had a very low outflow rate not only in relation to western economies, but also in relation to the other Visegrád[2] countries. One reason for this low outflow rate are certainly wage rigidities in some economic sectors as discussed in Section 2.1 above. The restrictive recruitment policies of large enterprises also affect the outflow rates of young school leavers as mentioned in our discussion of youth unemployment in this section. Obviously, qualifications mismatch is very high in the transition context. Another explanation for the low outflows from unemployment is that the low mobility of workers in Poland does not allow the regional mismatch between vacancies and unemployment to be eliminated. The regional dimension of the unemployment problem in Poland is the topic of the following section.

[2] The Visegrád countries are Poland, Hungary, and the Czech and Slovak Republics.

## 2.3 Unemployment in the Regional Context

The 18th century partitions and territorial changes of the 20th century have left their imprint on the regional structure of post-war Poland. Western Poland, which used to be under Prussian rule, is a traditionally industrialised area with Upper Silesia as one of the first industrial centres of continental Europe. Eastern Poland, on the other hand, which was under Russian rule for a long time, is economically and culturally dominated by agriculture. However, the central planners of the communist regime attempted to equalise the industrial development across Polish regions. The centralised governmental structure allowed for substantial regional transfers. However, industrial investments during the communist period were not only undertaken according to economic considerations. For example, a steel industry was built up near Crakow to 'develop a working class base next to one of the most bourgeois cities in the country' (OECD, 1992, p.41). However, Crakow neither has a coal reservoir nearby, nor is the local infrastructure particularly suited for the development of a steel industry. Although the communist policies diminished the regional disparities concerning industrial development in Poland, the transition to a market economy has necessarily had harsh consequences for regions where major investments were undertaken against their comparative advantage. In particular, regions with high employment shares in staple industries such as coal and steel face structural problems as the technology used there has been made obsolete by the opening to western markets. In addition, the former markets for these industries in eastern Europe and the former Soviet Union have collapsed.

New industries are mostly developing in areas with a good local infrastructure, such as transportation and telecommunication networks. In addition, the new technologies which come in from the west require a qualified labour force with high educational attainments. Thus large urban centres like Warsaw, Cracow, Gdansk, Lodz, Poznan, Wroclaw, and Szczecin act as major engines for economic revival (OECD 1992, Chapter 4).

Poland is divided into 49 voivodships (comparable to the French *départements*), which are purely administrative units with no political power of their own. Figure 1 displays a map of the Polish voivodships together with their official codes and names. Figure 2 displays a map of Poland where the voivodships are classified according to their unemployment rate in 1992. One can say that the north-western voivodships have the highest unemployment rates, whereas the south-eastern voivodships have the lowest ones. Finally, Figure 3 classifies the voivodships of Poland into *modern*, *industrial*, *agricultural*, and *other* types.

**Figure 1:** The Voivodships of Poland – Map, Codes and Names

| Code | Name | Code | Name | Code | Name |
|---|---|---|---|---|---|
| 1 | Stol. Warszawskie | 35 | Krakowskie | 69 | Rzeszowskie |
| 3 | Bialskopodlaskie | 37 | Krosnienskie | 71 | Siedleckie |
| 5 | Bialostockie | 39 | Legnickie | 73 | Sieradzkie |
| 7 | Bielskie | 41 | Leszczynskie | 75 | Skierniewickie |
| 9 | Bydgoskie | 43 | Lubelskie | 77 | Slupskie |
| 11 | Chelmskie | 45 | Lomzynskie | 79 | Suwalskie |
| 13 | Ciechanowskie | 47 | Lodzkie | 81 | Szczecinskie |
| 15 | Czestochowskie | 49 | Nowosadeckie | 83 | Tarnobrzeskie |
| 17 | Elblaskie | 51 | Olsztynskie | 85 | Tarnowskie |
| 19 | Gdanskie | 53 | Opolskie | 87 | Torunskie |
| 21 | Gorzowskie | 55 | Ostroleckie | 89 | Walbrzyskie |
| 23 | Jeleniogorskie | 57 | Pilskie | 91 | Wloclawskie |
| 25 | Kaliskie | 59 | Piotrkowskie | 93 | Wroclawskie |
| 27 | Katowickie | 61 | Plockie | 95 | Zamojskie |
| 29 | Kieleckie | 63 | Poznanskie | 97 | Zielonogorskie |
| 31 | Koninskie | 65 | Przemyskie | - | - |
| 33 | Koszalinskie | 67 | Radomskie | - | - |

*Note:* The voivodship codes are the standard codes used by the Polish Central Statistical Office (GUS).

Source: *Puhani and Steiner (1996); RegioGraph 2.0 software.*

**Figure 2:** Unemployment Across Polish Voivodships

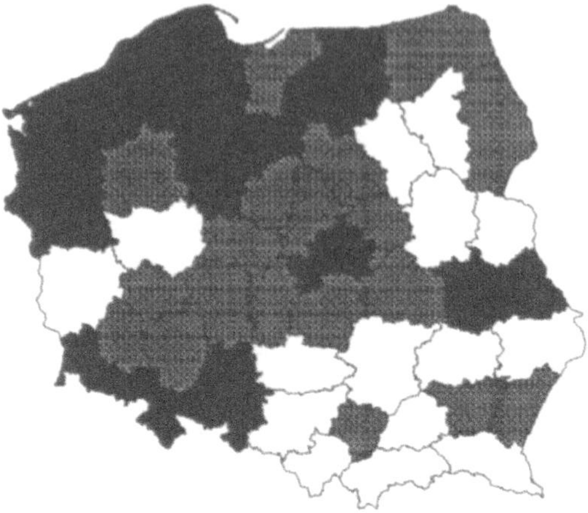

*Notes:* The black-(white-) shaded areas are the 15 voivodships with the highest (lowest) unemployment rates. The 19 hatched voivodships have unemployment rates between those two groups.

Source: *Polish Labour Force Survey May 1992; own calculations.*

**Figure 3:** Modern, Industrial, and Agricultural Voivodships

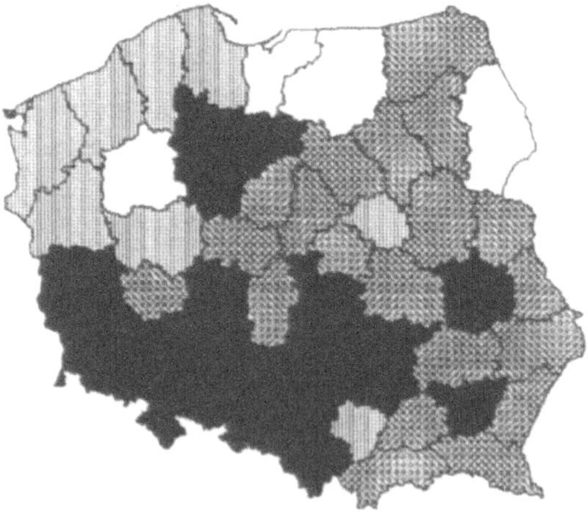

*Notes:* The striped voivodships are modern, the black ones industrial, the patterned ones agricultural, and the white ones belong to none of these categories.

Source: *Kwiatkowski and Gawronska (1995).*

The classification is taken from Kwiatkowski and Gawronska (1995) and is undertaken on the basis of employment shares in 1990. The modern voivodships are Warsaw and Cracow plus the voivodships in and around Pommerania. The industrial voivodships are found around Lodz, Bydgoszcz and Torun, and in and around Silesia. Central and Eastern Poland consists mainly of agricultural voivodships.

As can be seen from a comparison of Figure 2 and Figure 3, there is a weak relationship between the type of voivodship and the relative position concerning the unemployment rate. Roughly speaking, agricultural voivodships have lower unemployment rates, whereas modern and industrial regions have higher ones. The 're-evaluation' of regions that comes with the transition process to a market economy necessitates geographic flexibility, especially of labour. One would expect unemployed labour to migrate into regions with more active labour markets. Such migration should have an equalising tendency on regional unemployment rates.

However, as can be seen from Figure 4, the ranking of the voivodships in terms of unemployment does not seem to have changed much between 1992 and 1996. Voivodships with a comparatively high unemployment rate in 1992 still had a comparatively high unemployment rate in 1996. The coefficient of variation for the voivodship unemployment rates has been 0.30 in both years 1992 and 1996. Regional disparity has fallen in terms of unemployment-vacancy ratios, though. As Figure 5 shows, voivodships with a comparatively high unemployment-vacancy ratio in 1992 also had a comparatively high unemployment-vacancy ratio in 1996, but the correlation is less strong than the one between unemployment rates. Furthermore, there has been a fall in the regional disparity of vacancy rates. In 1992, the coefficient of variation for voivodship vacancy rates has been 0.64, by 1996 it had fallen to 0.45. However, it should be kept in mind that the vacancy data have to be interpreted carefully. Although there is a legal obligation for employers to report their vacancies to the local labour offices, there are no sanctions for failing to do so (Kwiatkowski and Gawronska, 1995). Especially in transition countries like Poland, where local labour offices are understaffed and probably overburdened by building up a network for job brokerage from scratch, the usefulness to employers of reporting vacancies to labour offices can be expected to be rather low. Instead, many job matches in Poland occur through alternative mechanisms like direct job-to-job transitions or trade unions (Boeri, 1994a; 1994b). Hence, actual vacancies are likely to be much higher than measured vacancies. Nevertheless, if the quality of the vacancy data has not changed over time, our conclusions on changes in regional vacancy dispersion are still valid.

**Figure 4:** Unemployment by Voivodship 1992 and 1996

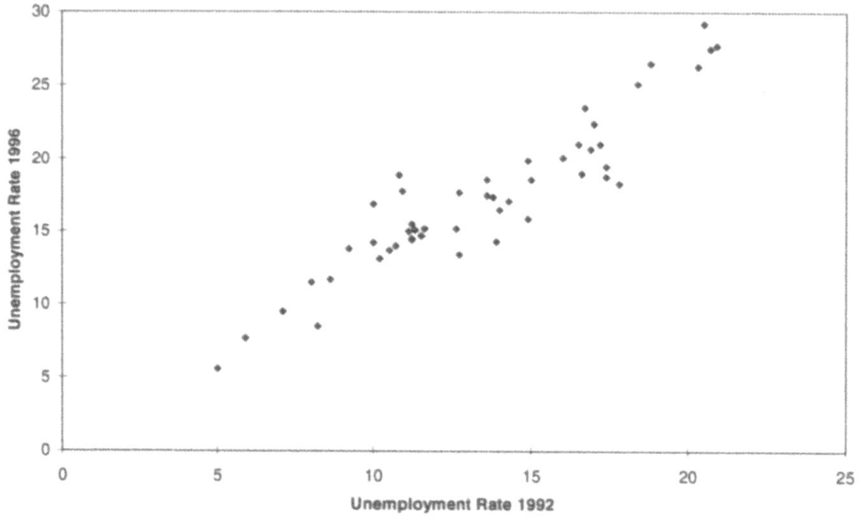


Source: *Polish Ministry of Labour and Social Policy.*

**Figure 5:** Unemployment-Vacancy Ratio by Voivodship 1992 and 1996

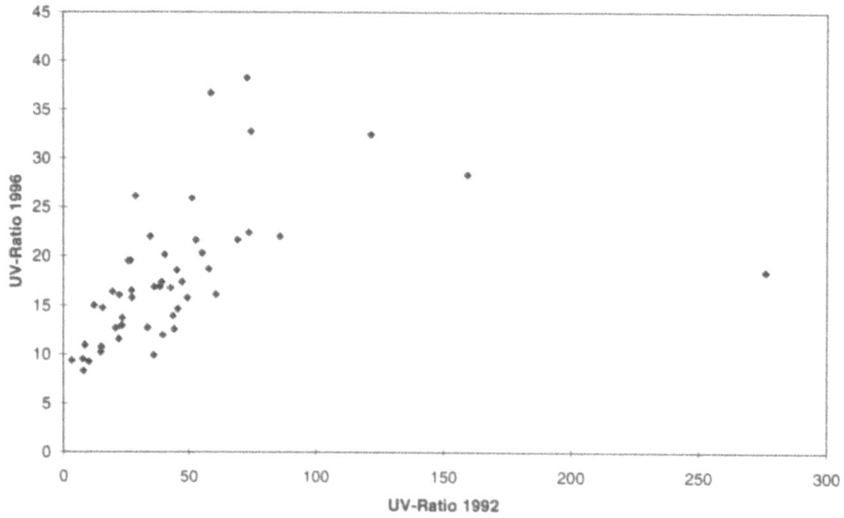


*Note:* UV-Ratio: unemployment-vacancy ratio.
Sources: *Polish Ministry of Labour and Social Policy; GUS (1994; 1995; 1996).*

Taking together the evidence from Figure 4 and Figure 5, we therefore come to the tentative conclusion that any equalising tendencies on regional labour markets between 1992 and 1996 have come from the regional distribution of new job creations rather than the mobility of the unemployment population.

The persistence in regional unemployment differentials can in essence have two reasons. On the one hand, the dynamic disequilibrium forces at work during the transition process may be so strong that any equilibrating forces like migration are being offset. On the other hand, there is reason to believe that regional mobility in Poland is insufficient to offset even a static disequilibrium. The underdevelopment of the housing market in Poland is well known and has been documented several times (OECD, 1992, Chapter 2; Boeri, 1994b; OECD, 1996, Chapter 3). The housing stock with 290 dwellings per 1000 inhabitants is small even in comparison with other transition countries (OECD, 1996). There is still a significant number of public flats which are rented out at subsidised prices. For the inhabitants of these flats, moving house would mean having to pay high rents in the private market. This market is very small and there are very limited opportunities to take out mortgages due to the lack of appropriate financial institutions. As a consequence, mobility is extremely costly for many Poles.

In sum, the restructuring process is relatively painless for those people who change their jobs directly without an intermittent unemployment spell. However, those people who become unemployed are confronted with a low chance of finding a new job and are in danger of becoming excluded from the labour market for a long time. It is the loss or lack of appropriate work habits and human capital which is key to the persistence of unemployment. To address these problems, the Polish government has implemented a set of active labour market policies which aim to break the vicious circle of long-term unemployment and loss of skills. These policies are described in the following section.

## 2.4 Active Labour Market Programmes (ALMPs) in Poland

The main active labour market programmes (ALMPs) that currently exist in Poland are the public employment service, training or retraining for the employed and unemployed, subsidies to employment in terms of wage subsidies (*intervention works*) or loans to enterprises, public works, and start-up loans to support self-employment. Table 4 puts the Polish ALMP programmes in the context of the classification used by the OECD (1993b). Poland has a similar range of ALMP programmes as other market economies. There are, however, no special youth measures except the apprenticeship programmes (Góra, 1994). Not listed here are special measures for the disabled (Kwiatkowski (1995a).

**Table 4:** Classification of ALMP Policies

| OECD ALMP category | Name of corresponding Polish institution |
|---|---|
| Public employment services (PES) and administration | Voivodship and Local Labour Offices (VLOs and LLOs) |
| Labour market training | (Re)Training for the employed and unemployed |
| Subsidies to employment | Intervention works<br>Loan schemes |
| Direct job creation | Public works |
| Youth measures | – |

Source*: Puhani and Steiner (1996).*

Right at the beginning of the transition process, Polish policy makers established a legal framework for the implementation of both active and passive labour market policies. ALMPs schemes are allocated to the unemployed through the public employment service. The duties of the public employment service are to support the unemployed in search for a new job and to register any job vacancies. At the beginning of the transition process in 1990, everybody could register as unemployed with the labour office in order to draw unemployment benefits. The entitlement period for the receipt of unemployment benefits was unlimited. At that time, unemployment benefits were seen also as an important factor of the social safety net, as the social assistance system was not fully developed yet.

In 1992, however, the unemployment benefit system underwent radical changes. The amount of benefit is now generally set at a flat rate of 36 percent of the average wage in the economy during the previous quarter. In December 1993, this would have been 86.1% of the minimum wage (World Bank, 1994). Also, the entitlement period has been curtailed to 12 months. There are exceptions, however. In crisis regions, unemployment benefits can be paid out for 18 months. The crisis regions have to be declared as such by the government and correspond to voivodships or smaller administrative districts within them. In general, benefit recipients are allowed to work for money, as long as their earned income does not exceed one-half of the minimum wage (Kwiatkowski, 1995b, Góra and Schmidt, 1997). Further, a benefit recipient disqualifies for entitlement if he or she refuses to accept a job offer or an offer to participate in training, intervention, or public works three times. There is, however, no evidence that Polish labour offices use ALMPs as a work test (Góra and Lehmann, 1995). It is up to the official in charge at the local labour office to propose an unemployed person to participate in any of the active labour market programmes described below.

**Training and Retraining**

The main aim of the Polish training programmes is to increase the employment chances of the unemployed. However, training courses may also be granted to workers who are in danger of losing their jobs due to lack of skills. There are training courses that take place in classrooms and are organised by the labour offices themselves. Others are delivered by private agencies which are paid for by the local labour offices. Or, as a third alternative, training can take place within firms (O'Leary, 1997a). The training courses usually last from three to six months. Prominent courses taught are using computers, accounting, secretarial work, working as a salesperson, and some craft trades, such as tailoring or welding. Whilst on a training course, an allowance is paid out to the participants which is equal to 115 percent of the amount of unemployment benefit. In order to make sure that the training participants take the programme seriously, they have to repay the costs of the course if it is not completed. There are not only incentives on the demand side of training, but also on the supply side. Partnership firms get a reduction on income tax since 1992 if they organise training courses in regions declared to be threatened by structural unemployment. This reduction is equal to six or nine times the minimum wage, depending on the length of the course (Kwiatkowski, Kubiak, and Kucharski, 1997).

**Intervention Works (Job Subsidies)**

As training courses, intervention works programmes seek to facilitate the re-integration of unemployed persons into the world of work. Intervention works participants can in principle choose to work in any type of job. The local labour office then pays out a subsidy to the employer. The employment subsidy can be paid out for 6 to 12 months. For 6 months' work contracts, the local labour office pays a subsidy equal to the unemployment benefit. The social security contributions are also covered by the labour office. If the employer decides to employ the intervention works participant for 12 months, the labour office pays out an amount equal to the minimum wage every second month, which is about 15 percent higher than the unemployment benefit. In addition, the social security contributions are covered by the labour office every second month. A further incentive to the employer is the possibility of receiving a grant of 150 percent of the average wage in the economy if the employer continues to employ the programme participant after the intervention works programme (Kwiatkowski, Kubiak, and Kucharski, 1997). The concept of intervention works programmes is that they allow the employer to gather information on the productivity of the unemployed worker very cheaply. This productivity might be higher than initially perceived by the allegedly prejudiced employer. In addition, the worker has the potential to acquire firm-specific human capital during his or her intervention works period so that he or she can raise his or her value to the employer. A rather different incentive to the unemployed worker to join intervention works is the fact that, up to the 1st of January 1997, the completion of an intervention works course led to a complete renewal of the 12 months' entitlement period to unemployment benefits.

**Public Works**

Public works are direct job creation programmes which are both targeted on the long-term unemployed and on certain regions to develop local infrastructure. The organisation of public works programmes is carried out by local labour offices in co-operation with the municipalities in question. Typical public works jobs are in construction or cleaning. As in the case of intervention works, the duration of the programmes lies between 6 and 12 months. The incentives for the organisation carrying out the public works programmes are similar to the ones for intervention works. For 6 months' contracts, the wage subsidy equals 75 percent of the average wage in the economy. For 12 months' contracts, a subsidy amounting to the average wage is paid out every second month. In both cases, the labour office pays the social security contribution monthly or every second month, respectively (Kwiatkowski, Kubiak, and Kucharski, 1997). In regions that are declared to be threatened by structural unemployment, the organiser of the public works programme may receive further subsidies for non-labour inputs. This subsidy may not exceed 25 percent of the total sum of wage subsidies, though. As in the case of intervention works, the completion of a public works course led to a complete renewal of the 12 months' entitlement period to unemployment benefits until the 1st of January 1997.

**Start-up Loans**

In Poland, as in western countries, capital market imperfections are generally used as a justification for loan schemes. The lack of an existing enterprise culture in former centrally planned economies deters many people from self-employment. Hence, the aim of start-up loans is to promote entrepreneurship amongst the unemployed and develop a network of small businesses. Anybody applying for a start-up loan has to present a business plan to the local labour office. The loan granted is a one-time lump sum of 20 times the average wage in the economy at the maximum. The interest rate on the loan is 60 percent of the market rate if the newly founded enterprise is operating in the field of manufacturing and 80 percent of the market rate if the business is in services. If the firm survives for more than 2 years, 50 percent of the loan may be turned into a grant and the borrower may be given up to 12 months grace (Kwiatkowski and Tokarski, 1997).

**Loans to Enterprises for the Creation of New Jobs**

A loan can be given to an enterprise for the creation of new jobs only when it has not reduced the number of its employees within the previous 12 months (Kwiatkowski and Tokarski, 1997). The enterprise has to take on people registered as unemployed and must specify the number of people who will be employed due to the loan (O'Leary, 1997a). The size of the loan is then determined on a per capita basis. As in the case of start-up loans, the sum lent is at the maximum 20 times the average monthly wage in the economy per unemployed person taken on by the enterprise. However, a reduced interest rate of 80 percent of the going rate is only granted if the jobs created are in the manufacturing industry. It is not possible to convert parts of the loan into grants and only up to 6 months of grace may be given.

The administrative structure of the public employment service is depicted in Figure 6. The delivery mechanism for ALMPs is in fact quite decentralised like in other transition countries, with local labour offices (LLOs) having in practice a lot of discretionary power over the resources allocated to them (Góra and Lehmann, 1995).

On the one hand, such a decentralised system is likely to perform better in face of the diverse regional developments during the transition to a market economy. Considering, on the other hand, the lack of expertise of labour offices which had to establish ALMP programmes without prior experience in that field, more centralised decision making or at least monitoring and education of local officials may be needed. For example, one reason for the alleged initial bad performance of public training are probably failures in the delivery mechanism. LLOs first had to go through a learning process and build up a network of training providers. Given that labour offices in transition countries are also heavily understaffed (World Bank, 1993, Annex 5), it seems no surprise that many regulations have not been well enforced.

**Figure 6:** The Institutional Structure of Labour Market Policies in Poland

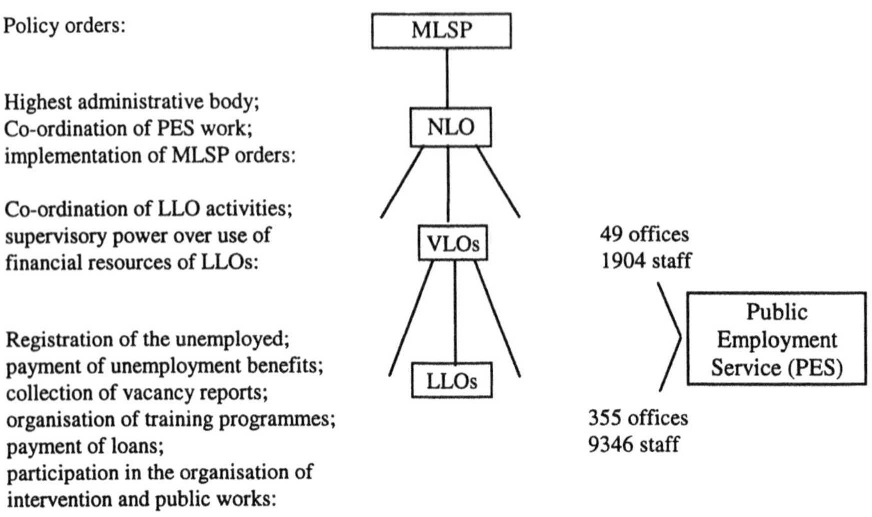


*Notes:* MLSP: Ministry of Labour and Social Policy; NLO: National Labour Office; VLO: Voivodship Labour Office; LLO: Local Labour Office; PES: public employment service; the figures refer to the end of April 1993.

Source: *Puhani and Steiner (1996).*

The Act on Employment and the Act on Group Layoffs which took effect at the beginning of 1990 established the Labour Fund as the main financial source for the funding of labour market policies. About one third of the Labour Fund's resources is drawn from employer's contributions. These are equal to 3 percent of the product wage. The other two thirds of the fund are drawn directly from the state budget. So far, employees do not have to pay directly into the fund.

The development of Labour Fund expenditures is described in Table 5.

**Table 5:** The Development of Labour Fund Expenditures 1990-1996

| | 1990 | 1991 | 1992 | 1993 | 1994 | 1995 | 1996 |
|---|---|---|---|---|---|---|---|
| Share of PLMP exp. in GDP | 0.34 | 1.38 | 1.71 | 1.72 | 1.72 | 1.93 | 1.75 |
| Share of ALMP exp. in GDP | 0.21 | 0.12 | 0.09 | 0.23 | 0.27 | 0.26 | 0.21 |
| Policy activism | 38.1 | 8.0 | 5.0 | 11.8 | 13.6 | 11.9 | 10.7 |
| Share of training in ALMP exp. | 1.3 | 9.5 | 18.0 | 12.7 | 12.7 | 9.19 | 13.5 |
| Share of IW in ALMP exp. | 17.6 | 47.8 | 43.7 | 38.5 | 40.7 | 44.8 | 40.1 |
| Share of PW in ALMP exp. | 0.0 | 0.0 | 16.2 | 33.7 | 36.8 | 36.5 | 34.6 |
| Share of loans in ALMP exp. | 81.0 | 42.7 | 22.1 | 15.1 | 9.7 | 9.6 | 13.5 |

*Notes:* policy activism is defined as the percentage share of ALMP (active labour market policy) expenditure in total Labour Fund expenditure;
loans include both start-up loans and loans to enterprises.
PLMP: passive labour market policy (unemployment benefits); IW: intervention works; PW: public works; exp.: expenditure.

Source: *Polish Ministry of Labour and Social Policy.*

It is shown that policy activism defined as the share of ALMP expenditures in total Labour Fund expenditures was as high as 38 percent right at the beginning of the transition period, but declined to 5 percent in 1992. After 1992, there was a rise in the activity rate again to between 11 and 14 percent. Although policy activism as just defined was never as high again as in 1990, the share of expenditures on ALMPs in GDP surpassed the level of 1990 as soon as 1993. What happened was that from 1990 to 1992, Polish unemployment skyrocketed from 0 to almost 14 percent (*cf.* Section 2.1) so that PLMP expenditures crowded out ALMP expenditures and reduced policy activism. Nevertheless, as can be seen from Table 5, policy makers renewed their commitment to active labour market policies in the subsequent period.

However, Table 5 also shows that the policy mix has changed dramatically between various labour market policies. In 1990, loans (mainly start-up loans) were the main tool of active labour market policy, but already in 1991, interventions works had increased their expenditure share above the one of start-up loans. Loans were then reduced to a tenth of total expenditures with the largest funds going to intervention and public works. Although only about one in eight zlotys of ALMP spending went into training in 1996, a quarter of all ALMP participants were in training as Table 6 shows.

**Table 6:** Participants Shares in ALMPs 1990-1996

| ALMP programme | 1990 | 1991 | 1992 | 1993 | 1994 | 1995 | 1996 |
|---|---|---|---|---|---|---|---|
| Training | 5.8 | 54.9 | 32.2 | 25.6 | 21.8 | 21.1 | 25.8 |
| Intervention works | 60.2 | 29.0 | 47.9 | 44.8 | 48.4 | 47.8 | 42.1 |
| Public works | 0.0 | 0.0 | 16.3 | 25.6 | 27.4 | 29.4 | 30.2 |
| Loans | 34.0 | 16.1 | 3.6 | 4.0 | 2.5 | 1.7 | 1.9 |
| Total | 100.0 | 100.0 | 100.0 | 100.0 | 100.0 | 100.0 | 100.0 |

*Notes*: numbers refer to percentages; loans include both start-up loans and loans to enterprises; ALMP: active labour market policy.

Source: *Polish Ministry of Labour and Social Policy.*

Comparing expenditure shares of Table 5 with participants shares of Table 6, one can see that loans and public works are relatively expensive, whereas training and intervention works are relatively cheap in terms of costs per participant.

In an international comparison for 1992, Poland is shown to have the least activist labour market policy of both the western OECD and the Visegrád countries. As can be seen from Table 7, the most activist western country is Sweden, where ALMPs have a strong tradition. Amongst the transition economies, eastern Germany has by far the highest expenditures on ALMPs in terms of its own GDP. The reason is of course the large transfer payments from western Germany, which allow massive interventions compared to the size of the economy. Although the Czech and Slovak Republics spend much less of their GDP on ALMPs than eastern Germany, their share of expenditures on ALMPs in total labour market expenditures is of similar magnitude.

Polish labour market policy activism and expenditure as a percentage of GDP is roughly at the level of Spain, a western country which also has a two-digit unemployment rate. It should be noted that even a liberal country like the United States with much lower unemployment spent only a little bit less of GDP on ALMPs than Poland. As can be seen from Table 5 above, though, ALMPs became more prominent in Poland after 1992.

**Table 7:** Polish Labour Market Policies in an International Comparison

| Economy | Unemployment rate | Expenditures on active measures [% of GDP] | Expenditures on passive measures [% of GDP] | Policy activism |
|---|---|---|---|---|
| Poland | 13.6 | 0.32 | 2.51 | 11.3 |
| Czech Republic | 3.2 | 0.32 | 0.19 | 62.7 |
| Slovak Republic | 12.1 | 1.37 | 0.65 | 67.8 |
| Hungary | 11.6 | 0.39 | 2.39 | 14.0 |
| Eastern Germany | 14.2 | 9.08 | 5.29 | 63.2 |
| Spain | 18.4 | 0.57 | 3.07 | 15.7 |
| Sweden | 5.3 | 3.21 | 2.78 | 53.6 |
| United States | 7.4 | 0.25 | 0.58 | 30.1 |

*Notes:* all data refer to 1992;
passive measures include unemployment benefits as well as early retirement for labour market reasons (see OECD 1993b, pp.73-78); the index for policy activism equals the percentage share of expenditures on active measures in total expenditures (active and passive);
the figures for Poland differ from Table 5 because active measures here also include expenditures on the public employment service as well as support of apprenticeship and passive measures also include early retirement for labour market reasons (see OECD 1993b, pp.73-78).

Sources: *Puhani and Steiner (1996); eastern Germany: Bundesanstalt für Arbeit (1993); Deutsche Bundesbank (1995); Statistisches Bundesamt (1994; 1997).*

In the following empirical analyses, we evaluate Polish active labour market programmes for the period 1992 to 1996. At that time, the new labour market institutions had already been operating for at least two years and gathered some experience. It has to be kept in mind, though, that during this period unemployment was very high in Poland (*cf.* Table 1 on page 8). On the one hand, such a situation is not a good precondition for trying to re-integrate unemployed people into the labour market. On the other hand, times of high unemployment are exactly those when ALMPs are most needed. Our observation period is thus well suited to put active labour market programmes to the test.

# 3 Macroeconometric ALMP Evaluation by Way of Augmented Matching Functions

This chapter will present the macroeconometric approach to ALMP evaluation using the augmented matching function as the basic modelling concept. The advantages of macroeconometric studies over microeconometric ones are that they are capable of capturing externalities by looking at aggregate data. ALMPs may not only have an effect on the participants themselves, but may very well have effects on the non-participant unemployment population or even the employment population. In Haskel and Jackman's (1986) terminology, substitution effects occur when the subsidised activity would have occurred even without the subsidy, but instead of employing an unemployed worker without subsidy, the employer now takes on somebody who receives a subsidy from the labour office. If substitution effects are prevalent, ALMPs do not increase the total outflows from unemployment into employment, but merely alter the composition of the outflows. Whereas microeconometric studies would only estimate the effect of ALMP programmes for the participants, macroeconometric studies based on regional or national data will estimate the employment effect net of substitution effects. The two approaches are thus complementary.

Furthermore, macroeconomic data can also identify displacement effects. Displacement effects occur when the hiring of a subsidised worker leads to a firing of a non-subsidised worker. With displacement effects, ALMPs may not lower unemployment in the economy as a whole, yet they benefit the participants and increase the turnover of the unemployment pool. Given the stagnancy of the unemployment pool in Poland (*cf.* Section 2.2 above), it has been argued that merely increasing its turnover would be a positive achievement for equity reasons (Boeri, 1996). Below we will test for the existence of displacement effects by estimating the dependence of the outflows from employment into unemployment on expenditures on active labour market policies. If displacement effects predominate, there should be both a positive effect of ALMPs on the outflows from unemployment into employment and on the outflows from employment into unemployment.

Of course, ALMPs may have no effects on the labour market at all. In this case, they just constitute a deadweight loss through the waste of taxpayers' money. If deadweight effects prevail, both macro- and microeconometric studies would estimate the effects of ALMPs on employment to be zero.

In the following sections, we will first present the economic theory behind the augmented matching function and summarise a selection of previous papers on the topic before presenting our own results. The concept of the (augmented) matching function is explained in Section 3.1. For the interested reader, Section 3.2 gives an overview of previous studies on the matching function for both western and eastern European countries. Section 3.3 then leads over to the empirical analysis by discussing the econometric issues that arise in our data sets which we present in Section 3.4. Section 3.5 discusses the estimation results for Poland and Section 3.6 concludes.

## 3.1 Economic Theory: The Matching Function Approach

New work contracts (matches) are the outcome of a complex search process, in which workers look for adequate jobs and firms look for adequate workers. The matching function is a macroeconomic concept which aims to summarise the outcome of this complex reality. This is done by relating hirings of workers to a minimum set of determining variables. The basic tenet of the matching function is to model matches of unemployed workers with vacancies as outcomes of a production process which has stocks of unemployed and vacancies as its main inputs (Blanchard and Diamond, 1989; 1990; Pissarides, 1990). Pissarides (1990) develops a macroeconomic model of equilibrium unemployment with the matching function as a main ingredient to it. In Pissarides's (1990, Chapter 4) model, constant returns to scale in the matching function are assumed to ensure the uniqueness of equilibrium. This simplification may seem rather arbitrary. However, as we shall see below, there is empirical evidence for the existence of a constant returns to scale matching function of a Cobb-Douglas form for many economies. The matching function has thus become an attractive tool for analysing labour market flows empirically.

The microeconomic foundation of the matching function is that both workers and firms have to search for their appropriate match in a world of uncertainty. The inclusion of uncertainty is an extension to the standard neoclassical model where all information in the economy permeates instantaneously through to all agents. With uncertainty and transaction costs, a worker will receive a number of job offers in a specific interval which is drawn from some known or unknown distribution. He or she then has to decide whether to accept that offer or wait for a better one to arrive. Similarly, a firm with a vacancy will receive a number of job applications and has to decide whether to employ somebody of the applicants or whether to leave the vacancy open and wait for a more qualified worker to apply for the job. Clearly, the more unemployed people and vacancies there are in the economy, the more contacts will be established between workers and vacancies. As a consequence, the expected number of matches (hirings) will increase. Constant returns to scale in the matching function means that if the labour market were twice as large in terms of unemployed people and vacancies, the number of matches would be twice as large, too. Increasing or decreasing returns to matching, on the other hand, would mean that there are positive or negative externalities with respect to the size of the labour market, which increase or decrease the matching efficiency, respectively.

A weakness of the matching function concept is that it does not consider job-to-job transitions. The assumption is that vacancies are filled only with unemployed people. However, there is some evidence for Hungary and the Czech and Slovak Republics that many workers move from the public to the private sector without any intervening unemployment spell (Boeri, 1994a; 1994b), which is also very common in western countries (*cf.* Franz, 1996, Chapter 6, on western Germany). This also seems plausible for Poland. Yet as data on job-to-job transitions are generally not available, previous empirical implementations of the matching function had to put up with ignoring this phenomenon. Although this is somewhat unsatisfactory, econometric estimates of the matching function will still be unbiased as long as the number of the employed persons searching for a job is proportional to the number of unemployed persons searching for a job. So far it has not been possible to test this assumption, though, because data on employed job searchers is not available to our knowledge.

**The Ordinary Matching Function**

Formally, the matching function can be written:

$$h = Am(U,V)$$

where $h$ are new hirings (matches, outflows from unemployment into employment), $U$ and $V$ are the stocks of unemployed persons and vacancies, respectively, and $m$ is a continuous non-constant function. $A$ is the mismatch parameter (the higher $A$, the smaller the mismatch between the unemployed and vacancies). Thus $A$ can capture a variety of factors. Amongst the most important are occupational mismatch, geographical mismatch, the efficiency of labour market institutions like the public employment service in creating matches, as well as preferences and institutionally set incentives which influence the search behaviour of the agents.

Specifying the matching process by a Cobb-Douglas production function we get

$$h = AU^{\beta}V^{\gamma}.$$

Taking logarithms on both sides and allowing for some random variation in hirings, we can formulate the following regression equation

$$\ln(h_t) = \alpha + \beta \ln(U_t) + \gamma \ln(V_t) + \delta t + \varepsilon_t$$

where $\ln(A_t) = \alpha + \delta t + \varepsilon_t$. $\delta$ is a deterministic time trend which accounts for changes in matching efficiency over time.

**The Augmented Matching Function**

In the ordinary matching function, the unemployed are treated as a homogenous pool of people. Lehmann (1995) taking up the concept of the search effectiveness of the unemployed by Layard, Nickell, and Jackman (1991, Chapters 5 and 10) formulates the augmented matching function as

$$h = A(\psi U)^{\beta} V^{\gamma}$$

where $\psi U$ denotes the search effective stock of the unemployed, and $\psi$ is the average search effectiveness of the unemployed people. The search effectiveness of the unemployment stock may be reduced by a higher share of the long-term unemployed in the total unemployment stock. ALMPs, on the other hand, can be viewed as measures to increase the search effectiveness of the unemployment stock. Following Lehmann (1995), we can thus decompose $\psi$ as

$$\psi = \psi_0(1+\kappa T), \textit{ with}$$
$$T = \sum_{r=1}^{R} w_r T_r, \textit{ and} \sum_{r=1}^{R} w_r = 1$$
$$\textit{so that } \psi = \psi_0 + \psi_0 \kappa w_1 T_1 + \psi_0 \kappa w_2 T_2 + \ldots + \psi_0 \kappa w_R T_R$$

where $\psi_0$ $(0 < \psi_0 \leq 1)$ is the search effectiveness index without any ALMP treatment, $T$ is a weighted ALMP index of the set of $R$ different ALMP programmes $T_r$. The $T_r$ variables can be expenditures on ALMPs, stocks or outflows of participants, or a combination of expenditures and participants in the programmes. $\psi_0 \kappa$ is the effect of the ALMP programmes on the search effectiveness of the unemployed.

Inserting the decomposition of $\psi$ into the Cobb-Douglas specification and taking logarithms we get:

$$\ln(h) = \ln(A) + \beta \ln(\psi_0(1+\kappa T)) + \beta \ln(U) + \gamma \ln(V)$$
$$= \ln(A) + \beta \ln(\psi_0) + \beta \ln(1+\kappa T) + \beta \ln(U) + \gamma \ln(V).$$

For small $\kappa T$ we can approximate the equation by

$$\ln(h) \approx \ln(A) + \beta \ln(\psi_0) + \beta \kappa T + \beta \ln(U) + \gamma \ln(V)$$

which is equal to

$$\ln(h) \approx \ln(A) + \beta \ln(\psi_0) + \beta \kappa w_1 T_1 + \beta \kappa w_2 T_2 + \ldots + \beta \kappa w_R T_R + \beta \ln(U) + \gamma \ln(V) .$$

We can therefore write the following regression equation:

$$\ln(h_t) \approx \alpha + \beta \ln(U_t) + \gamma \ln(V_t) + \phi_1 T_{1t} + \phi_2 T_{2t} + \ldots \phi_R T_{Rt} + \delta t + \varepsilon_t$$

where $\phi_r = \beta \kappa w_r$ and $\ln(A_t) = \alpha + \delta t + \varepsilon_t$. Thus we can estimate the effects $\phi_1, \ldots, \phi_R$, of the active labour market programmes 1 to $R$ on the outflows from unemployment to employment $h$. In the following section, we survey the previous literature on matching functions.

## 3.2 Literature Survey of Studies on the Matching Function

For the interested reader, we provide a summary of important studies on the matching function in this section. We hope to have included the most important studies on western countries and almost all studies on eastern Europe. The studies on ordinary matching function for western countries are surveyed in Section 3.2.1, the ones for eastern European transition economies in Section 3.2.2. Studies on augmented matching functions for transition economies are presented in Section 3.2.3.

For the reader who just wants to gain a quick overview of the previous studies, Table 8 and Table 9 summarise the evidence on ordinary and augmented matching functions, respectively. The conclusions we draw from these studies are then summarised in Section 3.2.4.

### 3.2.1 Studies on Ordinary Matching Functions for Western Countries

The first famous study on empirical matching functions was presented by Blanchard and Diamond (1989; 1990) for the United States. An important question addressed in these papers is whether there is empirical evidence for the existence of a matching function as outlined above and used in macroeconomic models like the one of Pissarides (1990). The assumption of a Cobb-Douglas functional form with constant returns to scale facilitates the mathematical tractability of the matching function in theoretical models. Therefore, issues of functional form, more specifically tests of Cobb-Douglas versus CES functions have dominated the previous empirical literature as well as the question of constant returns to scale to matching. In the following, we summarise study by study in chronological order.

We show that Blanchard and Diamond (1989) are mistaken in claiming that Pissarides (1986) attempted to estimate a matching function for Britain without success. An empirical matching function for Britain is presented in Layard, Nickell, and Jackman (1991). More evidence on the existence of an empirical matching function in western Europe can be found in Burda and Wyplosz (1994) and Entorf (1995).

#### Pissarides (1986)

Pissarides estimates outflows from unemployment in Britain using quarterly time-series data from 1967 to 1983. In fact, Pissarides does not report a matching function of the type that we have discussed above, but his article is still interesting for our purposes. The author reports that he '*failed to find any level effects from unemployment and vacancies*' (p.526) and that the '*best regressions, both for the logarithmic and the linear specifications, were the ones where the sum of the elasticities of vacancies and unemployment were restricted to zero*' (p.526) and so Pissarides chose to include the unemployment-vacancy ratio as the regressor.

Although Pissarides's paper is often quoted in the literature on matching functions, it should be noted that the focus of his paper was not to estimate a matching function of the type introduced above (Pissarides presents a general model of the British labour market). In their footnote n.17, Blanchard and Diamond (1989) claim that Pissarides estimates a matching function with 'less success' (p.21). We show that this is not true. The fact that Pissarides uses the outflow *rate* as his dependent variable may indeed explain the confusion. Suppose the true matching function was

$$\ln(h) = \ln(A) + 0.5\ln(U) + 0.5\ln(V).$$

This is a standard matching function with constant returns to scale. We can express this equation in terms of the outflow rate (as done by Pissarides) by writing

$$\ln(h / U) = \ln(A) - 0.5\ln(U) + 0.5\ln(V).$$

Pissarides reports that the coefficients of the unemployment and vacancy variables sum to zero, as is the case here. We have demonstrated that when the logarithm of the outflow *rate* is the dependent variable, this finding stands in no contradiction to the existence of a matching function.

**Blanchard and Diamond (1989; 1990)**

The authors estimate matching functions for the United States using a time series of monthly data from February 1968 up to December 1981. Their hirings variable incorporates both flows from unemployment and non-participation into employment as well as estimated employment-to-employment flows. Blanchard and Diamond thus take into account the fact that job-to-job transitions constitute an important share in flows into jobs. The authors' basic specification is derived from the Cobb-Douglas function as demonstrated above. Because the unemployment and vacancy data are collected at the middle and over the current month, respectively, Blanchard and Diamond in addition experiment with instrumenting these variables by their own lagged values. Unemployment is also instrumented by an industrial production index in one specification. A sensitivity analysis of various job-to-job transitions estimates is also carried out. Further, autoregressive models of order one AR(1) are estimated. Finally, the authors estimate a constant elasticity of substitution (CES) matching technology by nonlinear least squares.

In general, Blanchard and Diamond's evidence suggests that hires are driven by both unemployment and vacancies. In most specifications, the coefficient on vacancies is slightly above 0.5 whereas the coefficient on unemployment is slightly below that number. The results further suggest constant or mildly increasing returns to scale in matching. The elasticity of substitution in the CES specification is estimated to be 0.74 and significantly different from one at the 5 percent level. One may thus reject the Cobb-Douglas in favour of the CES functional form.

However, Blanchard and Diamond do not dwell any further on this point, probably because the difference between the CES and Cobb-Douglas estimates is not drastic.

In a further set of regressions, Blanchard and Diamond decompose the unemployment pool into the short-term and the long-term unemployed, respectively. The most interesting result from the decompositions is that the short-term and long-term unemployed turn out to have the same impact on hirings and can thus be regarded as perfect substitutes for the matching process. We will see below that this result is specific to the United States and has been rejected by studies on other countries.

**Layard, Nickell, and Jackman (1991)**

Layard, Nickell, and Jackman estimate matching functions using quarterly British time-series data from 1968 to 1988. The authors find constant returns to scale with a coefficient of 0.28 on the logarithm of vacancies. This number is not mentioned in the study, but can easily be derived by transforming the authors' specification with the logarithm of the outflow *rate* as the dependent variable into one with the logarithm of outflows as the dependent variable. In their model, Layard, Nickell, and Jackman include a lagged dependent variable which has a positive and significant estimated coefficient. The authors also experiment with including a mismatch index, an employment protection index, and lagged unemployment to allow for hysteresis effects. However, none of the just mentioned variables turn out to be significant.

**Burda and Wyplosz (1994)**

Burda and Wyplosz present time-series evidence for four major European economies using monthly data. The estimation periods are 1985 to 1993 for Britain, 1971 to 1993 for France, 1968 to 1991 for western Germany, and 1977 to 1992 for Spain. Testing for unit roots (see Section 3.3.1 on page 51) in their time series, the authors find that the logarithms of their hires, unemployment, and vacancies variables are integrated of order one. However, the authors stress that the tests for unit roots have very low power, and as a consequence they estimate both error correction models (ECMs, see Section 3.3.1) and models with a linear time trend. In their article, they only present the results of the ECMs with the Cobb-Douglas specification of the matching function. The large estimated coefficients on the error correction terms for all countries except Spain is evidence that labour markets adjust very rapidly. Moreover, Burda and Wyplosz find no evidence in favour of a CES specification of the matching function for any country except Spain. The estimation method used is OLS with an autoregressive error term of order one (AR(1)).

For all countries except western Germany, the authors reject constant returns to scale in favour of slightly decreasing returns to scale. This is mainly due to the small coefficient on the logarithm of vacancies, which varies between 0.09 for France and 0.27 for Germany. Burda and Wyplosz speculate that the low coefficients on vacancies may be due to a measurement error in that variable. The authors point out that firms report vacancies more frequently when the labour market is tight. In this case, *measured* vacancies will be disproportionately high when *total* vacancies are many. As a consequence, the coefficient on vacancies will be biased downwards.

**Entorf (1995)**

Entorf carries out a panel analysis for western Germany for 40 occupational groups using annual data from 1972 to 1992. The dependent variable is hirings arranged by the German labour offices. Both hirings, vacancies, and unemployment stock data are available on a disaggregated basis for the 40 occupations. Entorf's primary interest lies in identifying the development of mismatch in western Germany during the specified period. He finds a rise in mismatch or, in other words, a fall in the matching efficiency in the west German labour market over the sample period. The estimation results exhibit decreasing return to scale with a vacancies coefficient of 0.48 and an unemployment coefficient of 0.34 in the OLS equations. However, the AR(1) models suggest constant returns to scale with a coefficient on vacancies of 0.55.

### 3.2.2 Studies on Ordinary Matching Functions for Transition Economies

The studies by Burda (1993; 1994), Boeri (1994a; 1994b), Boeri and Scarpetta (1995) and Burda and Profit (1996) test the matching function concept on transition countries.

**Burda (1993)**

Burda uses both cross-sectional and panel data (with monthly information from October 1990 to May 1992) to estimate matching functions for the Czech and Slovak Republics. He tests the CES against the Cobb-Douglas functional form and finds that the Cobb-Douglas functional form cannot be rejected. Similar to Boeri's (1994a, 1994b) results which will be discussed below, Burda finds small coefficients on the logarithm of vacancies (between 0.24 and 0.44 for the Czech and between 0.08 and 0.23 for the Slovak Republic, respectively). The author's tests for constant returns to scale reveal that constant returns are rejected in favour of decreasing returns in the panel regressions, whereas constant returns cannot be rejected in the cross-section equations. Burda puts more weight on the cross-section estimates. He argues that the time dummies in the panel regression may capture not only technical progress, but also a downward trend in the reporting of vacancies that biases the coefficient on the vacancy variable.

**Burda (1994)**

In this paper, Burda carries out a comparative analysis of empirical matching functions in western Germany, eastern Germany, and the Czech Republic. The author uses monthly panel data, which go from February 1990 to December 1992, August 1990 to May 1992, and November 1990 to May 1992 for western Germany, eastern Germany, and the Czech Republic, respectively. Whereas Burda finds a constant returns to scale matching function for western Germany (coefficient on the logarithm of vacancies = 0.11), the matching function breaks down for eastern Germany (coefficient on the logarithm of unemployment = 1.75), and the Czech matching function exhibits decreasing returns to scale (as in Burda, 1993). Burda argues that the massive scale of state intervention in the east German labour market (*cf.* Table 7 on page 27) through active labour market programmes requires to control for ALMP effects in the east German matching function. The coefficients on the ALMP programmes are not reported, but Burda shows that when controlling for ALMP effects, the east German matching function is similar to the Czech one. For eastern Germany, decreasing returns to scale are thus found with a coefficient on the logarithm of unemployment equal to 0.72 and on the logarithm of vacancies equal to 0.07. As in his Burda (1993) paper on the Czech and Slovak Republics, Burda shows that constant returns to scale cannot rejected in cross-sectional regressions for eastern Germany. However, the cross-section estimates are only based on 35 observations.

**Boeri (1994a; 1994b)**

Boeri (1994b) estimates matching functions on regional monthly panel data for the Visegrád countries for the period 1991 to 1993. Boeri finds decreasing returns to scale for all countries except the Slovak Republic. As in Burda (1993) and Burda and Wyplosz (1994), it is mainly the small coefficients on vacancies that account for decreasing returns to scale. The estimated coefficients on the logarithm of the vacancy stock range between zero (!) and 0.24. One of Boeri's explanations for this finding is that many vacancies in the central and eastern European transition countries are filled by job-to-job transitions. This could explain the small impact of vacancies on outflows from unemployment into employment. Another explanation mentioned by Boeri is increasing regional mismatch of vacancies and the unemployed combined with low mobility due to malfunctioning housing markets.

Boeri also points to the spread of long-term unemployment which accompanied the increase in total unemployment in eastern Europe. If the search effectiveness of the long-term unemployed is lower than the one for the short-term unemployed, then the search effectiveness of the unemployed as a whole will decrease with a rising unemployment pool. Boeri (1994a; 1994b) therefore estimates matching functions with the short-term and long-term unemployed as separate regressors. It is shown that the long-term unemployed have a much smaller, if any, effect on hires than the short-term unemployed. This is at variance with the results by Blanchard and Diamond (1989; 1990), which we have discussed above. The different degrees of flexibility of the labour markets in the United States and the Visegrád countries probably account for this difference.

**Boeri and Scarpetta (1995)**

Boeri and Scarpetta like Boeri (1994a; 1994b) estimate matching functions on regional monthly panel data for the Visegrád countries. The authors use the same data as Boeri (1994a; 1994b) but with more recent observations from 1991 up to 1994. The prolonged observation period does not alter the main findings of decreasing returns to scale and small coefficients on the vacancy variables as presented in Boeri (1994a; 1994b).

Boeri and Scarpetta then estimate separate matching functions for agricultural, industrial, and diversified regions in the four countries, respectively. The typology of the regions is taken from Scarpetta and Huber (1995), who classify the regions according to their employment structure. It is shown that there is regional heterogeneity in the matching process. In general, the authors find that returns to scale are higher in diversified than in agricultural or industrial regions. Although constant returns to scale cannot be rejected for Slovakia as a whole, they can be rejected in favour of decreasing returns for the industrial regions of Slovakia. Also in Poland, where there are decreasing returns to scale for all regions, the smallest returns to scale are found in the industrial voivodships. The matching process exhibits increasing returns to scale in the diversified regions of the Czech Republic, but decreasing returns in the Czech agricultural and industrial regions. Only in Hungary Boeri and Scarpetta find no significant differences between regional matching functions.

**Burda and Profit (1996)**

Burda and Profit take up Boeri and Scarpetta's (1995) discussion of the regional stability of the matching function. The authors use a monthly panel for the 76 Czech labour market districts between 1990 and 1994 to estimate matching functions for the whole of the Czech Republic as well as its macro regions. As in previous studies, the authors find decreasing returns to scale with a very small coefficient on the logarithm of vacancies when estimating by OLS. Yet in an autoregressive model, the authors cannot reject constant returns to scale. Nevertheless, the coefficient on vacancies is still very small (0.13).

Burda and Profit then let the unemployment and vacancy elasticities of hirings vary across districts and time and find a considerable variation in the respective coefficients. This variation, however, decreases when the matching functions are estimated separately for the Czech macro regions. Therefore the authors suggest that spatial dependencies exist in the matching process which were not considered in the analysis of Boeri and Scarpetta (1995). The latter two authors have attributed the regional instability of the matching process to differences in the sectoral employment distribution between the regions. By including unemployment and vacancies of neighbouring districts as additional regressors, Burda and Profit show that spatial dependencies in matching remain even after controlling for sectoral heterogeneity as done by Boeri and Scarpetta (1995). Burda and Profit conclude that there is both sectoral and spatial heterogeneity in the matching function. Constant returns to scale are not rejected in the preferred specification.

**Table 8:** Summary of Studies on Ordinary Matching Functions

| Study | Country | Data | Main findings |
|---|---|---|---|
| | | *Studies on Western Countries* | |
| Pissarides (1986) | Britain | 1967-1983 quarterly time series | evidence consistent with constant returns to scale (CRS) |
| Blanchard and Diamond (1989; 1990) | United States | 1968-1981 monthly time series | Cobb-Douglas functional form rejected in favour of CES (constant elasticity of substitution) functional form; however no big differences in the results;<br>coefficient on *ln*(vacancies) slightly above 0.5 |
| Layard, Nickell, and Jackman (1991) | Britain | 1968-1988 quarterly time series | CRS not rejected;<br>coefficient on *ln*(vacancies) = 0.28 |
| Burda and Wyplosz (1994) | Britain | 1985-1993 monthly time series | Cobb-Douglas functional form not rejected in favour of CES; CRS rejected in favour of decreasing returns to scale;<br>coefficient on *ln*(vacancies) = 0.22; coefficient on *ln*(unemployment) = 0.67 |
| | France | 1971-1993 monthly time series | Cobb-Douglas functional form not rejected in favour of CES; CRS rejected in favour of decreasing returns to scale;<br>coefficient on *ln*(vacancies) = 0.09; coefficient on *ln*(unemployment) = 0.52 |
| | Western Germany | 1968-1991 monthly time series | Cobb-Douglas functional form not rejected in favour of CES; CRS not rejected ;<br>coefficient on *ln*(vacancies) = 0.27 |
| | Spain | 1977-1992 monthly time series | Cobb-Douglas functional form rejected in favour of CES; CRS rejected in favour of decreasing returns to scale;<br>coefficient on *ln*(vacancies) = 0.14; coefficient on *ln*(unemployment) = 0.12 |

**Table 8:** Summary of Studies on Ordinary Matching Functions (ctd.)

| Study | Country | Data | Main findings |
|---|---|---|---|
| Entorf (1995) | Western Germany | 1972-1992 annual panel for 40 occup. groups | CRS not rejected in AR(1) model, but rejected in OLS model; coefficient on *ln*(vacancies) in AR(1) model = 0.55 |
| | | *Studies on Transition Economies* | |
| Burda (1993) | Czech Republic | 1991 cross-section for 76 labour office districts | Cobb-Douglas functional form not rejected in favour of CES; CRS not rejected; coefficient on *ln*(vacancies) = 0.27 |
| | | 1990-1992 monthly panel for 76 labour office districts | Cobb-Douglas functional form not rejected in favour of CES; CRS rejected in favour of decreasing returns to scale; coefficient on *ln*(vacancies) = 0.24; coefficient on *ln*(unemployment) = 0.65 |
| | Slovak Republic | 1991 cross-section for 38 labour office districts | Cobb-Douglas functional form not rejected in favour of CES; CRS not rejected; coefficient on *ln*(vacancies) = 0.10 |
| | | 1990-1991 monthly panel for 38 labour office districts | Cobb-Douglas functional form not rejected in favour of CES; CRS rejected in favour of decreasing returns to scale; coefficient on *ln*(vacancies) = 0.23; coefficient on *ln*(unemployment) = 0.53 |

**Table 8:** Summary of Studies on Ordinary Matching Functions (ctd.)

| Study | Country | Data | Main findings |
|---|---|---|---|
| Burda (1994) | Eastern Germany | 1990-1992 monthly panel for 35 labour office districts | no empirical matching function found unless ALMP effects are controlled for; after controlling for ALMP effects (which are not reported), CRS are rejected in favour of decreasing returns to scale; coefficient on *ln*(vacancies) = 0.72; coefficient on *ln*(unemployment) = 0.07 |
| | (Western Germany) | (1990-1992 monthly panel for 141 labour office districts) | (CRS not rejected; coefficient on *ln*(vacancies) = 0.11) |
| | Czech Repulic | 1990-1992 monthly panel for 76 labour office districts | CRS rejected in favour of decreasing returns to scale; coefficient on *ln*(vacancies) = 0.70; coefficient on *ln*(unemployment) = 0.09 |
| Boeri (1994b) | Czech Republic | 1991-1993 monthly panel for 8 regions | CRS rejected in favour of decreasing returns to scale; coefficient on *ln*(vacancies) = 0.15; coefficient on *ln*(unemployment) = 0.77 (Boeri, 1994a) |
| | Slovak Republic | 1990-1993 monthly panel for 4 regions | CRS not rejected; coefficient on *ln*(vacancies) = - 0.03 |
| | Hungary | 1991-1993 monthly panel for 20 counties | CRS rejected in favour of decreasing returns to scale; coefficient on *ln*(vacancies) = 0.06; coefficient on *ln*(unemployment) = 0.93 |
| | Poland | 1992-1993 monthly panel for 49 voivodships | CRS rejected in favour of decreasing returns to scale; Coefficient on *ln*(vacancies) = 0.14; coefficient on *ln*(unemployment) = 0.65 |

**Table 8:** Summary of Studies on Ordinary Matching Functions (ctd.)

| Study | Country | Data | Main findings |
|---|---|---|---|
| Boeri and Scarpetta (1995) | Czech Republic | 1991-1994 monthly panel for 76 labour office districts | CRS rejected in favour of decreasing returns to scale for whole country; decreasing returns to scale in agricultural and industrial districts, increasing returns to scale in diversified districts;<br>coefficient on *ln*(vacancies) = 016; coefficient on *ln*(unemployment) = 0.78 (for whole country) |
| | Slovak Republic | 1990-1993 monthly panel for 38 labour office districts | CRS not rejected for whole country, agricultural, and diversified districts; decreasing returns to scale in industrial districts;<br>coefficient on *ln*(vacancies) = 0.28 (for whole country) |
| | Hungary | 1991-1994 monthly panel for 20 counties | CRS rejected in favour of decreasing returns to scale for whole country and regions (agricultural, industrial, diversified);<br>coefficient on *ln*(vacancies) = 0.05; coefficient on *ln*(unemployment) = 0.52 (for whole country) |
| | Poland | 1992-1993 monthly panel for 49 voivodships | CRS rejected in favour of decreasing returns to scale for whole country and regions (agricultural, industrial, diversified);<br>coefficient on *ln*(vacancies) = 0.16; coefficient on *ln*(unemployment) = 0.59 (for whole country) |
| Burda and Profit (1996) | Czech Republic | 1990-1994 monthly panel for 76 labour office districts | CRS not rejected; regional heterogeneity in the matching function due to both sectoral and spatial effects;<br>coefficient on *ln*(vacancies) = 0.13 (for whole country) |

*Notes*: CRS: constant returns to scale; CES: constant elasticity of substitution; AR(1) model: autoregressive model of order 1; when the CRS are not rejected, only the coefficient on ln vacancies is reported.

### 3.2.3 Studies on Augmented Matching Functions for Transition Economies

The literature on augmented matching functions that estimate the effects of active labour market programmes has so far mainly concentrated on transition economies, although there are related approaches for western Germany and Britain (Haskel and Jackman, 1988; Disney *et al.*, 1992). In the following, we concentrate on the results obtained for transition economies. There are studies on the Czech and Slovak Republics (Burda and Lubyova, 1995; Svejnar, Terrell, and Münich, 1995; and Boeri and Burda, 1996) and there is also some evidence on Poland in Lehmann (1995), Góra, Lehmann, Socha, and Sztanderska (1996), Puhani and Steiner (1996; 1997), and Kwiatkowski and Tokarski (1997). We have found one study on Bulgaria by Lenkova (1997), one on eastern Germany by Steiner *et al.* (1998), but have seen no evidence on Hungary so far. As in the previous two sections, the just-mentioned empirical studies will be summarised in chronological order. Where possible, we have calculated the estimated costs of increasing the outflow from unemployment into employment by one person through ALMP programmes in euro.[3] Table 9 on page 48 above summarises the main findings of the surveyed articles.

**Burda and Lubyova (1995)**

Burda and Lubyova use monthly panel data to estimate augmented matching functions for the Czech and the Slovak Republics. The panels have 76 and 38 observations for the district labour offices of the Czech and Slovak Republics, respectively. The time-series dimension goes from the beginning of 1992 to mid-1994 for the Czech Republic and to the end of 1993 for the Slovak Republic. Apart from the ALMP spending data, which the authors have for both countries, Burda and Lubyova in addition have monthly information on the participants in publicly useful jobs (PUJs, direct job creation) and socially purposeful jobs (SPJs, mostly job subsidies) for the Czech Republic, whereas they have the staff of district and local labour offices for the Slovak Republic. All estimates are obtained by OLS with fixed district and time effects. Some specifications include lagged dependent variables.

Estimating ordinary (not augmented) matching functions first, Burda and Lubyova do not reject constant returns to scale in their preferred specifications with lagged dependent variables for both countries. We calculate the long-run coefficient on the logarithm of vacancies to be 0.14 for the Czech and 0.08 for the Slovak Republic, respectively.

---

[3] At the time of writing, the euro does not exist yet. We assume that € 1 is equal to ECU1.

As to the augmented matching function estimates, the estimated coefficients on the logarithm of current ALMP expenditure are positive and significant for both countries (although only at the 10 percent level for Slovakia in the specification with lagged dependent variables). The logarithms of participants in PUJs and SPJs in the previous month in the preferred dynamic specification for the Czech Republic as well as the staff variables in the preferred dynamic specification for Slovakia turn out to be insignificant. So the evidence from Burda and Lubyova's study remains somewhat inconclusive, although the authors interpret the positive coefficient on ALMP expenditures as evidence for the effectiveness of ALMPs. According to the authors' estimates, the costs to get an unemployed worker back into employment by ALMP programmes is € 3,428 in the Czech and € 1,052 in the Slovak Republic, respectively.

**Svejnar, Terrell, and Münich (1995)**

Svejnar, Terrell, and Münich estimate outflows from unemployment for the Czech and Slovak Republics using annual cross-sections for the years 1992 and 1993. The authors do not adopt a strict matching function framework, as they include - apart from vacancies, the stock of the unemployed, and per capita ALMP expenditures - the real value of industrial production (and some other variables) as regressors. As a consequence, not much can be said on returns to scale. Estimating the equations for the two years as seemingly unrelated regression models (SURE), Svejnar, Terrell, and Münich find no effects of ALMPs on outflows from unemployment in Slovakia, but a significant and positive effect for the Czech Republic. From the authors' estimation results, we conclude that the estimated costs to get an unemployed worker back into employment by ALMP programmes is around € 1,808.

**Lehmann (1995); Góra, Lehmann, Socha, and Sztanderska (1996)**

Both papers report the estimation results of Lehmann (1995) where an augmented matching function is estimated on a panel of 49 Polish voivodships for six quarters in 1993 to 1994. The unemployed enter the matching function through the stock of short-term and long-term unemployed, respectively. As in the other studies on Poland, the estimated coefficient on the logarithm of vacancies is very small (0.07). The coefficient on the logarithm of the number of short-term unemployed is 0.76 whereas the coefficient on the long-term unemployed is only 0.16. Hence, as in Boeri (1994a; 1994b), there is evidence that the search effectiveness of the unemployment reduces with the duration of unemployment.

The matching function is augmented with the lagged stock of participants in training. However, no significant impact of training can be detected. The coefficient on training is even negative, although insignificant. Lehmann concludes that training is either ineffective in placing the unemployed into jobs and/or displacement effects net out the positive gross effects on the unemployed.

**Puhani and Steiner (1996; 1997)**

Although Puhani and Steiner do not estimate matching functions as they do not include the unemployment stock nor vacancies in their regressions, their approach is related to the augmented matching function in that the authors investigate the effect of ALMP expenditures on the outflows from unemployment. Puhani and Steiner use the quarterly outflow *rate* from unemployment for the 49 Polish voivodships for the years 1993 and 1994 as their dependent variable. The outflow rates are calculated from various waves of the Polish Labour Force Survey. The regressors are the lagged logarithms of expenditures on public works (direct job creation), intervention works (subsidised employment), training, and fixed time effects. This data was obtained from official sources. Both fixed and random effects models are estimated, but in no case do Puhani and Steiner find any effects of expenditure on any ALMP on the outflow rate from unemployment. In addition, the authors test whether ALMPs cause any displacement effects (see our discussion at the beginning of Chapter 3). This is done by regressing the outflow rate from employment on the ALMP expenditure variables. In their 1997 article, the authors distinguish between outflows from public and private sector employment, respectively. The idea behind this distinction is that public works programmes may be more likely to displace public sector workers, whereas training and intervention works programmes may predominantly displace workers in the private sector. The results indicate displacement effects of training in the private, and of public works programmes in the public sector, respectively. However, the authors state that the significance of the respective coefficients is not robust with respect to the specification of the functional form of their equations.

**Boeri and Burda (1996)**

Boeri and Burda use a panel of quarterly data for the 76 Czech district labour offices to estimate augmented matching functions for the period 1991 to 1994. In their specification, the authors pay special attention to the possible endogeneity of ALMP expenditures. Their specification looks as follows

$$[1-f(L)]\ln(h_{it}) = \alpha + \beta\ln(U_{it-1}) + \gamma\ln(V_{it-1}) + \phi T_{it} + \varepsilon_{it}$$

$$[1-g(L)]T_{it} = a + b\ln(U_{it-1}) + c\ln(V_{it-1}) + d\ln(h_{it}) + \mathbf{S}_{it}'\varphi + \eta_{it}$$

where $f(L)$ and $g(L)$ are lag polynomials, *i.e.* the authors include lagged dependent variables in their estimations. **S** is a vector of variables influencing ALMP expenditure $T$, but not directly outflows from unemployment. **S** is also not correlated with $\varepsilon$. In Boeri and Burda's model, endogeneity will lead to biased estimates of $\phi$ if $d$ is nonzero and/or $\varepsilon$ is correlated with $\eta$. A plausible explanation for a nonzero $d$ would be that more people take the chance to join ALMPs when outflows from unemployment are low. A correlation between outflows and ALMP spending due to this line of causation is more likely to occur when the frequency of the data is low. If labour offices react to low outflows by increasing ALMP expenditure within a quarter, then using quarterly data bears the potential danger of endogeneity bias. Using a non-parametric estimator, the authors show that district ALMP expenditure is highly correlated with local unemployment rates in the Czech Republic. This finding gives reason to take care of potential endogeneity. Hence, besides estimating simple fixed effects models by OLS, Boeri and Burda also estimate fixed effects models with variables from the vector **S** as instruments. The instruments used are average quarterly ALMP spending over the year, the fitted values of the authors' non-parametric regression of ALMP expenditure, ALMP spending according to the formula used in Slovakia for the allocation of ALMP funds among districts, and the variables in the matching function other than ALMP expenditure. Apart from ALMP expenditures, Boeri and Burda also use new ALMP placements as well as the creation of new ALMP positions for the ALMP variable. The results show that although the estimated coefficients on ALMP expenditures hardly differ in the OLS and instrumental variable (IV) estimates, the coefficients on new ALMP placements as well as new ALMP positions are much higher when using IV. All coefficients on the ALMP variables are positive and significant at the 5 or 10 percent level. The authors estimate that an additional outflow out of the unemployment pool costs € 1,250.

**Lenkova (1997)**

Lenkova uses monthly time-series data to estimate ordinary and augmented matching functions for Bulgaria for the years 1994-1996. The author tests the CES against the Cobb-Douglas functional form. It turns out that the Cobb-Douglas specification cannot be rejected. The augmented matching function includes the number of people who have finished a training programme amongst the regressors, yet the coefficient on this variable is not significantly different from zero.

The matching function exhibits increasing returns to scale when one looks at the point estimates (the coefficient on the logarithm of vacancies is 0.84, the one on unemployment 1.00). However, no test is being carried out for constant returns to scale, so not much can be said on this issue. Indeed, Lenkova's separate estimates for 3 educational groups (unskilled workers, skilled workers, and people with higher education) exhibit decreasing returns to scale for people with higher education and skilled workers, and increasing returns to scale for unskilled workers. Again, no tests on constant returns to scale are carried out. The low number of observations (34) probably makes it difficult to draw any firm conclusions on the issue

**Kwiatkowski and Tokarski (1997)**

Kwiatkowski and Tokarski estimate augmented matching functions using a quarterly panel of 49 Polish voivodships. Their data span the time period from the

1st quarter of 1992 up to the 1st quarter of 1996. However, although outflows to employment (including employment in ALMPs) are available for the whole sample period, outflows to regular jobs are only available from the 1st quarter of 1994 onwards. Kwiatkowski and Tokarski's ALMP variables are (real) expenditures on public works (direct job creation), intervention works (wage subsidies), training for unemployed persons, loans for enterprises, and start-up loans. The authors adopt a Cobb-Douglas specification, where they also distinguish between the short-term and the long-term unemployed in some specifications. Kwiatkowski and Tokarski estimate pooled OLS regressions without controlling for fixed or random voivodship effects. Although no test is carried out for constant returns to scale, the estimated coefficients on the logarithms of vacancies and unemployment roughly sum up to one. This is valid for both specifications of the dependent variable (outflows to employment and outflows to regular jobs). The estimated outflow elasticity of vacancies is around 0.28. It is also shown that the search effectiveness of the long-term unemployed is far lower than the one of the short-term unemployed. The ALMP variables are insignificant except intervention works, which has a positive impact on outflows and public works, which has a negative impact (we do not consider Kwiatkowski and Tokarski's estimation results without a time trend here). In the case where outflows to employment is the dependent variable, loans to enterprises also have a significantly negative coefficient. The estimated cost to increase the number of outflows from unemployment by one person through intervention works is € 446.

**Steiner *et al.* (1998)**

Steiner *et al.* estimate augmented matching functions for eastern Germany using monthly panel data between January 1992 and January 1997. The matching function is augmented by the outflows from *Fortbildungs- und Umschulungsmaßnahmen* (*FuU*, publicly-financed training programmes). Steiner *et al.* present two estimates, one for the subperiod January 1992 to December 1992, the other for the subperiod January 1994 to January 1997. It is shown that the matching function has been rather stable over time. Constants returns to scale are not rejected, and the estimated coefficient on the logarithm of vacancies is 0.16-0.17. As to the effect of training programmes, Steiner *et al.* estimate that an increase in the outflows from training of 10 percent would only effect an increase in the outflows from the unemployment pool of one percent. Hence, the estimated training effects are very small.

**Table 9:** Summary of Studies on Augmented Matching Functions for Transition Economies

| Study | Country | Data | Main findings |
|---|---|---|---|
| Burda and Lubyova (1995) | Czech Republic | 1992-1994 monthly panel for 76 labour office districts | positive effects of ALMP expenditure, positive effects of participants in ALMPs only in specification without lagged dependent variables; CRS not rejected; estimated costs of an additional outflow: CSK 132,000 ≈ € 3,428 |
| | Slovak Republic | 1992-1993 monthly panel for 38 labour office districts | Positive effects of ALMP expenditure; no effects of labour office staff; CRS not rejected; estimated costs of an additional outflow: CSK 40,500 ≈ € 1,052 |
| Svejnar, Terrell, and Münich (1995) | Czech Republic | 1992-1993 annual cross sections | positive effect of ALMP expenditure per capita; estimated costs of an additional outflow: CSK 69,616 ≈ € 1,808 |
| | Slovak Republic | 1992-1993 annual cross sections | no effect of ALMP expenditure per capita |
| Lehmann (1995); and Góra, Lehmann, Socha, and Sztandersk a (1996) | Poland | 1993-1994 quarterly panel for 49 voivodships | no effect of training expenditure |
| Puhani and Steiner (1996; 1997) | Poland | 1993-1994 quarterly panel for 49 voivodships | no effects of expenditure on training, intervention works, nor public works |
| Boeri and Burda (1996) | Czech Republic | 1991-1994 quarterly panel for 76 labour office districts | positive effect of ALMP expenditure; estimated costs of an additional outflow: CSK 43,000 ≈ € 1,250 (both numbers given by authors) |

**Table 9:** Summary of Studies on Augmented Matching Functions for Transition Economies (ctd.)

| Study | Country | Data | Main findings |
|---|---|---|---|
| Lenkova (1997) | Bulgaria | 1994-1996 monthly time series | no effects of training; Cobb-Douglas functional form not rejected in favour of CES; increasing returns to scale, although CRS not tested |
| Kwiatkowski and Tokarski (1997) | Poland | 1992-1996 quarterly panel for 49 voivodships | positive effects of intervention works, negative effects of public works and loans to enterprises, no effects of training and start-up loans;<br>estimated costs of an additional outflow through intervention works: new PLZ 1,318 ≈ € 446 |
| Steiner *et al.* (1998) | Eastern Germany | 1992-1997 monthly panel for 35 labour office districts | very small positive effect of outflows from training programmes (*Fortbildungs- und Umschulungsmaßnahmen, FuU*) on outflows from unemployment; elasticity = 0.1<br>CRS not rejected |

*Notes:* CRS: constant returns to scale; CES: constant elasticity of substitution; CSK: Czech(oslovakian) crowns; PLZ: Polish Zlotys; €: euro/ECU.

Source: *exchange rates are taken from Deutsche Bundesbank (1992).*

### 3.2.4 Conclusions from Previous Work on the Matching Function

The research carried out so far on empirical matching functions in both western and eastern European countries suggests that the Cobb-Douglas specification of the matching process provides an adequate description in most cases. The assumption of a constant returns to scale matching function is in many cases empirically rejected. However, Burda (1993) argues that this might be due to measurement bias, as firms report vacancies more frequently when the labour market is tight. In addition, the articles by Entorf (1995) as well as Burda and Profit (1996) show that misspecification of the dynamics can lead to a rejection of the constant returns to scale hypothesis.

Some authors have extended the standard specification by including the short-term and the long-term unemployment pool as separate regressors. Here the results differ between the United States and the central and eastern European transition economies. Whereas the long-term unemployed exhibit the same search effectiveness as the short-term unemployed in the United States (Blanchard and Diamond, 1989; 1990), the long-term unemployed seem to be much more detached and/or excluded from the labour market in central and eastern Europe (Boeri, 1994a; 1994b; Lehmann; 1995; Góra, Lehmann, Socha, and Sztanderska, 1996; Kwiatkowski and Tokarski, 1997). Moreover, it has been shown that the matching mechanism works differently in various types of regions (diversified/modern, industrial, and agricultural ones), although no clear pattern has emerged from these results (Boeri and Scarpetta, 1995; Burda and Profit, 1996).

As to the effects of ALMPs estimated from augmented matching functions, the general results for the Czech Republic, Slovakia, Bulgaria, and Poland seem to be mixed. Some studies find significant positive effects (Burda and Lubyova, 1995; Svejnar, Terell, and Münich, 1995; Boeri and Burda, 1996; Kwiatkowski and Tokarski, 1997), others cannot detect any impacts (Lehmann, 1995; Góra, Lehmann, Socha, and Sztanderska, 1996; Puhani and Steiner, 1996; 1997; Lenkova, 1997). Kwiatkowski and Tokarski (1997) even find negative effects of public works and loans to enterprises on outflows from unemployment. When positive effects of ALMPs show up, the estimated costs to get an unemployed worker back into employment by way of ALMP programmes range between € 1,250 and € 3,430 for the Czech Republic (Burda and Lubyova, 1995; Svejnar, Terrell, and Münich, 1995; Boeri and Burda, 1996). Further, these costs were estimated to be € 1,052 for Slovak ALMPs (Burda and Lubyova, 1995) and € 446 for Polish intervention works (Kwiatkowski and Tokarski, 1997).

An important econometric issue addressed in Burda and Wyplosz (1994) is the potential non-stationarity of the time series, which can lead to spurious regression results. Further, the dynamics of labour market flows have been modelled econometrically by experimenting with lagged dependent and independent variables (Blanchard and Diamond, 1989; 1990; Entorf, 1995; Boeri and Burda,

1996). As pointed out by Boeri and Burda (1996), the question of endogeneity of the ALMP variables is very important. Expenditures on ALMPs are in most countries allocated to regional units according to the severity of the local labour market situation. As a consequence, ALMP expenditure or participants variables may themselves be dependent on outflows from unemployment. This endogeneity will most likely lead to biased estimation results. Therefore, we address issues of dynamics and the possible endogeneity of ALMPs in the empirical analysis below. Before we come to our own results, some econometric issues will be discussed in the next section, though.

## 3.3 Econometric Issues

The following two sections will highlight the main econometric issues that arise in our empirical analysis of augmented matching functions. When working with time series, we have to test whether some of our variables exhibit stochastic trends that can lead to spurious regression results (Granger and Newbold, 1974). Section 3.3.1 briefly outlines how to address the problem of non-stationarity in time series econometrically. Recently, some analyses on non-stationary variables in panel data have been undertaken. However, no consensus has been achieved so far on a standard testing procedure. Estimation methods on panel data are presented in Section 3.3.2. We briefly discuss the fixed and random effects approaches that are most frequently employed in the literature.

Following Puhani and Steiner (1996; 1997), the endogeneity problem will be addressed by lagging the ALMP variables. Lagging the ALMP expenditure variables also accounts for the fact that it takes some time until these expenditures can have an effect on the labour market. As will be seen in Section 3.5 below, we also check the sensitivity of the results with respect to the inclusion of current ALMP expenditure in the panel estimations.

### 3.3.1 The Issue of Non-Stationarity in Time Series

A time series is called non-stationary if it has some time trend. This trend can be deterministic or stochastic. A simple example for a series with a stochastic time trend is the random walk process

$$x_t = x_{t-1} + \eta_t$$

where $\eta_t$ is white noise (*i.e.* has zero mean, a constant variance, and no autocorrelation). Clearly, any shocks to this system through $\eta$ persist indefinitely. This means that the process has infinite memory. Processes of this sort are called integrated or said to have a unit root (see, for example, Banerjee, Dolado, Galbraith, and Hendry, 1993, Chapter 1). As shown by Granger and Newbold (1974), a regression of two independent time series which are integrated may produce spurious results in that a significant relationship between the two variables may be obtained, although no such relationship exists. It is therefore important to test whether time series are integrated, or in other words, have a unit root. This can be done by a unit root test like the Augmented Dickey-Fuller (ADF) test of order $k$ which runs the following regression

$$\Delta x_t = \mu + \varsigma t + \delta x_{t-1} + \sum_{i=1}^{k} \lambda_k \Delta x_{t-k} + \eta_t$$

(Maddala, 1992, Chapter 14). One tests whether $\delta$ is zero against the alternative that $\delta$ is smaller than zero. If $\delta$ equals zero, the process is integrated of order one or higher. If $\delta$ is smaller than zero, the process is stationary or stationary around a deterministic time trend. The Augmented Dickey-Fuller test of order $k$ includes lagged differences of the series ($\Delta x_{t-k}$) to catch up any potential serial correlation in the error term. Critical values for the distribution of $\delta$ have been presented in Fuller (1976) and Dickey and Fuller (1979), and are implemented in econometric software packages like *EViews* or *Microfit.*

Regressing integrated series (say $y$ and $x$) on each other is only valid if they are cointegrated. To check whether a cointegrating relationship exists between two series of a regression one first tests whether the series are integrated of the same order and then estimates an ADF regression on the residuals $\hat{\varepsilon}$ of the regression of $y$ on $x$

$$\Delta \hat{\varepsilon}_t = \delta \hat{\varepsilon}_{t-1} + \sum_{i=1}^{k} \lambda_k \Delta \hat{\varepsilon}_{t-k} + \eta_t$$

The critical values for the distribution of $\delta$ in this case have been found by Engle and Yoo (1987), and are also reported automatically in *EViews* or *Microfit.* They differ from the ones reported in Dickey and Fuller (1976) because the $\hat{\varepsilon}$ is unknown and has to be estimated ($\hat{\varepsilon}$).

Economically, one interprets the cointegrating equation (regression of $y$ on $x$) as the long-run relationship between the series in question. The deviation $\hat{\varepsilon}_t$ from this long-run equilibrium can thus be interpreted as a measure for disequilibrium at time $t$. The short-run dynamics of the dependent variable can then be modelled as an error correction model (ECM)

$$\Delta y_t = \alpha + \sum_{i=1}^{I} \rho_i \Delta y_{t-i} + \sum_{j=0}^{J} \beta_j \Delta x_{t-j} + \vartheta \hat{\varepsilon}_{t-1} + \xi_t$$

An application of ECMs in the matching function context can be found in Burda and Wyplosz (1994).

It is well known that the unit root and cointegration tests have low power (Maddala, 1992, Chapter 14; Banerjee, Dolado, Galbraith, and Hendry, 1993, Chapter 4). It is thus difficult to distinguish between a process that has a unit root and a process which has very long, but not infinite memory. For this reason, the applied researcher is often forced to rely on other information apart from statistical tests, too, when deciding whether he or she regards a process as integrated or not.

Such information can be *a priori* reasoning from economic theory. To give an example, high and growing unemployment has been a persistent phenomenon in western Europe since the 1970s. Hence, unit root tests on unemployment data from the 1970s onwards often do not reject that unemployment is integrated of order one. However, neoclassical economic theory and observation of longer historical time periods suggest that unemployment does not grow unboundedly and that it falls back to some equilibrium level once the effects of some economic shock have subsided. This suggests that unemployment does not have a unit root. Our empirical analysis will take up such arguments later on in Section 3.5.1.

### 3.3.2 Estimating the Augmented Matching Function Using Panel Data

Panel data are data on a cross-section of individual units observed over a period of time. Alternatively, one may view panel data as a collection of time series for a set of individuals units. There are significant advantages in estimating the augmented matching function by panel data. First, the times series and cross-section dimensions jointly provide a larger number of observations than either one of them alone. In the transition context, this is very important, because the number of observations is naturally very small as the transition process has only begun eight years ago. Second, panel data allow to control for fixed time and individual effects which are not identifiable in pure time-series or cross-sectional data sets. This way, the ALMP effect on outflows from unemployment can still be estimated without bias in fixed effects models (see below) even if the ALMP variables are correlated with the fixed time or individual effects. This is not the case with pure time-series or cross-sectional models.

In traditional panel data analysis, the issue of stationarity is not addressed as in the time-series literature. The general argument is that the cross-sectional dimension in panel data eliminates the problem of non-stationarity in the time-series dimension. Recently, some papers have been written on unit root tests in panel data, though (Levin and Lin, 1992; 1993; Breitung and Meyer, 1994; Breitung, 1997; Entorf, 1997). But no general consensus on testing procedures nor the necessity of unit roots tests in panel data has emerged yet. In our study, the cross-sectional dominates the time-series dimension, so we will follow the traditional approach and not test for unit roots in the panel data. However, we will shortly discuss the issue of stationarity in Section 3.5.2 by referring to our time-series results of Section 3.5.1.

In the empirical part of this Chapter, we will make use of the two most widely applied models for panel data sets, namely the fixed and random effects estimators. Consider the following model

$$y_{it} = \boldsymbol{\beta}'\mathbf{x}_{it} + \varepsilon_i + \xi_{it}$$

where $y_{it}$ in our case denotes the logarithm of the outflows from unemployment and the $\mathbf{x}_{it}$-vector is the set of independent variables that also includes time-specific effects. For the error term $\xi_{it}$ one makes the standard Gauss-Markov assumptions, which will not be repeated here (*cf.* Greene, 1997, Chapters 6 and 14). In the empirical analysis below, the individual units $i$ will be Polish voivodships. Thus the $\varepsilon_i$ signify constant voivodship-specific differences in matching efficiency. These may arise because some voivodships have more efficient labour offices than others, so that they can create more matches for a given number of unemployed persons and vacancies. Other explanations for voivodship-specific effects are differences in mobility, qualifications mismatch, or other characteristics of the unemployed. Differences in the proportion of measured vacancies may also be captured in the voivodship-specific effects $\varepsilon_i$. The proportion of reported vacancies can vary if employers judge the quality of labour offices differently between voivodships. It is a philosophical question whether one sees these voivodship-specific effects as fixed in repeated samples or whether one regards them as random. Nevertheless, these two views lead to rather different econometric models, as shown in the following.

**The Fixed Effects Estimator**

If one regards the voivodship-specific effects as fixed in repeated samples they can be estimated by including a dummy variable $d_i$ for each voivodship (except for the one which acts as the base category). We can hence write

$$y_{it} = \beta' \mathbf{x}_{it} + \varepsilon_i d_i + \xi_{it}. \tag{3. 1}$$

In this model, the $\varepsilon_i$ are fixed voivodship-specific effects which are to be estimated as coefficients. The Frisch-Waugh-Lovell theorem (see, for example, Davidson and MacKinnon, 1993, Chapter 1) gives an additional insight into the fixed effects model, as it states that it can be rewritten in the following transformed form

$$(y_{it} - \bar{y}_{i.}) = \beta' (\mathbf{x}_{it} - \bar{\mathbf{x}}_{i.}) + (\xi_{it} - \bar{\xi}_{i.}) \tag{3. 2}$$

where, for example, $\bar{y}_{i.}$ denotes the mean of $y_{it}$ over time for unit $i$. One can thus estimate $\beta$ by subtracting from all variables their mean over time by unit and estimate OLS on the transformed data. As by the Frisch-Waugh-Lovell theorem the regressions [3. 1] and [3. 2] are identical, we see from equation [3. 2] that the fixed effects estimator only uses information from the time variation of the panel data. In other words, all the information in the variation of the variables *between* voivodships is discarded and only the variation of the variables over time, *i.e.* *within* voivodships is considered. For this reason, the fixed effects estimator is also called the *within estimator*. As demonstrated in the following, the random effects estimator makes use of both the *within* and *between* variation in the data.

**The Random Effects Estimator**

By treating the voivodship-specific effects as random and thus part of the error term, the random effects model has an error structure at variance with the Gauss-Markov assumptions. The error term is given by

$$\omega_{it} = \varepsilon_i + \xi_{it}$$

where the assumption is made that the random effects $\varepsilon_i$ are uncorrelated with the error component $\xi_{it}$ (*i.e.* $Cov(\varepsilon_i, \xi_{it}) = 0$). As in the standard OLS model, this error term fulfils the conditions

$$E[\omega_{it}] = 0 \text{ and}$$

$$V[\omega_{it}] = V(\varepsilon_i + \xi_{it}) = V(\varepsilon_i) + V(\xi_{it}) + 2Cov(\varepsilon_i, \xi_{it}) = \sigma_\varepsilon^2 + \sigma_\xi^2 = \text{constant.}$$

However, the covariance of two error terms for the same person for two different points in time is not equal to zero:

$$Cov(\omega_{it}, \omega_{is}) = E[(\varepsilon_i + \xi_{it})(\varepsilon_i + \xi_{is})] - E[\varepsilon_i + \xi_{it}]E[\varepsilon_i + \xi_{is}] = \sigma_\varepsilon^2, \quad t \neq s.$$

This is a violation of the Gauss-Markov assumptions. For voivodship $i$, the variance-covariance matrix of the errors for the observation period of $N_t$ time units is

$$\underset{N_t \times N_t}{\Omega} = \left[\begin{array}{cc|cc} \sigma_\varepsilon^2 + \sigma_\xi^2 & \sigma_\varepsilon^2 & \sigma_\varepsilon^2 & \sigma_\varepsilon^2 \\ \sigma_\varepsilon^2 & \sigma_\varepsilon^2 + \sigma_\xi^2 & \sigma_\varepsilon^2 & \sigma_\varepsilon^2 \\ \hline \sigma_\varepsilon^2 & \sigma_\varepsilon^2 & \sigma_\varepsilon^2 + \sigma_\xi^2 & \sigma_\varepsilon^2 \\ \sigma_\varepsilon^2 & \sigma_\varepsilon^2 & \sigma_\varepsilon^2 & \sigma_\varepsilon^2 + \sigma_\xi^2 \end{array}\right].$$

The variance-covariance matrix of the errors for the panel of $N_i N_t$ observations is then given by

$$\mathbf{V} = \mathbf{I} \otimes \Omega$$

where $\otimes$ denotes the Kronecker product. In principle, this model can be estimated by generalised least squares (GLS). GLS amounts to estimating OLS on a transformed model with transformation matrix

$$\mathbf{P} = \mathbf{V}^{-1/2} = \mathbf{I} \otimes \Omega^{-1/2}.$$

It can be shown that the transformed model is (Greene, 1997, Chapter 14)

$$(y_{it} - \theta \bar{y}_{i.}) = \beta'(\mathbf{x}_{it} - \theta \bar{\mathbf{x}}_{i.}) + [(\varepsilon_i - \theta \varepsilon_i) + (\xi_{it} - \theta \bar{\xi}_{i.})] \qquad [3.\ 3]$$

with

$$\theta = 1 - \frac{\sigma_\xi}{\sqrt{\sigma_\xi^2 + T\sigma_\varepsilon^2}}.$$

As can be seen from equation [3. 3], the random effects estimator makes use of both the *within*- and the *between*-voivodship variation in the data. If the variance of the voivodship-specific effects $\varepsilon_i$ is very large in relation to the variance of the residual component $\xi_{it}$, $\theta$ will approach one and the random effects estimator converges to the fixed effects estimator. If, on the other hand, the variance of the residual component $\xi_{it}$ is very large compared to the variance of the voivodship-specific effects $\varepsilon_i$, $\theta$ will approach zero and the random effects estimator converges to the pooled regression, *i.e.* a standard OLS regression without voivodship-specific effects. Because the variances $\sigma_\varepsilon$ and $\sigma_\xi$ are generally unknown, they have to be estimated. *Stata5.0*, which is the econometric package we will use, obtains estimates of $\sigma_\varepsilon$ and $\sigma_\xi$ from the fixed effects and the *between* estimates (a 'cross-section' regression of the unit means of the variables over time), respectively. Equation [3. 3] is then estimated by feasible GLS using the estimate of $\theta$.

In the case where $N_t$ varies between the $N_i$ units, one speaks of an unbalanced panel. In our case, the panels will sometimes be unbalanced due to missing observations. On the assumption that observations are missing randomly, the fixed and random effects models can be estimated on unbalanced panels as on balanced panels with some technical qualifications to the calculation of $\theta_i$, which then varies between the individual units (Baltagi, 1995, Chapter 9). These qualifications are implemented in *Stata5.0* (Stata Corp., 1997).

To test for the existence of voivodship-specific effects, one can carry out a standard $F$-test (Greene, 1997, Chapter 14) for the fixed effects model, and a Lagrange Multiplier test for random effects as developed by Breusch and Pagan (1980) and adapted to unbalanced panel data by Baltagi and Le (1990). Calculation of the corresponding test statistics is implemented in *Stata5.0*. Furthermore, one can test the assumption made in the random effects model that the random effects $\varepsilon_i$ are uncorrelated with the regressors $\mathbf{x}_{it}$. A widely-used test of this hypothesis has been suggested by Hausman (1978). The null hypothesis of this test is that the difference between the coefficients of the random and the fixed effects models is zero. The test statistic is

$$H = \left(\hat{\beta}_{FE} - \hat{\beta}_{RE}\right)' \left[\hat{\mathbf{Var}}\left(\hat{\beta}_{FE}\right) - \hat{\mathbf{Var}}\left(\hat{\beta}_{RE}\right)\right]^{-1} \left(\hat{\beta}_{FE} - \hat{\beta}_{RE}\right)$$

where $H$ has a $\chi_k^2$ distribution, $k$ being the number of estimated parameters per model. If the models are otherwise correctly specified, a rejection of the null hypothesis of no differences between the fixed and random effects coefficients must mean that the random effects are correlated with the regressors. In this case, the random effects model is not consistent. Otherwise, if the random effects are uncorrelated with the regressors, fixed effects estimation is still consistent, but the random effects estimator is more efficient.

**Inconsistency due to Lagged Dependent Variables in Panel Estimations**

Above it has been shown that both fixed and random effects estimators can be expressed as OLS estimators on the transformed models [3. 2] and [3. 3]. It can be seen from equations [3. 2] and [3. 3] that the inclusion of a lagged dependent variable amongst the regressors $\mathbf{x}_{it}$ will induce a correlation between the error term and the regressors, because the mean of the error terms over time $\bar{\xi}_{i.}$ is by definition correlated with every $y_{it}$. In the random effects case, the problem is even more severe, as the lagged dependent variables are also correlated with the error term through the unit-specific effects $\varepsilon_i$. Therefore, estimates with lagged dependent variables in panel data will be inconsistent for fixed $N_t$ and $N_i \rightarrow \infty$.

As a solution to this problem, instrumental variable estimators on a model in first differences have been proposed in the literature (*cf.* Greene, 1997, Chapter 14). Moreover, generalised method of moments estimators have been developed (Ahn and Schmidt, 1995). However, Monte Carlo evidence suggests that the fixed effects estimator, although biased, has a relatively small variance compared to the instrumental variable and generalised method of moments estimators and therefore does not necessarily perform worse in terms of mean square error (Kiviet, 1995). The induced correlation through the inclusion of a lagged dependent variable is of order $1/N_t$. That is to say, the greater $N_t$, the lower the induced correlation. As in our matching function analyses below, $N_t$ will always be greater than eleven, we hope that the problem of induced autocorrelation is attenuated in the fixed effects models. But as we generally work in a small sample context, all proposed panel estimators in the face of lagged dependent variables must be expected to yield biased results.

Weighing up the Monte Carlo research by Kiviet (1995) we choose to apply the fixed effects estimator because of its comparatively small dispersion (the random effects estimates are also reported for comparative purposes). This has been the approach in all studies surveyed above which include lagged dependent variables in panel settings (Burda and Lubyova, 1995; Boeri and Burda, 1996; and Burda and Profit, 1996). Although we will see below that the inclusion of lagged dependent variables does not make a qualitative difference to the estimation results obtained, it must be stressed that the estimation results with lagged dependent variables have to be interpreted with a *caveat*.

## 3.4 Data and Variables

We use three types of data. First, we have monthly time-series information on outflows from registered unemployment, stocks of unemployment and vacancies, and stocks and flows of ALMP participants in training, intervention works, and public works. Second, we use quarterly panel data from the Polish Ministry of Labour and Social Policy on outflows from unemployment, unemployment stocks and vacancy stocks, as well as expenditures on the Polish ALMP programmes (training, intervention works, public works, loans for the unemployed, loans for employers). Third, we calculate outflows from unemployment and employment, as well as stock of unemployed people from the Polish Labour Force Survey. In the following, we give a description of these data sets.

### Time-Series Data

Various publications of the Polish Central Statistical Office (GUS 1994; 1995; 1996) provide monthly time series data on registered unemployment, vacancies, and training, intervention, and public works participants. We do not use any information on intervention or public works, though. The reason is that the *total outflow* as well as *outflows to jobs* variables include outflows to intervention and public works. Therefore, by definition an inflow into a works programme leads to an outflow from the unemployment register. Regressing any type of *outflows* on *works* programmes variables must consequently yield upward-biased estimates. As trainees, unlike works programme participants, stay on the unemployment register, training effects are identifiable from our data. Descriptive Statistics for the time series are presented in Table 10.

**Table 10:** Descriptive Statistics for Time-Series Data

| Variable | Mean | S.d. | Min. | Max. | Obs. |
|---|---|---|---|---|---|
| *ln* total outflows | 5.14 | 0.28 | 4.50 | 5.62 | 43 |
| *ln* outflows to jobs | 4.44 | 0.33 | 3.85 | 5.00 | 43 |
| *ln* unemployment stock | 7.92 | 0.05 | 7.83 | 8.00 | 43 |
| *ln* vacancy stock | 3.54 | 0.26 | 3.02 | 3.96 | 43 |
| Training expenditure | 5.72 | 1.59 | 3.37 | 9.43 | 37 |
| Training participant stock | 13.57 | 5.44 | 4.30 | 32.50 | 43 |
| Training participant outflows | 7.47 | 2.69 | 2.30 | 12.90 | 42 |

*Note:* the outflow, unemployment and vacancy data are in logarithms (*ln*) of thousands, training expenditure is in million real new PLZ (1995), and the training participant data are in thousands; S.d.: standard deviation; obs.: number of observations.

Source: *GUS (1994; 1995; 1996); except quarterly expenditure data (Polish Ministry of Labour and Social Policy).*

Table 10 shows that the variation of *outflows* and *vacancies* over time is much higher than the variation in *unemployment*. The *training* variables also exhibit a large variation over time. As the transition process has only started in 1990, the observation period naturally is somewhat short. Generally, the series start in December 1992 and end in June 1996. Exceptions are the training outflows data, which starts in January 1993, and the training expenditure data, which ends in December 1995. The training expenditure data has been received from the Polish Ministry of Labour and Social Policy. As the training expenditure data is only available on a quarterly basis, we assume that quarterly expenditure is spread equally over the three months of each quarter.

**Panel Data**

Our second data source is quarterly panel data from the Polish Ministry of Labour and Social Policy[4] on outflows from unemployment, unemployment and vacancy stocks, as well as expenditures on the Polish ALMP programmes (training, intervention works, public works, start-up loans, and loans for enterprises). The data are available for all 49 voivodships between the first quarter of 1992 until the last quarter of 1995. Some series also start during the last quarter of 1991 and/or end at the first quarter of 1996. We discuss this data in relation to the labour force survey data which is our third source of information.

The Polish Labour Force Survey (PLFS) is a quarterly survey of the Polish labour force which started in May 1992. The sample size is around 50,000 persons each wave. Sampling in the PLFS takes place by randomly drawing a number of households from Poland's territorial statistical units (TSUs) proportional to the population share of the TSUs. From the households drawn, all members aged 15 and above are interviewed. Excluded from the possibility of interview are the non-housing population (essentially the homeless, people in group quarters, soldiers doing compulsory military service and the prison population) and people living abroad at the time of interview. The PLFS is thus only representative for the Polish population that does not fall into any of these categories. Another factor limiting the representative character of the PLFS is the fact that the non-interview rate varies with the size of the place of residence. Whereas this rate was 6.5 percent in August 1993 for the whole of Poland, it was 24 percent in Warsaw, but only 1.6 percent in rural communities (Szarkowski and Witkowski, 1994). However, for the other place-of-residence categories mentioned in Szarkowski and Witkowski (1994), the highest non-interview rate is 8.2 percent and the lowest 4.5 percent, so that the PLFS may show some, but hopefully not too severe distortions in terms of representative character.

---

[4] We thank Professor Eugeniusz Kwiatkowski, University of Lodz, for sending us this data.

We can use the PLFS to calculate outflow rates from unemployment into employment and *vice versa*. The advantage of using PLFS data lies in the fact that the classification of individuals into the three labour force states employment, unemployment, and non-participation follows the definitions of the International Labour Office (ILO). Accordingly, classified as employed are people who during the week of interview earn money for at least one hour or who hold a job, but do not work temporarily (*e.g.* because they are ill). Additionally, so-called unpaid family workers are also classified as employed. Those people not employed are classified as unemployed if they actively search for a job and are also ready to start work in the week of interview or the following one. Anybody not falling into either of the two labour force states employment or unemployed is classified as not being in the labour force.

In order to estimate the total numbers of *unemployed* people and *outflows from unemployment* from the PLFS, we divide the figures in the PLFS by the share of people interviewed out of the total voivodship population. To calculate this share, we need figures for the population aged 15 and above. Unfortunately, we were not able to obtain this series, but only figures for the total population of Poland. Yet as far as the population share of this age group did not change very much over the observation period, the scaling error in our data will not bias any econometric estimates except constant terms.

Figure 7 and Figure 8 compare the developments of the *unemployment stock* as well as *outflows from unemployment* variables as measures in the register and PLFS data, respectively. The figures depict the time series for the whole of Poland, which was obtained by adding up the data for the 49 voivodships.

**Figure 7:** The Development of Unemployment in Poland

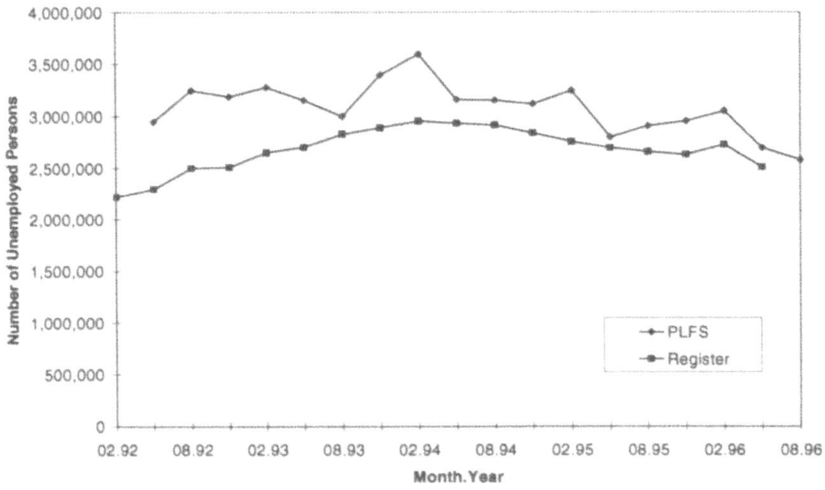


Sources: *Polish Labour Force Survey (PLFS); Polish Ministry of Labour and Social Policy (Register); own calculations.*

**Figure 8:** The Development of Outflows from Unemployment in Poland

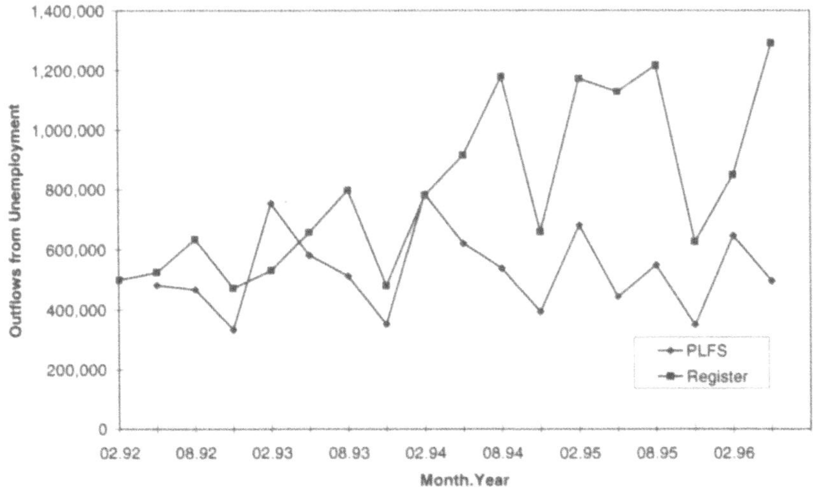


Sources: *Polish Labour Force Survey (PLFS); Polish Ministry of Labour and Social Policy (Register); own calculations.*

Figure 7 shows that the unemployment stock is generally higher in the PLFS than in the register data. This, however, is almost surely due to the just mentioned scaling effect which occurs through the inclusion of people under 15 years of age in the calculation of the population shares sampled in the PLFS. Kalaska and Witkowski (1997) demonstrate that unemployment figures obtained from the PLFS are generally lower than those from the register. Furthermore, the PLFS data show a greater seasonal variation in unemployment than the register data. This is not an unexpected result, as the register data are likely to be stronger driven by institutional factors such as entitlement to unemployment benefit for a fixed period of usually 12 months. The PLFS data can be expected to reflect the search behaviour of the unemployed more accurately due to the application of the ILO definition of unemployment.

An even greater difference between the PLFS and register data emerges when looking at the *outflows from unemployment* in Figure 8. The fact that the register data exhibits higher *outflows* for most months is not surprising, as the register data measures *total outflows* from the registers, whereas the PLFS data only measures *outflows to employment*. Of course, outflows to employment is what we are interested in. When using the *total outflows* data from the register (because *outflows to jobs* are not available to us on the voivodship level) we hope the movements in the two series to be proportional. In this case, any estimation results would still be unbiased. However, as can be seen from Figure 8, this proportionality assumption does not seem to hold between the two data sources we observe here. Unfortunately, though, we cannot make a clear statement on the validity of the proportionality assumption, as the difference in the two series may stem from many factors. One is the just mentioned difference in the type of *outflow* measures. Another one is the different definition of unemployment. Further, the different data source *per se* may play a role. And finally, there might be estimation errors when inferring from the PLFS on the total population.

The just discussed differences in concepts and measurements between the data sources at hand warrant a sensitivity analysis with respect to the data set used. Descriptive statistics for the data from both the Polish Ministry of Labour and Social Policy and the Polish Labour Force Survey are presented in Table 11.

**Table 11:** Descriptive Statistics for Panel Data

| Variable | Data | Mean | S.d. | Min. | Max. | Observations | |
|---|---|---|---|---|---|---|---|
| *ln* outflows from | *overall* | 2.149 | 0.745 | 0.352 | 4.377 | $N_{it}$ | 818 |
| unemployment | *between* | | 0.473 | 1.044 | 3.461 | $N_i$ | 49 |
| (PLFS) | *within* | | 0.583 | 0.033 | 4.311 | $\bar{N}$ | 16.69 |
| *ln* unemployment stock | *overall* | 4.020 | 0.490 | 2.437 | 5.519 | $N_{it}$ | 882 |
| (PLFS) | *between* | | 0.463 | 2.890 | 5.418 | $N_i$ | 49 |
| | *within* | | 0.172 | 3.395 | 4.587 | $N_t$ | 18 |
| *ln* outflows from | *overall* | 2.088 | 0.604 | -0.223 | 3.813 | $N_{it}$ | 833 |
| unemployment | *between* | | 0.437 | 1.146 | 3.365 | $N_i$ | 49 |
| (register) | *within* | | 0.421 | 0.198 | 3.251 | $N_t$ | 17 |
| *ln* unemployment stock | *overall* | 3.903 | 0.427 | 2.451 | 5.179 | $N_{it}$ | 882 |
| (register) | *between* | | 0.417 | 2.786 | 5.037 | $N_i$ | 49 |
| | *within* | | 0.111 | 3.459 | 4.184 | $N_t$ | 18 |
| *ln* outflows from | *overall* | 1.853 | 0.685 | 0.353 | 4.377 | $N_{it}$ | 799 |
| employment | *between* | | 0.413 | 1.036 | 2.856 | $N_i$ | 49 |
| (PLFS) | *within* | | 0.554 | -0.063 | 4.300 | $\bar{N}$ | 16.31 |
| *ln* employment stock | *overall* | 5.847 | 0.498 | 4.732 | 7.569 | $N_{it}$ | 882 |
| (PLFS) | *between* | | 0.499 | 4.845 | 7.478 | $N_i$ | 49 |
| | *within* | | 0.063 | 5.627 | 6.071 | $N_t$ | 18 |
| *ln* vancancy stock | *overall* | 0.927 | 0.827 | -2.303 | 3.211 | $N_{it}$ | 833 |
| (register) | *between* | | 0.684 | -0.364 | 2.734 | $N_i$ | 49 |
| | *within* | | 0.475 | -1.185 | 2.312 | $N_t$ | 17 |
| Expenditure on training | *overall* | 0.308 | 0.441 | 0.000 | 3.808 | $N_{it}$ | 784 |
| (register) | *between* | | 0.343 | 0.015 | 1.816 | $N_i$ | 49 |
| | *within* | | 0.282 | -1.342 | 2.300 | $N_t$ | 16 |
| Expenditure on | *overall* | 1.109 | 0.955 | 0.034 | 6.038 | $N_{it}$ | 784 |
| intervention works | *between* | | 0.673 | 0.255 | 3.141 | $N_i$ | 49 |
| (register) | *within* | | 0.684 | -1.483 | 4.638 | $N_t$ | 16 |
| Expenditure on public | *overall* | 0.887 | 1.019 | 0.000 | 6.252 | $N_{it}$ | 784 |
| works | *between* | | 0.630 | 0.108 | 2.705 | $N_i$ | 49 |
| (register) | *within* | | 0.805 | -1.818 | 4.867 | $N_t$ | 16 |

**Table 11:** Descriptive Statistics for Panel Data (ctd)

| Variable | Data | Mean | S.d. | Min. | Max. | Observations | |
|---|---|---|---|---|---|---|---|
| Expenditure on loans for | *overall* | 0.156 | 0.256 | 0.000 | 4.554 | $N_{it}$ | 784 |
| the unemployed | *between* | | 0.116 | 0.002 | 0.730 | $N_i$ | 49 |
| (register) | *within* | | 0.229 | -0.573 | 3.980 | $N_t$ | 16 |
| Expenditure on loans for | *overall* | 0.117 | 0.270 | 0.000 | 3.225 | $N_{it}$ | 784 |
| enterprises | *between* | | 0.161 | 0.001 | 0.840 | $N_i$ | 49 |
| (register) | *within* | | 0.217 | -0.723 | 2.587 | $N_t$ | 16 |

*Notes:* The *between* data are formed by calculating the means over time by voivodship $\bar{x}_{i.}$; the *within* data are defined as $x_{it} - \bar{x}_{i.} + \bar{\bar{x}}$, where the overall mean $\bar{\bar{x}}$ is added to equate the mean of all data (*overall, between,* and *within*); the unemployment and vacancy data are in logarithms (*ln*) of thousands, and ALMP expenditure is in million real new PLZ (1995); S.d.: standard deviation.

Sources: *Polish Labour Force Survey (PLFS); Polish Ministry of Labour and Social Policy (Register); own calculations.*

For some voivodships in the PLFS, we measure zero flows from unemployment to employment or *vice versa* between two quarters. As in these voivodships only a small number of people is sampled, zero flows in the sample should not be inferred for the whole population. We therefore drop such observations. As a consequence, the panel becomes unbalanced. Although the missing values are not random, they will be treated as such, as their number is small and any method to model the occurrence of missing values has to invoke additional assumptions.

The observation period generally goes from the first quarter of 1992 (second quarter for PLFS data) to the last quarter of 1995. The register data are identical to those of Kwiatkowski and Tokarski (1997). Boeri (1994a; 1994b) has a shorter observation period from January 1992 to March 1993, but more observations, as his panel has monthly time-series information. He states an OECD database as his data source which is probably obtained from the Polish registers. Lehmann (1995), and Góra, Lehmann, Socha, and Sztanderska (1996) also have a shorter observation period than us: they use quarterly register data from the first quarter of 1993 to the second quarter of 1994. The only other studies on Poland also using PLFS data are the ones by Puhani and Steiner (1996; 1997), who use PLFS data for the outflow variable and combine them with administrative data on ALMP expenditures. The observation period in these studies (1992 to 1993) is also shorter than in this work.

Again as with the time-series data, we have the conceptual problem that *outflows* into any ALMP apart from training are measured as *outflows into employment.* This is true both for the register and PLFS data. Therefore we can only identify training effects in the panel data, too.

Table 11 not only reports standard deviations for the pooled panel data (*overall*), but also for the *between* (means over time) and *within* (deviation from means over time) data. Glancing over the sizes of the standard deviations, we find both large *within* and *between* variation in all variables. As mentioned in Section 3.3.2, the fixed effects estimator only makes use of the *within* information. However, the existence of a considerable *between* variation in the data makes the random effects estimator potentially more attractive, because it also makes use of the *between* information in the data. Therefore, we estimate both fixed and random effects model in the following section.

## 3.5 Estimation Results for Poland

In the following three sections we report the estimation results. As mentioned in the discussion of the data sets, we can only estimate the effect of *training* measures on the *outflows from unemployment*. Sections 3.5.1 and 3.5.2 present the time-series and panel evidence, respectively. We can however, estimate the effects of all five ALMP programmes on the *outflows from employment*. These are presented in Section 3.5.3.

### 3.5.1 Time-Series Evidence

#### Unit Root Tests

In order to avoid spurious regressions, we first carry out unit root tests for the time series. The test statistics and critical values for the Dickey-Fuller and Augmented Dickey-Fuller tests of order one are shown in Table 12. Estimation results for the time-series data were obtained using the econometric software packages *EViews 2.0* and *MICROFIT 3.0* (Pesaran and Pesaran, 1991).

In most cases, the Dickey-Fuller test does not reject the null hypothesis of a unit root. However, we have found serial correlation in the Dickey-Fuller regressions. As no serial correlation has been found in the ADF(1) regressions, these tests are appropriate (see Section 3.3.1 above). The Dickey-Fuller regressions themselves are not reported here, but can be obtained from the author upon request.

**Table 12:** Unit Root Tests for Time-Series Data

| Variable | Test type | Without trend | | With trend | |
|---|---|---|---|---|---|
| | | $\delta$ | $c_{0.05}$ | $\delta$ | $c_{0.05}$ |
| *ln* outflows | DF | -2.13 | -2.93 | -2.86 | -3.52 |
| | ADF(1) | -3.14 | -2.93 | -4.54 | -3.52 |
| *ln* outflows to jobs | DF | -2.46 | -2.93 | -3.26 | -3.52 |
| | ADF(1) | -3.35 | -2.93 | -4.91 | -3.52 |
| *ln* unemployment stock | DF | -1.37 | -2.93 | -1.95 | -3.52 |
| | ADF(1) | -1.60 | -2.93 | -2.03 | -3.52 |
| *ln* vacancies | DF | -2.41 | -2.93 | -2.29 | -3.52 |
| | ADF(1) | -3.51 | -2.93 | -3.44 | -3.52 |
| Training participants outflow | DF | -5.56 | -2.93 | -5.62 | -3.52 |
| | ADF(1) | -3.76 | -2.93 | -3.78 | -3.52 |
| Training participants stock | DF | -1.51 | -2.93 | -2.26 | -3.52 |
| | ADF(1) | -1.67 | -2.93 | -2.55 | -3.52 |
| Training expenditure | DF | -3.55 | -3.15 | -3.25 | -3.87 |
| | ADF(1) | -3.31 | -3.18 | -2.45 | -3.93 |

*Note:* $\delta$ is the test statistic as described in Section 3.3.1 on page 51. $c_{0.05}$ is the 5 percent critical value; the null hypothesis of a unit root is rejected if $\delta < c_{0.05}$ (shaded $\delta$ values); DF: Dickey-Fuller test; ADF(1): Augmented Dickey-Fuller test of order 1.

Source: *Polish Ministry of Labour and Social Policy; own calculations.*

Although we cannot reject the existence of a unit root in the regressions with trend for *vacancies* and *training expenditures*, the trend variable has not been significant in the ADF(1) regressions. The ADF(1) regressions without trend reveal that the unit root can be rejected for both *vacancies* and *training expenditures*. In all other cases, except *unemployment* and *training participants stocks*, we can also reject the null hypothesis of a unit root.

However, it is well known that the Dickey-Fuller test has low power (Maddala, 1992, Chapter 14). This is all the more true the closer the alternative hypothesis is to the null hypothesis of a unit root. To take the *unemployment stock* as an example, it is quite probable that an increase in the *unemployment stock* will persistent for a very long time. Persistence means an autocorrelation coefficient of close to one. This case will be very hard to distinguish from the case of hysteresis (unit root case) where the autocorrelation coefficient is exactly equal to one. Tschernig and Zimmermann (1992) illustrate this point for western Germany. We therefore infer from the Augmented Dickey-Fuller tests that there might be a high degree of persistence in the *unemployment stock*. For theoretical reasons, we do not infer that the *unemployment stock* has a unit root, as we believe that labour markets in the long run tend towards equilibrium. Hence any shocks to the economy which increase unemployment should be reversed in the long run, when unemployment tends back towards its natural rate. Our statistical result for Polish unemployment between 1992 and 1995 can easily be explained by the fact that we only have a relatively short observation period so that these long-run trends are not observable in our data. The same type of reasoning is applied to the *stock of training participants*. Indeed, the *stock of training participants* is very likely to be closely related to the *unemployment stock*. For these reasons, our time-series matching functions will be estimated in levels and not in differences as error correction models (ECMs).

**Matching Function Estimates**

Table 13 reports estimates of ordinary matching functions using both *total outflows from registered unemployment* as well as *outflows from registered unemployment into regular jobs* as the dependent variable. Although *outflow to jobs* should be the dependent variable according to the theory on matching functions, often in empirical studies only *total outflows from unemployment* can be observed. As both variables are available here as time series, we have the opportunity to check what difference it makes to use *total outflows from unemployment* as the dependent variable. However, our results will have to remain tentative, because the observation period is very short.

As the estimates of the ordinary matching functions in Table 13 show, there is almost no qualitative difference between the estimation results using either of the *outflow* measures as the dependent variable. Constant returns to scale are not rejected and the significant coefficients are of similar size in both equations. There is evidence for serial correlation of order 12, though, in the regression with *outflows to jobs* as the dependent variable. Because the number of observations is fairly small, we were not able to get rid off this serial correlation by changing the dynamic structure of the model. The results therefore have to be interpreted with caution, as in the presence of serial correlation and lagged dependent variables, OLS estimates are no longer unbiased nor consistent (Greene, 1997, Chapter 13). However, as the comparison of the two regression results on ordinary matching functions in Table 13 suggests, the bias induced through serial correlation does not seem to be too large. This follows from the fact that the estimation results of the two equations – one with, the other without serial correlation – are fairly similar. It would be an unlikely coincidence if the regression with *outflows to jobs* were severely biased and still yielded similar results to the unbiased regression with *total outflows* as the dependent variable.

Unlike the previous studies on Poland (Boeri, 1994a; 1994b; Boeri and Scarpetta, 1995; Lehmann, 1995; and Kwiatkowski and Tokarski, 1997), we find that *outflows* are exclusively driven by *vacancies* and not by *unemployment*. These studies, however, use panel data. Our result can be explained economically: in the current situation of mass unemployment in Poland, the pool of the unemployed may be so 'crowded' that adding another unemployed worker to the pool may have no effect on the search effectiveness with which firms fill their vacancies. However, below we will see that our panel estimates are more in line with the previous results on Poland as far the relative importance of *unemployment* and *vacancies* in the matching function are concerned.

**Table 13:** Ordinary and Augmented Matching Function Estimates (Training Expenditure)

| Variable | Ordinary matching functions | | | | Augmented matching functions | | | |
|---|---|---|---|---|---|---|---|---|
| | Total outflows | | Outflows to jobs | | Total outflows | | Outflows to jobs | |
| | Coeff. | t-value | Coeff. | t-value | Coeff. | t-value | Coeff. | t-value |
| *ln* outfl. (t-6) | 0.38 | 3.55 | 0.43 | 4.49 | 0.261 | 1.53 | 0.391 | 2.24 |
| *ln* unemp stock (t-1) | -0.30 | -0.58 | 0.50 | 0.86 | 0.389 | 0.77 | 0.738 | 1.10 |
| *ln* vac. (t-1) | 0.94 | 7.67 | 0.97 | 7.00 | 0.767 | 5.49 | 0.866 | 5.38 |
| Train.exp.(t-1) | - | - | - | - | -0.017 | -0.98 | -0.005 | -0.26 |
| Train.exp.(t-2) | - | - | - | - | -0.025 | -1.20 | -0.048 | -2.05 |
| Train.exp.(t-3) | - | - | - | - | 0.05 | 2.05 | 0.032 | 1.10 |
| Train.exp.(t-4) | - | - | - | - | -0.021 | -1.02 | -0.012 | -0.51 |
| Train.exp.(t-5) | - | - | - | - | 0.025 | 1.53 | 0.006 | 0.30 |
| Month | 0.00 | 0.67 | 0.01 | 1.40 | 0.009* | 1.66 | 0.006 | 0.83 |
| First quarter | 0.27 | 3.58 | 0.38 | 4.56 | 0.128 | 1.25 | 0.333 | 2.63 |
| Sec. Quarter | 0.19 | 4.19 | 0.45 | 8.03 | 0.123 | 2.87 | 0.374 | 5.66 |
| Third quarter | -0.01 | -0.20 | 0.09 | 1.40 | -0.098 | -1.63 | 0.052 | 0.66 |
| Constant | 2.08 | 0.54 | -5.15 | -1.17 | -2.301 | -0.65 | -6.366 | -1.35 |
| Adjusted $R^2$ | 0.85 | | 0.87 | | 0.906 | | 0.908 | |
| Observations | 37 | | 37 | | 32 | | 32 | |
| CRS test | 0.96 | | 0.10 | | 0.32 | | 0.067 | |
| Ser. Corr. test | 0.38 | | 0.03 | | 0.002 | | 0.004 | |
| Joint train. test | - | | - | | 0.076 | | 0.213 | |
| Costs in PLZ | - | | - | | 472 | | - | |
| Costs in € | - | | - | | 160 | | - | |

*Note:* shaded coefficients are significant at the 5 percent level, and asterisked coefficients are significant at the 10 percent level; CRS: constant returns to scale; the serial correlation test is the LM test as implemented in *EViews 2.0* and tests for serial correlation of order 12; test results are reported in terms of p-values, which means that the null hypothesis is rejected at the 5 percent significance level if the p-value is smaller than 0.05;
the null hypotheses are *constant returns to scale, no serial correlation, all training variables equal to zero*; the *costs in PLZ* and *costs in €* are the estimated costs to increase the outflow from unemployment by one person (at the mean).

Source: *Polish Ministry of Labour and Social Policy; own calculations.*

**Table 14:** Augmented Matching Function Estimates (Training Participants)

| Variable | With Participants Stocks | | | | With Participants Outflows | | | |
|---|---|---|---|---|---|---|---|---|
| | Total outflows | | Outflows to jobs | | Total outflows | | Outflows to jobs | |
| | Coeff. | t-value | Coeff. | t-value | Coeff. | t-value | Coeff. | t-value |
| *ln* outfl. (t-6) | 0.543 | 2.25 | 0.388 | 2.00 | 0.281 | 2.22 | 0.28 | 2.42 |
| *ln* unempl. Stock (t-1) | 1.078 | 0.82 | 1.661 | 1.22 | 0.24 | 0.37 | 1.186* | 1.68 |
| *ln* vac. (t-1) | 1.072 | 3.99 | 1.024 | 3.76 | 0.863 | 5.38 | 0.888 | 5.42 |
| Tr. part. (t) | - | - | - | - | -0.011 | -1.26 | -0.014 | -1.55 |
| Tr. part. (t-1) | -0.032* | -1.65 | -0.022 | -1.04 | 0.002 | 0.29 | -0.004 | -0.53 |
| Tr. part. (t-2) | 0.018 | 1.15 | 0.014 | 0.82 | -0.008 | -1.03 | -0.02 | -2.42 |
| Tr. part. (t-3) | 0.000 | -0.03 | -0.018 | -1.10 | 0.005 | 0.61 | 0.006 | 0.69 |
| Tr. part. (t-4) | 0.011 | 0.58 | 0.013 | 0.67 | 0.005 | 0.65 | 0.005 | 0.71 |
| Tr. part. (t-5) | -0.004 | -0.23 | 0.004 | 0.21 | 0.002 | 0.26 | -0.004 | -0.51 |
| Tr. part. (t-6) | -0.016 | -0.96 | -0.017 | -0.97 | - | - | - | - |
| Tr. part. (t-7) | 0.006 | 0.32 | -0.009 | -0.48 | - | - | - | - |
| Tr. part. (t-8) | 0.027* | 1.73 | 0.028* | 1.69 | - | - | - | - |
| Tr. part. (t-9) | -0.024 | -1.38 | -0.018 | -0.91 | - | - | - | - |
| Tr. part.(t-10) | 0.019 | 1.04 | 0.008 | 0.40 | - | - | - | - |
| Tr. part.(t-11) | -0.014 | -0.87 | -0.009 | -0.51 | - | - | - | - |
| Tr. part.(t-12) | 0.006 | 0.45 | 0.007 | 0.55 | - | - | - | - |
| Month | 0.005 | 0.75 | 0.013* | 1.87 | 0.006 | 1.52 | 0.011 | 2.44 |
| First quarter | 0.133 | 0.75 | 0.274 | 1.41 | 0.210* | 1.79 | 0.316 | 2.59 |
| Sec. Quarter | 0.159 | 1.15 | 0.464 | 2.87 | 0.187 | 3.38 | 0.449 | 7.25 |
| Third quarter | -0.346* | -1.92 | -0.11 | -0.54 | -0.043 | -0.63 | 0.073 | 0.99 |
| Constant | -10.047 | -0.90 | -14.352 | -1.27 | -1.448 | -0.31 | -9.589* | -1.86 |

**Table 14:** Augmented Matching Function Estimates (Training Participants) (ctd)

| Variable | With Participants Stocks | | With Participants Outflows | |
|---|---|---|---|---|
| | Total outflows | Outflows to jobs | Total outflows | Outflows to jobs |
| Adjusted $R^2$ | 0.8196 | 0.8633 | 0.834 | 0.888 |
| Observations | 31 | 31 | 37 | 37 |
| CRS test | 0.275 | 0.181 | 0.484 | 0.031 |
| Ser. corr. test | 0.000 | 0.001 | 0.765 | 0.072 |
| Joi. train. test | 0.620 | 0.687 | 0.67 | 0.197 |

*Note:* shaded coefficients are significant at the 5 percent level, and asterisked coefficients are significant at the 10 percent level;
CRS: constant returns to scale; the serial correlation test is the LM test as implemented in *EViews 2.0* and tests for serial correlation of order 12; test results are reported in terms of p-values, which means that the null hypothesis is rejected at the 5 percent significance level if the p-value is smaller than 0.05;
Tr. part.: Training participation
the null hypotheses are *constant returns to scale, no serial correlation, all training variables equal to zero.*

Source: *Polish Ministry of Labour and Social Policy; own calculations.*

The second half of Table 13 and Table 14 report augmented matching functions using data on *training expenditure*, *training participants*, and *outflows from training programmes*, respectively. The general features of the matching function are hardly changed by the augmentation. In all cases, the coefficients on *unemployment* is not significantly different from zero. Although the point estimates on the returns to scale are way above *one* in all cases, the constant returns to scale hypothesis cannot be rejected at the 5 percent significance level, except in the specification with *training participants outflows* in Table 14 with *outflows to jobs* as the dependent variable. Unfortunately, all regressions except the ones with *training participants outflows* in Table 14 are potentially contaminated by serial correlation. Again, it was not possible to eliminate the serial correlation through a different specification of the model dynamics. One probably has to wait until data for a longer time period are available before this problem can be resolved.

Joint tests on the *training* variables show insignificance in most specifications. The only exception is *training expenditure* when *total outflows* are used as the dependent variable. Here the cost of letting a worker leave the unemployment pool is estimated to be € 160, which is very low compared to the estimates of other studies summarised in Table 9.[5] On the other hand, when using the more appropriate measure of *outflows into regular jobs*, the *training expenditure* variables are not statistically significant. Moreover, the effect of training is estimated to be negative.

To conclude, we have found only weak evidence for positive effects of training expenditure on the outflows from unemployment. The small number of observations in the time-series data does not allow to draw strong conclusions, though, and makes an analysis of augmented matching functions by panel data attractive. The estimation results for the panel data are discussed in the following section.

### 3.5.2 Panel Evidence on the Effects of Training on the Outflows from Unemployment

In the following, we present estimates of augmented matching functions on our panel data sets. We first discuss the results on the data from the Polish registers and then compare them with the ones from the Polish Labour Force Survey (PLFS). As outlined in Section 3.4, only training programmes are evaluated here, because participation in any other programme is measured as an outflow into employment. Thus estimates on the other programmes would be biased. Because of the large enough sample size, we will nevertheless include current expenditures on the other ALMP programmes as control variables. Some of them turn out to be significant, but they will not be discussed any further because it is difficult to make a statement on the size of the bias.

The results from the unit root tests on the time-series data suggests that we can treat our variables as stationary in the panel context as well. Furthermore, the cross-section dimension dominates the time-series dimension in the panels at hand (*cf.* Breitung, 1997). Therefore, we can be confident that the estimation results will not be spurious due to unit roots.

#### Estimates Based on Register Data

Table 15 and Table 16 show the augmented matching function estimates on the panel data from the Polish registers. The specifications in Table 16 unlike those in

---

[5] This cost is calculated as follows: $\partial T/\partial h \approx 1/(\phi \bar{h})$, where $\phi = \left(1/\left(1-\sum_{i=1}^{l} \rho_i\right)\right) \times (\partial \ln h/T)$. Here, $\phi$ is the estimated long-run training semi-elasticity of outflows from unemployment $h$, $T$ is training expenditure, $l$ is the number of lagged dependent variables, and $\rho_i$ is the coefficient on the lagged dependent variable $h_{t-i}$. $\bar{h}$ indicates the sample mean of $h$. Note that because $\partial \ln h \approx \partial h/h$, we have $\partial T/\partial h \approx 1/(\phi h)$.

Table 15 include lagged dependent variables. Each table reports four regression results: because of the potential endogeneity of training expenditures and the fact that it takes time for these expenditures to become effective, we check whether the exclusion of current expenditure makes any difference to the results. Furthermore, we estimate each specification by both fixed and random effects models. In case the Hausman test does not reject the random effects model, the random effects estimates are more efficient than the fixed effects estimates as outlined in Section 3.3.2.

Unlike in the time-series estimates of the previous section, the coefficient on *unemployment* is significant in all specifications and even larger than the one on *vacancies*. This has also been found in the other studies on Poland using panel data (see Boeri, 1994a; 1994b; Boeri and Scarpetta, 1995; Lehmann, 1995; and Kwiatkowski and Tokarski, 1997). Random effects are rejected in favour of fixed effects in all equations by the Hausman test.

Constant returns to scale in matching are not rejected in the specifications without lagged dependent variables (Table 15). However, they are rejected in favour of increasing returns to scale when lagged dependent variables are included (Table 16). Increasing returns to scale have not been found in previous studies on Poland. However, the difference between our results and those of the other studies summarised above has an econometric explanation. Neither Boeri (1994b), Boeri and Scarpetta (1995), Lehmann (1995), nor Kwiatkowski and Tokarski (1997) control for voivodship effects. They simply estimate pooled panel regressions. Only Boeri (1994a) estimates a random effects model, but he rejects this specification by the Hausman test. Another difference to the other studies on Poland is that they do not include lagged dependent variables.

**Table 15:** Augmented Matching Function Estimates with Register Data without Lagged Dependent Variables

| Variable | With current training expenditure | | | | Without current training expenditure | | | |
|---|---|---|---|---|---|---|---|---|
| | Fixed effects | | Random effects | | Fixed effects | | Random effects | |
| | Coeff. | t-value | Coeff. | t-value | Coeff. | t-value | Coeff. | t-value |
| *ln* unemp.(t-1) | 0.940 | 7.547 | 0.673 | 13.96 | 0.930 | 7.48 | 0.670 | 13.97 |
| *ln* vac. (t-1) | 0.122 | 4.596 | 0.192 | 9.02 | 0.124 | 4.66 | 0.190 | 8.94 |
| Train. exp. | -0.043 | -1.219 | -0.020 | -0.60 | - | - | - | - |
| Train.exp.(t-1) | 0.110 | 3.445 | 0.086 | 2.69 | 0.098 | 3.23 | 0.078 | 2.70 |
| Train.exp.(t-2) | -0.047 | -1.514 | -0.045 | -1.43 | -0.045 | -1.45 | -0.046 | -1.45 |
| Train.exp.(t-3) | 0.052* | 1.759 | 0.055* | 1.95 | 0.062 | 2.15 | 0.057 | 2.04 |

**Table 15**: Augmented Matching Function Estimates with Register Data without Lagged Dependent Variables (ctd)

| Variable | With current training expenditure | | | | Without current training expenditure | | | |
|---|---|---|---|---|---|---|---|---|
| | Fixed effects | | Random effects | | Fixed effects | | Random effects | |
| | Coeff. | t-value | Coeff. | t-value | Coeff. | t-value | Coeff. | t-value |
| IW exp. | -0.021 | -1.072 | -0.021 | -1.20 | -0.024 | -1.27 | -0.023 | -1.30 |
| PW exp. | 0.054 | 3.221 | 0.012 | 0.80 | 0.053 | 3.17 | 0.013 | 0.87 |
| Start-up loans exp. | 0.246 | 6.419 | 0.212 | 5.55 | 0.238 | 6.30 | 0.207 | 5.58 |
| Loans to ent. exp. | -0.005 | -0.138 | -0.032 | -0.90 | -0.016 | -0.48 | -0.038 | -1.13 |
| (fixed time effects omitted) | | | | | | | | |
| Constant | -1.928 | -4.024 | -0.917 | -5.27 | -1.905 | -3.98 | -0.909 | -5.23 |
| $R^2$ overall | 0.831 | | 0.869 | | 0.832 | | 0.869 | |
| $N_i$ | 49 | | 49 | | 49 | | 49 | |
| $N_t$ | 13 | | 13 | | 13 | | 13 | |
| F/LM test | 0.000 | | 0.000 | | 0.000 | | 0.000 | |
| Hausman test | - | | 0.000 | | - | | 0.000 | |
| CRS test | 0.622 | | 0.002 | | 0.670 | | 0.001 | |
| Joint train. test | 0.006 | | 0.023 | | 0.005 | | 0.001 | |
| Costs in PLZ | 1,434 | | 1,371 | | 906 | | 1,167 | |
| Costs in € | 485 | | 464 | | 306 | | 395 | |

*Notes:* shaded coefficients are significant at the 5 percent level; asterisked coefficients are significant at the 10 percent level;
IW.: intervention works; PW.: public works; Ent.: enterprises; CRS: constant returns to scale;
'$R^2$ overall' (as *Stata* calls it) is the correlation between the actual and predicted outflows;
the null hypothesis of the F/LM test is the non-existence of voivodship-specific effects; test results are reported in terms of p-values, which means that the null hypothesis is rejected at the 5 percent significance level if the p-value is smaller than 0.05;
the null hypotheses are *non-existence of voivodship-specific effects; equality of random and fixed effects estimates; constant returns to scale; all training variables equal to zero*;
the *costs in PLZ* and *costs in €* are the estimated costs to increase the outflow from unemployment by one person (at the mean);
the time effects are quarterly dummies.

Source: *Polish Ministry of Labour and Social Policy; own calculations.*

**Table 16:** Augmented Matching Function Estimates with Register Data with Lagged Dependent Variables

| Variable | With current training expenditure | | | | Without current training expenditure | | | |
|---|---|---|---|---|---|---|---|---|
| | Fixed effects | | Random effects | | Fixed effects | | Random effects | |
| | Coeff. | t-value | Coeff. | t-value | Coeff. | t-value | Coeff. | t-value |
| *ln* outfl. (t-1) | 0.315 | 7.78 | 0.376 | 9.92 | 0.315 | 7.78 | 0.376 | 9.94 |
| *ln* outfl. (t-2) | 0.129 | 3.59 | 0.130 | 3.60 | 0.130 | 3.69 | 0.130 | 3.64 |
| *ln* outfl. (t-3) | -0.027 | -0.88 | -0.034 | -1.13 | -0.027 | -0.88 | -0.034 | -1.13 |
| *ln* outfl. (t-4) | 0.141 | 5.72 | 0.131 | 5.55 | 0.141 | 5.72 | 0.131 | 5.57 |
| *ln* unemp.(t-1) | 1.425 | 9.87 | 0.338 | 10.42 | 1.424 | 9.87 | 0.339 | 10.44 |
| *ln* vac. (t-1) | 0.038 | 1.37 | 0.072 | 4.03 | 0.038 | 1.38 | 0.072 | 4.05 |
| Train.exp. | -0.007 | -0.20 | 0.001 | 0.04 | - | - | - | - |
| Train.exp.(t-1) | 0.076 | 2.37 | 0.046 | 1.43 | 0.074 | 2.49 | 0.046 | 1.80 |
| Train.exp.(t-2) | -0.062 | -2.15 | -0.083 | -2.83 | -0.062 | -2.15 | -0.083 | -2.84 |
| Train.exp.(t-3) | 0.065 | 2.39 | 0.042 | 1.68 | 0.067 | 2.52 | 0.042 | 1.68 |
| IW exp. | -0.012 | -0.63 | -0.009 | -0.69 | -0.013 | -0.67 | -0.009 | -0.69 |
| PW exp. | 0.026 | 1.57 | -0.014 | -1.28 | 0.026 | 1.56 | -0.014 | -1.29 |
| Start-up loans exp. | 0.160 | 2.94 | 0.059 | 1.13 | 0.160 | 2.94 | 0.059 | 1.14 |
| Loans to enterpr. exp. | -0.024 | -0.69 | -0.026 | -0.79 | -0.026 | -0.77 | -0.026 | -0.82 |
| | (fixed time effects omitted) | | | | | | | |
| Constant | -4.915 | -8.20 | -0.791 | -7.91 | -4.914 | -8.21 | -0.791 | -7.92 |

**Table 16**: Augmented Matching Function Estimates with Register Data with Lagged Dependent Variables (ctd)

| Variable | With current training expenditure | | Without current training expenditure | |
|---|---|---|---|---|
| | Fixed effects | Random effects | Fixed effects | Random effects |
| $R^2$ overall | 0.8204 | 0.9205 | 0.8204 | 0.9205 |
| $N_i$ | 49 | 49 | 49 | 49 |
| $N_t$ | 12 | 12 | 12 | 12 |
| F/LM test | 0.000 | 0.247 | 0.000 | 0.247 |
| Hausman test | - | 0.000 | - | 0.000 |
| CRS test | 0.000 | 0.565 | 0.000 | 0.559 |
| Joint train. test | 0.020 | 0.076 | 0.009 | 0.037 |
| Costs in PLZ | 638 | 7,206 | 587 | 7,645 |
| Costs in € | 216 | 2,437 | 199 | 2,586 |

*Notes:* shaded coefficients are significant at the 5 percent level; asterisked coefficients are significant at the 10 percent level; IW.: intervention works; PW.: public works; Ent.: enterprises; CRS: constant returns to scale; '$R^2$ overall' (as *Stata* calls it) is the correlation between the actual and predicted outflows;
the null hypothesis of the F/LM test is the non-existence of voivodship-specific effects; test results are reported in terms of p-values, which means that the null hypothesis is rejected at the 5 percent significance level if the p-value is smaller than 0.05; the null hypotheses are *non-existence of voivodship-specific effects; equality of random and fixed effects estimates; constant returns to scale; all training variables equal to zero*; the *costs in PLZ* and *costs in €* are the estimated costs to increase the outflow from unemployment by one person; the time effects are quarterly dummies.

Source: *Polish Ministry of Labour and Social Policy; own calculations.*

The estimates without lagged dependent variables in Table 15 show that *training* has a positive influence on the outflow rate from unemployment. Although the Hausman test always rejects the random effects model in favour of the fixed effects model, the impact of training on outflows from unemployment does not vary very much between the fixed and the random effects models. According to the estimation results without lagged dependent variables, it costs about € 300 to € 500 to reduce unemployment by one person through public training programmes. These estimates are much lower than those for the Czech and Slovak Republics. There, the numbers range between € 1,000 and € 3,500 (*cf.* Burda and Lubyova, 1995; Svejnar, Terrell, and Münich, 1995; Boeri and Burda, 1996).

In the specifications with lagged dependent variables (Table 16), the estimated costs get even smaller down to about € 200 in the fixed effects specifications. The random effects models which estimate a cost around € 2,500 are rejected by the Hausman test. As the lagged dependent variables are significant in all specifications, one may infer that the cost for getting an additional worker into employment through training is around € 200. This estimate is fairly robust to the inclusion of *current training expenditure* amongst the set of regressors. However, as noted in Section 3.3.2, the estimates with lagged dependent variables may be biased. But even if we infer that the costs per outflow through training lie between € 300 to € 500, the conclusion will be that training is comparatively effective.

Given the short observation period, we do not test for structural stability over time. However, the persistent economic diversity of the Polish regions (see Section 2.3 above) warrants to test for structural stability between types of regions. Following Boeri and Scarpetta (1995) and Burda and Profit (1996), we estimate the just presented regressions separately for *modern*, *industrial*, and *agricultural* voivodships, respectively. The geographical distribution of these groups of voivodships has been depicted in the map of Figure 3 in Section 2.3 above. Regression results are presented in Table 17 to Table 22. Except in Table 17 and in the last equation of Table 21, the random effects model is rejected by the Hausman test.

As in our regressions for the whole of Poland, but unlike in Boeri and Scarpetta (1995), constant returns to scale are not rejected in the specifications without lagged dependent variables (Table 17, Table 19, and Table 21). Our coefficients on *unemployment* and *vacancies* for *modern* (diversified) and *agricultural* voivodships are similar to those found in Boeri and Scarpetta (1995) despite of their slightly different classification of the voivodships. In both cases, the coefficient on *unemployment* is around four times as large as the one on *vacancies.* However, for the *industrial* voivodships, the coefficients on the two 'inputs' for the matching process are about equal in Boeri and Scarpetta's (1995) regression, whereas we find the coefficient on *unemployment* to be about eleven times as large as the one on *vacancies.*

When lagged dependent variables are included in the equations, the hypothesis of constant returns to scale is rejected for all types of regions (see, Table 18, Table 20, and Table 22). We can thus substantiate the findings by Boeri and Burda (1996) and Burda and Profit (1996) that a dynamic specification of the matching function can make a decisive difference to the estimation results obtained. For *modern* voivodships (Table 18), the coefficients on the *vacancy* variable are positive again. Yet in the *industrial* voivodships, they are only marginally significantly different from zero.

**Table 17**: Augmented Matching Function Estimates with Register Data without Lagged Dependent Variables - Modern Voivodships

| Variable | With current training expenditure | | | | Without current training expenditure | | | |
|---|---|---|---|---|---|---|---|---|
| | Fixed effects | | Random effects | | Fixed effects | | Random effects | |
| | Coeff. | t-value | Coeff. | t-value | Coeff. | t-value | Coeff. | t-value |
| *ln* unem.(t-1) | 1.070 | 4.36 | 0.611 | 4.31 | 1.070 | 4.36 | 0.625 | 4.51 |
| *ln* vac. (t-1) | -0.017 | -0.21 | 0.175 | 2.96 | -0.028 | -0.36 | 0.176 | 2.99 |
| Train. exp. | 0.081 | 0.97 | 0.056 | 0.58 | - | - | - | - |
| Train.exp.(t-1) | -0.064 | -0.66 | -0.097 | -0.84 | -0.020 | -0.23 | -0.058 | -0.62 |
| Train.exp.(t-2) | 0.087 | 0.89 | 0.046 | 0.39 | 0.085 | 0.87 | 0.048 | 0.41 |
| Train.exp.(t-3) | 0.101 | 1.19 | 0.072 | 0.70 | 0.098 | 1.16 | 0.075 | 0.74 |
| IW exp. | 0.123 | 2.69 | -0.012 | -0.31 | 0.121 | 2.65 | -0.017 | -0.42 |
| PW exp. | 0.054 | 1.07 | 0.002 | 0.03 | 0.052 | 1.04 | 0.000 | 0.00 |
| Start-up loans exp. | 0.302 | 2.05 | -0.031 | -0.20 | 0.313 | 2.13 | -0.026 | -0.17 |
| Loans to enterpr. exp. | -0.035 | -0.32 | -0.213* | -1.80 | -0.001 | -0.01 | -0.190* | -1.72 |
| | (fixed time effects omitted) | | | | | | | |
| Constant | -2.386 | -2.47 | -0.494 | -0.97 | -2.333 | -2.42 | -0.527 | -1.04 |
| $R^2$ overall | 0.417 | | 0.787 | | 0.400 | | 0.786 | |
| $N_i$ | 8 | | 8 | | 8 | | 8 | |
| $N_t$ | 13 | | 13 | | 13 | | 13 | |
| F/LM test | 0.000 | | 0.147 | | 0.000 | | 0.166 | |
| Hausman test | - | | 0.610 | | - | | 0.425 | |
| CRS test | 0.824 | | 0.058 | | 0.861 | | 0.069 | |
| Joint train. test | 0.324 | | 0.788 | | 0.290 | | 0.707 | |

*Notes:* shaded coefficients are significant at the 5 percent level; asterisked coefficients are significant at the 10 percent level;
IW: intervention works; PW: public works; CRS: constant returns to scale;
'$R^2$ overall' (as *Stata* calls it) is the correlation between the actual and predicted outflows;
the null hypothesis of the F/LM test is the non-existence of voivodship-specific effects; test results are reported in terms of p-values, which means that the null hypothesis is rejected at the 5 percent significance level if the p-value is smaller than 0.05;
the null hypotheses are *non-existence of voivodship-specific effects; equality of random and fixed effects estimates; constant returns to scale; all training variables equal to zero*;
the time effects are modelled by quarterly dummies.

Source*: Polish Ministry of Labour and Social Policy; own calculations.*

**Table 18:** Augmented Matching Function Estimates with Register Data with Lagged Dependent Variables - Modern Voivodships

| Variable | With current training expenditure | | | | Without current training expenditure | | | |
|---|---|---|---|---|---|---|---|---|
| | Fixed Effects | | Random Effects | | Fixed Effects | | Random Effects | |
| | Coeff. | t-value | Coeff. | t-value | Coeff. | t-value | Coeff. | t-value |
| *ln* outfl. (t-1) | 0.448 | 4.33 | 0.520 | 4.65 | 0.443 | 4.347 | 0.522 | 4.715 |
| *ln* outfl. (t-2) | 0.216 | 2.79 | 0.168* | 1.71 | 0.216 | 2.81 | 0.168* | 1.72 |
| *ln* outfl. (t-3) | 0.106 | 1.29 | -0.097 | -1.01 | 0.106 | 1.31 | -0.098 | -1.03 |
| *ln* outfl. (t-4) | 0.200 | 2.80 | 0.044 | 0.58 | 0.195 | 2.80 | 0.046 | 0.62 |
| *ln* unem.(t-1) | 2.719 | 6.90 | 0.406 | 2.95 | 2.692 | 7.01 | 0.411 | 3.08 |
| *ln* vac. (t-1) | -0.162 | -2.21 | 0.003 | 0.05 | -0.158 | -2.20 | 0.003 | 0.04 |
| Train.exp. | -0.026 | -0.35 | 0.015 | 0.16 | - | - | - | - |
| Train.ex.(t-1) | -0.029 | -0.36 | -0.095 | -0.94 | -0.044 | -0.63 | -0.085 | -1.07 |
| Train.ex.(t-2) | 0.063 | 0.78 | 0.090 | 0.89 | 0.064 | 0.80 | 0.091 | 0.90 |
| Train.ex.(t-3) | 0.046 | 0.66 | 0.009 | 0.10 | 0.047 | 0.68 | 0.009 | 0.11 |
| IW exp. | 0.027 | 0.62 | -0.004 | -0.12 | 0.029 | 0.67 | -0.005 | -0.15 |
| PW exp. | 0.035 | 0.79 | -0.054 | -1.03 | 0.036 | 0.81 | -0.055 | -1.06 |
| Start-up loans exp. | -0.057 | -0.40 | -0.138 | -0.84 | -0.059 | -0.42 | -0.136 | -0.84 |
| Loans to enterpr. exp. | 0.092 | 0.91 | 0.140 | 1.12 | 0.080 | 0.84 | 0.148 | 1.31 |
| (fixed time effects omitted) | | | | | | | | |
| Constant | -10.551 | -6.08 | -0.769 | -1.53 | -10.438 | -6.16 | -0.787 | -1.62 |

**Table 18:** Augmented Matching Function Estimates with Register Data with Lagged Dependent Variables - Modern Voivodships (ctd)

| Variable | With current training expenditure | | Without current training expenditure | |
|---|---|---|---|---|
| | Fixed Effects | Random Effects | Fixed Effects | Random Effects |
| $R^2$ overall | 0.5731 | 0.8492 | 0.574 | 0.849 |
| $N_i$ | 8 | 8 | 8 | 8 |
| $N_t$ | 12 | 12 | 12 | 12 |
| F/LM test | 0.000 | 0.303 | 0.000 | 0.301 |
| Hausman test | - | 0.016 | - | 0.0001 |
| CRS test | 0.000 | 0.710 | 0.000 | 0.655 |
| Joint train. test | 0.714 | 0.824 | 0.571 | 0.680 |

*Notes:* shaded coefficients are significant at the 5 percent level; asterisked coefficients are significant at the 10 percent level; IW: intervention works; PW: public works; CRS: constant returns to scale; '$R^2$ overall' (as *Stata* calls it) is the correlation between the actual and predicted outflows;

the null hypothesis of the F/LM test is the non-existence of voivodship-specific effects; test results are reported in terms of p-values, which means that the null hypothesis is rejected at the 5 percent significance level if the p-value is smaller than 0.05;

the null hypotheses are *non-existence of voivodship-specific effects; equality of random and fixed effects estimates; constant returns to scale; all training variables equal to zero*;

the time effects are modelled by quarterly dummies.

Source: *Polish Ministry of Labour and Social Policy; own calculations.*

**Table 19:** Augmented Matching Function Estimates with Register Data without Lagged Dependent Variables - Industrial Voivodships

| Variable | With current training expenditure | | | | Without current training expenditure | | | |
|---|---|---|---|---|---|---|---|---|
| | Fixed Effects | | Random Effects | | Fixed Effects | | Random Effects | |
| | Coeff. | t-value | Coeff. | t-value | Coeff. | t-value | Coeff. | t-value |
| *ln* unemp.(t-1) | 1.111 | 5.10 | 0.697 | 7.32 | 0.981 | 4.53 | 0.708 | 6.93 |
| *ln* vac. (t-1) | 0.098 | 2.07 | 0.179 | 4.19 | 0.080* | 1.67 | 0.146 | 3.43 |
| Train. exp. | -0.116 | -2.81 | -0.047 | -1.20 | - | - | - | - |
| Train.exp.(t-1) | 0.065 | 2.02 | 0.072 | 2.17 | 0.050 | 1.533 | 0.058* | 1.85 |
| Train.exp.(t-2) | -0.059* | -1.82 | -0.034 | -1.03 | -0.049 | -1.50 | -0.037 | -1.14 |
| Train. xp.(t-3) | -0.007 | -0.21 | 0.044 | 1.39 | 0.027 | 0.86 | 0.046 | 1.53 |
| IW exp. | -0.063 | -2.34 | -0.060 | -2.30 | -0.086 | -3.28 | -0.075 | -3.04 |
| PW exp. | 0.078 | 3.86 | 0.029 | 1.57 | 0.077 | 3.72 | 0.043 | 2.27 |
| Start-up loans exp. | 0.174 | 4.56 | 0.192 | 4.88 | 0.162 | 4.21 | 0.178 | 4.66 |
| Loans to enterpr. exp. | 0.025 | 0.72 | 0.007 | 0.21 | -0.003 | -0.08 | -0.004 | -0.12 |
| (fixed time effects omitted) | | | | | | | | |
| Constant | -2.484 | -2.80 | -0.929 | -2.56 | -1.996 | -2.25 | -0.957 | -2.43 |

**Table 19:** Augmented Matching Function Estimates with Register Data without Lagged Dependent Variables - Industrial Voivodships (ctd)

| Variable | With current training expenditure | | Without current training expenditure | |
|---|---|---|---|---|
| | Fixed Effects | Random Effects | Fixed Effects | Random Effects |
| $R^2$ overall | 0.853 | 0.860 | 0.806 | 0.854 |
| $N_i$ | 17 | 17 | 17 | 17 |
| $N_t$ | 13 | 13 | 13 | 13 |
| F/LM test | 0.000 | 0.000 | 0.000 | 0.000 |
| Hausman test | - | 0.0202 | - | 0.472 |
| CRS test | 0.348 | 0.165 | 0.782 | 0.120 |
| Joint train. test | 0.020 | 0.120 | 0.271 | 0.160 |
| Costs in PLZ | -894 | 3,063 | 3,838 | 1,540 |
| Costs in € | -302 | 1,036 | 1,298 | 521 |

*Notes:* shaded coefficients are significant at the 5 percent level; asterisked coefficients are significant at the 10 percent level;
IW: intervention works; PW: public works; CRS: constant returns to scale;
'$R^2$ overall' (as *Stata* calls it) is the correlation between the actual and predicted outflows;
the null hypothesis of the F/LM test is the non-existence of voivodship-specific effects; test results are reported in terms of p-values, which means that the null hypothesis is rejected at the 5 percent significance level if the p-value is smaller than 0.05;
the null hypotheses are *non-existence of voivodship-specific effects; equality of random and fixed effects estimates; constant returns to scale; all training variables equal to zero*;
the *costs in PLZ* and *costs in €* are the estimated costs to increase the outflow from unemployment by one person (at the mean);
the time effects are modelled by quarterly dummies.

Source: *Polish Ministry of Labour and Social Policy; own calculations.*

**Table 20**: Augmented Matching Function Estimates with Register Data with Lagged Dependent Variables - Industrial Voivodships

| Variable | With current training expenditure | | | | Without current training expenditure | | | |
|---|---|---|---|---|---|---|---|---|
| | Fixed effects | | Random effects | | Fixed effects | | Random effects | |
| | Coeff. | t-value | Coeff. | t-value | Coeff. | t-value | Coeff. | t-value |
| *ln* outfl. (t-1) | 0.256 | 3.74 | 0.375 | 5.94 | 0.265 | 3.83 | 0.372 | 5.92 |
| *ln* outfl. (t-2) | 0.022 | 0.37 | 0.067 | 1.12 | 0.052 | 0.90 | 0.075 | 1.28 |
| *ln* outfl. (t-3) | -0.002 | -0.04 | 0.020 | 0.38 | -0.004 | -0.08 | 0.016 | 0.30 |
| *ln* outfl. (t-4) | 0.108 | 2.75 | 0.118 | 3.10 | 0.104 | 2.64 | 0.115 | 3.05 |
| *ln* unemp.(t-1) | 1.218 | 4.81 | 0.316 | 5.78 | 1.117 | 4.45 | 0.313 | 5.75 |
| *ln* vac. (t-1) | 0.085* | 1.75 | 0.102 | 3.15 | 0.073 | 1.49 | 0.099 | 3.09 |
| Train. exp. | -0.091 | -2.07 | -0.025 | -0.69 | - | - | - | - |
| Train.exp.(t-1) | 0.073 | 2.05 | 0.079 | 2.26 | 0.053 | 1.53 | 0.066 | 2.25 |
| Train.exp.(t-2) | -0.080 | -2.44 | -0.081 | -2.54 | -0.074 | -2.24 | -0.083 | -2.60 |
| Train.exp.(t-3) | 0.017 | 0.51 | 0.056 | 2.02 | 0.043 | 1.41 | 0.058 | 2.09 |
| IW exp. | -0.032 | -1.13 | -0.032 | -1.54 | -0.045* | -1.65 | -0.036* | -1.82 |
| PW exp. | 0.043 | 1.96 | 0.002 | 0.13 | 0.037* | 1.67 | 0.003 | 0.25 |
| Start-up loans exp. | 0.070 | 1.11 | 0.027 | 0.45 | 0.069 | 1.09 | 0.025 | 0.41 |
| Loans to enterpr. exp. | -0.009 | -0.26 | -0.036 | -1.08 | -0.031 | -0.91 | -0.044 | -1.37 |
| (fixed time effects omitted) | | | | | | | | |
| Constant | -3.969 | -3.71 | -0.711 | -3.79 | -3.639 | -3.40 | -0.690 | -3.74 |

**Table 20:** Augmented Matching Function Estimates with Register Data with Lagged Dependent Variables - Industrial Voivodships (ctd)

| Variable | With current training expenditure | | Without current training expenditure | |
|---|---|---|---|---|
| | Fixed effects | Random effects | Fixed effects | Random effects |
| $R^2$ overall | 0.8312 | 0.9307 | 0.845 | 0.931 |
| $N_i$ | 17 | 17 | 17 | 17 |
| $N_t$ | 12 | 12 | 12 | 12 |
| F/LM test | 0.008 | 0.389 | 0.024 | 0.393 |
| Hausman test | - | 0.021 | - | 0.079 |
| CRS test | 0.014 | 0.959 | 0.030 | 0.808 |
| Joint train. test | 0.027 | 0.031 | 0.080 | 0.017 |
| Costs in PLZ | -791 | 1,527 | 2,752 | 1,069 |
| Costs in € | -268 | 516 | 931 | 362 |

*Notes:* shaded coefficients are significant at the 5 percent level; asterisked coefficients are significant at the 10 percent level; IW: intervention works; PW: public works; CRS: constant returns to scale; '$R^2$ overall' (as *Stata* calls it) is the correlation between the actual and the predicted outflows;
the null hypothesis of the F/LM test is the non-existence of voivodship-specific effects; test results are reported in terms of p-values, which means that the null hypothesis is rejected at the 5 percent significance level if the p-value is smaller than 0.05; the null hypotheses are *non-existence of voivodship-specific effects; equality of random and fixed effects estimates; constant returns to scale; all training variables equal to zero*;
the *costs in PLZ* and *costs in €* are the estimated costs to increase the outflow from unemployment by one person (at the mean); the time effects are modelled by quarterly dummies.

Source: *Polish Ministry of Labour and Social Policy; own calculations.*

**Table 21**: Augmented Matching Function Estimates with Register Data without Lagged Dependent Variables - Agricultural Voivodships

| Variable | With current training expenditure | | | | Without current training expenditure | | | |
|---|---|---|---|---|---|---|---|---|
| | Fixed effects | | Random effects | | Fixed effects | | Random effects | |
| | Coeff. | t-value | Coeff. | t-value | Coeff. | t-value | Coeff. | t-value |
| *ln* unemp.(t-1) | 0.803 | 3.57 | 0.628 | 11.84 | 0.811 | 3.62 | 0.614 | 9.53 |
| *ln* vac. (t-1) | 0.182 | 3.88 | 0.179 | 5.46 | 0.182 | 3.88 | 0.176 | 4.81 |
| Train. exp. | 0.067 | 0.61 | -0.033 | -0.30 | - | - | - | - |
| Train.exp.(t-1) | 0.215* | 1.68 | 0.160 | 1.18 | 0.253 | 2.24 | 0.183* | 1.66 |
| Train.exp.(t-2) | -0.091 | -0.71 | -0.092 | -0.68 | -0.102 | -0.81 | -0.094 | -0.73 |
| Train.exp.(t-3) | 0.124 | 1.11 | 0.007 | 0.06 | 0.118 | 1.06 | 0.048 | 0.44 |
| IW exp. | -0.004 | -0.07 | 0.049 | 1.20 | 0.001 | 0.02 | 0.032 | 0.73 |
| PW exp. | 0.025 | 0.60 | -0.013 | -0.42 | 0.023 | 0.54 | -0.008 | -0.23 |
| Start-up loans exp. | 0.381 | 2.58 | 0.108 | 0.77 | 0.375 | 2.55 | 0.209 | 1.50 |
| Loans to enterpr. exp. | -0.218 | -1.32 | -0.178 | -1.06 | -0.203 | -1.25 | -0.183 | -1.13 |
| (fixed time effects omitted) | | | | | | | | |
| Constant | -1.468* | -1.83 | -0.752 | -4.17 | -1.482* | -1.85 | -0.735 | -3.30 |

**Table 21:** Augmented Matching Function Estimates with Register Data without Lagged Dependent Variables - Agricultural Voivodships (ctd)

| Variable | With current training expenditure | | Without current training expenditure | |
|---|---|---|---|---|
| | Fixed effects | Random effects | Fixed effects | Random effects |
| $R^2$ overall | 0.797 | 0.824 | 0.799 | 0.8216 |
| $N_i$ | 20 | 20 | 20 | 20 |
| $N_t$ | 13 | 13 | 13 | 13 |
| F/LM test | 0.000 | 0.000 | 0.000 | 0.000 |
| Hausman test | - | 0.001 | - | 0.259 |
| CRS test | 0.951 | 0.001 | 0.979 | 0.002 |
| Joint train. test | 0.177 | 0.810 | 0.114 | 0.413 |
| Costs in PLZ | 330 | 2,509 | 389 | 761 |
| Costs in € | 112 | 849 | 131 | 257 |

*Notes:* shaded coefficients are significant at the 5 percent level; asterisked coefficients are significant at the 10 percent level;
IW: intervention works; PW: public works; CRS: constant returns to scale;
'$R^2$ overall' (as *Stata* calls it) is the correlation between the actual and the predicted outflows;
the null hypothesis of the F/LM test is the non-existence of voivodship-specific effects; test results are reported in terms of p-values, which means that the null hypothesis is rejected at the 5 percent significance level if the p-value is smaller than 0.05;
the null hypotheses are *non-existence of voivodship-specific effects; equality of random and fixed effects estimates; constant returns to scale; all training variables equal to zero*;
the *costs in PLZ* and *costs in €* are the estimated costs to increase the outflow from unemployment by one person (at the mean);
the time effects are modelled by quarterly dummies.

Source: *Polish Ministry of Labour and Social Policy; own calculations.*

**Table 22**: Augmented Matching Function Estimates with Register Data with Lagged Dependent Variables - Agricultural Voivodships

| Variable | With current training expenditure | | | | Without current training expenditure | | | |
|---|---|---|---|---|---|---|---|---|
| | Fixed effects | | Random effects | | Fixed effects | | Random effects | |
| | Coeff. | t-value | Coeff. | t-value | Coeff. | t-value | Coeff. | t-value |
| *ln* outfl. (t-1) | 0.257 | 3.60 | 0.301 | 4.89 | 0.260 | 3.63 | 0.301 | 4.89 |
| *ln* outfl. (t-2) | 0.122* | 1.93 | 0.119 | 2.03 | 0.115* | 1.82 | 0.114* | 1.96 |
| *ln* outfl. (t-3) | 0.006 | -0.12 | -0.011 | -0.24 | -0.003 | -0.06 | -0.010 | -0.21 |
| *ln* outfl. (t-4) | 0.171 | 3.99 | 0.168 | 4.30 | 0.171 | 3.98 | 0.169 | 4.31 |
| *ln* unemp.(t-1) | 1.311 | 4.87 | 0.351 | 6.10 | 1.336 | 4.96 | 0.359 | 6.32 |
| *ln* vac. (t-1) | 0.105 | 2.10 | 0.050 | 1.62 | 0.106 | 2.11 | 0.051* | 1.66 |
| Train. exp. | 0.152 | 1.41 | 0.079 | 0.75 | - | - | - | - |
| Train.exp.(t-1) | 0.133 | 1.11 | 0.092 | 0.74 | 0.219 | 2.11 | 0.147 | 1.47 |
| Train.exp.(t-2) | -0.097 | -0.82 | -0.116 | -0.94 | -0.124 | -1.06 | -0.129 | -1.06 |
| Train.exp.(t-3) | 0.066 | 0.64 | -0.054 | -0.54 | 0.051 | 0.50 | -0.052 | -0.53 |
| IW exp. | 0.046 | -0.84 | 0.012 | 0.36 | -0.038 | -0.70 | 0.013 | 0.37 |
| PW exp. | 0.025 | 0.62 | -0.033 | -1.27 | 0.020 | 0.49 | -0.033 | -1.27 |
| Start-up loans exp. | 0.518 | 3.40 | 0.242* | 1.73 | 0.505 | 3.31 | 0.244* | 1.75 |
| Loans to enterpr. exp. | 0.207 | -1.08 | -0.156 | -0.83 | -0.197 | -1.03 | -0.147 | -0.79 |
| (fixed time effects omitted) | | | | | | | | |
| Constant | -4.287 | -4.09 | -0.897 | -5.76 | -4.358 | -4.15 | -0.913 | -5.93 |

**Table 22:** Augmented Matching Function Estimates with Register Data with Lagged Dependent Variables - Agricultural Voivodships (ctd)

| Variable | With current training expenditure | | Without current training expenditure | |
|---|---|---|---|---|
| | Fixed effects | Random effects | Fixed effects | Random effects |
| $R^2$ overall | 0.7429 | 0.8758 | 0.743 | 0.876 |
| $N_i$ | 20 | 20 | 20 | 20 |
| $N_t$ | 12 | 12 | 12 | 12 |
| F/LM test | 0.006 | 0.383 | 0.010 | 0.3671 |
| Hausman test | - | 0.002 | - | 0.002 |
| CRS test | 0.007 | 0.660 | 0.0054 | 0.721 |
| Joint train. test | 0.171 | 0.400 | 0.220 | 0.323 |
| Costs in PLZ | 187 | 37,380 | 325 | -1,315 |
| Costs in € | 63 | 12,643 | 110 | -445 |

*Notes:* shaded coefficients are significant at the 5 percent level; asterisked coefficients are significant at the 10 percent level; IW: intervention works; PW: public works; CRS: constant returns to scale; '$R^2$ overall' (as *Stata* calls it) is the correlation between the actual and the predicted outflows;
the null hypothesis of the F/LM test is the non-existence of voivodship-specific effects; test results are reported in terms of p-values, which means that the null hypothesis is rejected at the 5 percent significance level if the p-value is smaller than 0.05; the null hypotheses are *non-existence of voivodship-specific effects; equality of random and fixed effects estimates; constant returns to scale; all training variables equal to zero*;
the *costs in PLZ* and *costs in €* are the estimated costs to increase the outflow from unemployment by one person (at the mean); the time effects are modelled by quarterly dummies.
Source: *Polish Ministry of Labour and Social Policy; own calculations.*

There is also a difference in the estimated effects of *training* between the three types of regions. The joint test on the *training* variables suggests that there are no effects of training expenditure on the outflows from unemployment in the *modern* voivodships.

For the *industrial* voivodships, the estimates are rather sensitive with respect to the model specification. When *current expenditure on training* is included as a regressor, the fixed effects model estimates a negative training effect, irrespective of whether lagged dependent variables are included or not. Potential endogeneity problems on the one hand, and time lags until training expenditure becomes effective on the other, are reasons why one might want to leave out *current training expenditure* from the set of regressors. We have seen in Table 15 and Table 16, that the inclusion of *current training expenditure* does not make a real difference to the estimation results for the whole of Poland. However, for the *industrial* voivodships (Table 19 and Table 20), the inclusion of *current training expenditure* of the estimates becomes decisive. The estimates with *current training expenditure* suggest that on average, every € 300 spent on training programmes reduce the outflows from unemployment by one person. By contrast, the estimates without *current training expenditure* reveal that training can increase the number of outflows from unemployment. The estimated cost to reduce unemployment by one person through training varies between € 500 (random effects model without lagged dependent variables in Table 19) and € 900 (fixed effect model with lagged dependent variables in Table 20).

In the *agricultural* voivodships, the training variables are jointly (but not necessarily individually) insignificant even at the 10 percent level in all specifications. Only if one is willing to accept statistical significance at lower levels, positive training effects can be detected. Indeed, the point estimates in the fixed effects models with lagged dependent variables in Table 22 are rather astonishing. They would suggest that reducing unemployment by one person in the agricultural voivodships only costs between € 60 and € 110. Although we know that these estimates may be biased due to the inclusion of lagged dependent variables (*cf.* Section 3.3.2), the specifications without lagged dependent variables lead to similar conclusions. At the 12 percent significance level, the fixed effects model without current training expenditure in Table 21 estimates the costs of and additional outflow to be € 130. In the corresponding random effects specification, the estimated costs are higher (€ 260, which is still low), but insignificant.

McCloskey and Ziliak (1996) argue that econometricians should not exclusively focus on the statistical significance of the variables in their models, but concentrate on what is economically significant. The estimates for the agricultural voivodships are a good example for the potential conflict between the two concepts of significance: at standard levels of *statistical* significance, training has no effects at all. However, the 5 or 10 percent significance level, albeit common practice, are arbitrary thresholds for the rejection of a null hypothesis. The point estimates of the costs to reduce unemployment in the agricultural areas of Poland through training programmes are very low. Hence they are of high *economic* significance. It has to be left to the reader whether he or she is willing to accept estimates which are only safe at a 12 percent significance level or lower.

We have not reported the training effects for *modern* voivodships in euro. In the modern areas of Poland, the training variables are not even significantly different from zero at the 50(!) percent significance level (if one ignores the fixed effect estimates of Table 17, which are not efficient according to the Hausman test statistics). We therefore believe that the training variables cannot be given a positive interpretation for the modern voivodships.

Table 23 shows that the differences in the estimated training effects between the *modern*, *industrialised*, and *agricultural* voivodships are not very sharp. We have estimated joint regressions for pairs of two regions. In addition to the set of regressors used above, we have included either all or only the training variables multiplied by a dummy variable with value *one* for the second region and *zero* otherwise. We then use the test on the joint significance of these compound variables as a test on the equality of the coefficients between the two regions in question. A *plus* sign in Table 23 signifies that the coefficients are statistically different at least at the 10 percent level between the two regions. A minus sign stands for no statistical difference.

**Table 23**: Tests of the Equality of Coefficients between Modern, Industrial, and Agricultural Voivodships

| Test | Without lagged dependent variables | | | | With lagged dependent variables | | | |
|---|---|---|---|---|---|---|---|---|
| | With current training | | Without current training | | With current training | | Without current training | |
| | FE | RE | FE | RE | FE | RE | FE | RE |
| *Test of the equality of all coefficients* | | | | | | | | |
| Modern-industrialised | + | (+) | - | (+) | + | + | + | + |
| Modern-agricultural | (+) | + | (+) | + | + | + | + | + |
| Industrialised-agricultural | - | - | - | - | - | - | - | - |
| *Test of the equality of the training coefficients - all other coefficients restricted to be equal between regions* | | | | | | | | |
| Modern-industrialised | + | + | (+) | + | (-) | - | (-) | - |
| Modern-agricultural | - | - | - | - | - | - | - | - |
| Industrialised-agricultural | + | - | - | - | + | (-) | - | (-) |

*Notes:* FE: fixed effects; RE: random effects;
'+' means that the coefficients are significantly different between the specified types of regions at the 5 percent level; '(+)', '(-)', and '-' signify that the coefficients are different at the 10 percent level, just not different at the 10 percent level, and not significantly different, respectively.

Source: *Polish Ministry of Labour and Social Policy; own calculations.*

It is shown that the matching functions as a whole differ between *modern* and *industrialised* regions on the one hand, and *modern* and *agricultural* regions on the other. The matching function for the industrialised and agricultural regions seem not to be statistically distinguishable from each other. If one restricts the matching functions between the regions to be equal in all respects except the training coefficients, one does at least for the specifications without lagged dependent variables hardly observe any difference in the training effect between the regions. These test results suggest that the above-reported differences in the training effects between the modern, industrialised, and agricultural voivodships might be exaggerated. In particular, we cannot say that the training effect differs significantly between the industrialised and agricultural voivodships.

**Table 24**: Tests of the Equality of Coefficients between High, Medium and Low Unemployment Voivodships

| Test | Without lagged dependent variables | | | | With lagged dependent variables | | | |
|---|---|---|---|---|---|---|---|---|
| | With current training | | Without current training | | With current training | | Without current training | |
| | FE | RE | FE | RE | FE | RE | FE | RE |
| *Test of the equality of all coefficients* | | | | | | | | |
| Low U-medium U | - | - | - | - | - | - | - | - |
| Low U-high U | (-) | - | (-) | - | - | - | - | - |
| Medium U-high U | - | - | - | - | - | - | - | - |
| *Test of the equality of the training coefficients – all other coefficients restricted to be equal between regions* | | | | | | | | |
| Low U-medium U | - | - | - | - | - | - | - | - |
| Low U-high U | - | - | - | - | - | - | - | - |
| Medium U-high U | - | - | - | - | - | - | - | - |

*Note:* FE: fixed effects; RE: random effects; U: unemployment.
'+' would mean that the coefficients are significantly different between the specified types of regions at the 5 percent level; '(+)', '(-)', and '-' signify that the coefficients are different at the 10 percent level, just not different at the 10 percent level, and not significantly different, respectively.

Source: *Polish Ministry of Labour and Social Policy; own calculations.*

We have also classified the voivodships into groups of high, medium, and low unemployment regions as shown in Figure 2 of Section 2.3 above. The estimation results for these subgroups are not reported here, but available from the author upon request. Instead, we report the test results for the equality of coefficients between these subgroups in Table 24. As the table shows, there are no significant differences between these types of regions. This is valid for both the tests on all coefficients of the matching function as well as the tests on the training coefficient only.

### Estimates Based on Polish Labour Force Survey Data

Table 25 and Table 26 report the estimation results for the whole of Poland where the *outflow from unemployment* and the *stock of the unemployed* variables are taken from the Polish Labour Force Survey (PLFS). In contrast to the estimates from the register data (Table 15), the Hausman test does not reject the random effects model in the specifications without lagged dependent variables (Table 25). Including lagged dependent variables leads to a rejection, though (Table 26).

Constant returns to scale are generally rejected in favour of decreasing returns, in contrast to our results based on the register data, where we have found constant or increasing returns (Table 15 and Table 16). However, decreasing returns have been found in the previous studies on Poland which have carried out tests on the issue (Boeri, 1994a; Boeri and Scarpetta, 1995).

An interesting finding arises from the comparison between the results with lagged dependent variables in the two data sets (Table 16 and Table 26). The estimated long-run elasticity of outflows with respect to unemployment is much smaller when using labour force survey (PLFS) data than when using register data. Indeed, the significance of the unemployment variable is even called into question from the PLFS data. Our estimation results suggest that the registered unemployed have a higher search effectiveness than the unemployed according to the ILO criteria (not working, looking for work, ready to start work). This finding is consistent with the hypothesis that there are many people on the register who draw unemployment benefits until their entitlement to benefits runs out and then find a job fairly quickly. As the unemployment entitlement period generally lasts 12 months in Poland, one may expect that, on the other hand, many long-term unemployed persons drop off the register after that period and look for jobs through different channels (Boeri, 1994a). If this was true, then the registered unemployed would have a lower long-term unemployment share than the unemployed according to the ILO definition in the PLFS. That the two definitions of unemployment lead to rather distinct unemployment populations has already been demonstrated in Figure 7 on page 61. There it is shown that the number of unemployed according to the ILO definition has a much greater cyclical component than the number of registered unemployed people.

For our purposes, the most important finding from the regressions in Table 25 and Table 26 is that the *training* variables become insignificant at the 5 percent level in all specifications. The insignificance of the training variables is a robust result for the PLFS data: like with the register data, we have also estimated separate regressions for *modern*, *industrial*, *agricultural*, and low, medium, and high unemployment voivodships. In none of the regressions were the training variables significant. The results are not reported here, but can be obtained from the author upon request.

**Table 25**: Augmented Matching Function Estimates with PLFS Data without Lagged Dependent Variables

| Variable | With current training expenditure | | | | Without current training expenditure | | | |
|---|---|---|---|---|---|---|---|---|
| | Fixed effects | | Random effects | | Fixed effects | | Random effects | |
| | Coeff. | t-value | Coeff. | t-value | Coeff. | t-value | Coeff. | t-value |
| *ln* unemp.(t-1) | 0.213 | 1.368 | **0.600** | 6.09 | 0.218 | 1.40 | **0.574** | 5.71 |
| *ln* vac. (t-1) | **0.253** | 2.785 | **0.229** | 3.74 | **0.260** | 2.86 | **0.231** | 3.71 |
| Train. exp. | -0.198* | -1.669 | -0.107 | -1.04 | - | - | - | - |
| Train.exp.(t-1) | 0.103 | 0.946 | 0.138 | 1.33 | 0.048 | 0.46 | 0.085 | 0.93 |
| Train.exp.(t-2) | 0.008 | 0.074 | 0.027 | 0.26 | 0.017 | 0.16 | 0.020 | 0.20 |
| Train.exp.(t-3) | -0.138 | -1.359 | -0.070 | -0.78 | -0.094 | -0.96 | -0.066 | -0.73 |
| IW exp. | -0.026 | -0.400 | -0.017 | -0.33 | -0.042 | -0.65 | -0.023 | -0.45 |
| PW exp. | -0.051 | -0.898 | -0.063 | -1.44 | -0.055 | -0.97 | -0.058 | -1.31 |
| Start-up loans exp. | -0.058 | -0.445 | -0.011 | -0.09 | -0.093 | -0.73 | -0.047 | -0.40 |
| Loans to enterpr. exp. | 0.161 | 1.346 | 0.135 | 1.21 | 0.107 | 0.93 | 0.101 | 0.96 |
| | | | (fixed time effects omitted) | | | | | |
| Constant | **1.531** | 2.389 | -0.096 | -0.26 | **1.438** | 2.25 | -0.019 | -0.05 |
| $R^2$ overall | 0.340 | | 0.431 | | 0.378 | | 0.430 | |
| $N_i$ | 49 | | 49 | | 49 | | 49 | |
| $\bar{N}$ | 12.71 | | 12.68 | | 12.71 | | 12.68 | |
| F/LM test | 0.000 | | 0.000 | | 0.000 | | 0.000 | |
| Hausman test | - | | 0.813 | | - | | 0.933 | |
| CRS test | 0.002 | | 0.030 | | 0.003 | | 0.015 | |
| Joint train. test | 0.392 | | 0.629 | | 0.724 | | 0.679 | |

*Notes:* shaded coefficients are significant at the 5 percent level; asterisked coefficients are significant at the 10 percent level;
IW: intervention works; PW: public works; CRS: constant returns to scale;
'$R^2$ overall' (as *Stata* calls it) is the correlation between the actual and the predicted outflows;
the null hypothesis of the F/LM test is the non-existence of voivodship-specific effects; test results are reported in terms of p-values, which means that the null hypothesis is rejected at the 5 percent significance level if the p-value is smaller than 0.05;
the null hypotheses are *non-existence of voivodship-specific effects; equality of random and fixed effects estimates; constant returns to scale; all training variables equal to zero*;
the time effects are modelled by quarterly dummies.

Source: *Polish Ministry of Labour and Social Policy; own calculations.*

**Table 26:** Augmented Matching Function Estimates with PLFS Data with Lagged Dependent Variables

| Variable | With current training expenditure | | | | Without current training expenditure | | | |
|---|---|---|---|---|---|---|---|---|
| | Fixed effects | | Random effects | | Fixed effects | | Random effects | |
| | Coeff. | t-value | Coeff. | t-value | Coeff. | t-value | Coeff. | t-value |
| *ln* outfl. (t-1) | -0.133 | -2.92 | 0.024 | 0.54 | -0.136 | -2.98 | 0.023 | 0.51 |
| *ln* outfl. (t-2) | -0.099 | -2.33 | 0.029 | 0.67 | -0.100 | -2.34 | 0.027 | 0.64 |
| *ln* outfl. (t-3) | -0.050 | -1.17 | 0.066 | 1.56 | -0.048 | -1.13 | 0.065 | 1.53 |
| *ln* outfl. (t-4) | 0.023 | 0.53 | 0.124 | 2.88 | 0.026 | 0.60 | 0.124 | 2.90 |
| *ln* unemp.(t-1) | 0.282 | 1.63 | 0.486 | 4.25 | 0.299* | 1.73 | 0.484 | 4.23 |
| *ln* vac. (t-1) | 0.188* | 1.94 | 0.159 | 2.73 | 0.196 | 2.02 | 0.153 | 2.64 |
| Train. exp. | -0.207* | -1.69 | -0.127 | -1.14 | - | - | - | - |
| Train.exp.(t-1) | 0.131 | 1.15 | 0.137 | 1.21 | 0.058 | 0.55 | 0.061 | 0.66 |
| Train.exp.(t-2) | 0.028 | 0.27 | 0.026 | 0.25 | 0.036 | 0.35 | 0.013 | 0.13 |
| Train.exp.(t-3) | -0.116 | -1.18 | -0.065 | -0.72 | -0.075 | -0.78 | -0.065 | -0.73 |
| IW exp. | 0.010 | 0.15 | -0.011 | -0.23 | -0.009 | -0.14 | -0.014 | -0.31 |
| PW exp. | -0.084 | -1.42 | -0.068* | -1.69 | -0.090 | -1.52 | -0.063 | -1.58 |
| Start-up loans exp. | 0.010 | 0.06 | 0.074 | 0.40 | 0.007 | 0.04 | 0.058 | 0.31 |
| Loans to enterpr. exp. | 0.242* | 1.95 | 0.146 | 1.24 | 0.184 | 1.54 | 0.104 | 0.92 |
| (fixed time effects omitted) | | | | | | | | |
| Constant | 1.648 | 2.32 | -0.298 | -0.76 | 1.529 | 2.16 | -0.289 | -0.74 |

**Table 26:** Augmented Matching Function Estimates with PLFS Data with Lagged Dependent Variables (ctd)

| Variable | With current training expenditure | | Without current training expenditure | |
|---|---|---|---|---|
| | Fixed effects | Random effects | Fixed effects | Random effects |
| $R^2$ overall | 0.2289 | 0.4386 | 0.280 | 0.437 |
| $N_i$ | 48 | 48 | 48 | 48.000 |
| $\bar{N}_{.}$ | 11.15 | 10.64 | 11.15 | 10.64 |
| F/LM test | 0.000 | 0.002 | 0.000 | 0.003 |
| Hausman test | - | 0.000 | - | 0.000 |
| CRS test | 0.000 | 0.136 | 0.000 | 0.095 |
| Joint train. test | 0.398 | 0.695 | 0.752 | 0.821 |

*Notes:* shaded coefficients are significant at the 5 percent level; asterisked coefficients are significant at the 10 percent level; IW.: intervention works; PW.: public works; CRS: constant returns to scale; '$R^2$ overall' (as *Stata* calls it) is the correlation between the actual and the predicted outflows;
the null hypothesis of the F/LM test is the non-existence of voivodship-specific effects; test results are reported in terms of p-values, which means that the null hypothesis is rejected at the 5 percent significance level if the p-value is smaller than 0.05; the null hypotheses are *non-existence of voivodship-specific effects; equality of random and fixed effects estimates; constant returns to scale; all training variables equal to zero*;

Source: *Polish Ministry of Labour and Social Policy; own calculations.*

To sum up, there is some evidence that training programmes can reduce unemployment in the Polish labour market. However, this result is not very robust. It depends both on the analysed data set and the type of voivodship. Doubts on whether training programmes are of any use at all arise from the Polish Labour Force Survey data. Using this data source we find no effects of training expenditure on outflows to jobs. This is what has been argued in previous papers on Poland (Lehmann, 1995; Puhani and Steiner, 1996; 1997; Kwiatkowski and Tokarski, 1997).

Augmented matching functions for the whole of Poland on register data suggest that the cost of reducing unemployment by one person through training programmes lies between € 300 to € 500. Compared to the estimates of studies on the Czech and Slovak Republics, these figures seem rather low: Burda and Lubyova (1995), Svejnar, Terrell, and Munich (1995), and Boeri and Burda (1996) have estimated this cost to be between € 1,000 and € 3,500. In the previous literature on Poland no positive effects of training could be detected. By identifying positive effects from the register data, we differ from Lehmann (1995), Puhani and Steiner (1996; 1997), and Kwiatkowski and Tokarski (1997). Our analysis by region, however, shows that the positive training effects are mainly to be found in the *industrialised* voivodships, and perhaps also in the *agricultural* ones. It might be an encouraging result that training programmes are effective in those areas where the need to restructure the economy away from the old staple industries and low-tech agriculture is most urgent. These voivodships are not necessarily the ones with the highest unemployment rates, however. Classifying voivodships into three groups according to their unemployment rate shows no differences in the effects of training between low and high unemployment regions.

### 3.5.3 Panel Evidence on the Effects of ALMP Programmes on the Outflows from Employment

In this section, we investigate whether the Polish active labour market programmes have any effects on the outflows from employment to unemployment. On the one hand, ALMPs might encourage outflows from employment through displacement effects as mentioned in the discussion at the beginning of Chapter 3: employers might want to sack workers who are employed without a subsidy in order to take on unemployed people whose wage is partly subsidised. Such displacement effects are therefore most likely to occur due to intervention works, public works, or loans to enterprises.

On the other hand, ALMPs might have a negative impact on outflows from employment to unemployment by preventing workers from being sacked in the first place. *A priori* consideration suggests that such effects may occur through training programmes, intervention and public works schemes, as well as loans to enterprises. Of course, displacement effects can overlap with the prevention of job losses. Hence we are at best able to identify the net result of these two effects with the data at hand.

In order to estimate the effects of ALMPs on the outflows from employment into unemployment, we use data from the PLFS on outflows from employment into unemployment as well as the stock of the employed in each voivodship. Summary statistics for the data have been presented in Table 11 in Section 3.4. Our model specification does not have a compelling theoretical basis as the matching function, but we use a comparable model regressing the outflows from employment into unemployment on the current and past stocks of employment, as well as expenditures on active labour market policies. As before, we also estimate the models with lagged dependent variables. Fixed and random effects models are estimated to control for any time-invariant unexplained heterogeneity between voivodships which cannot be explained otherwise with our data.

The estimation results are presented in Table 27 and Table 34. In all models, the specifications with lagged dependent variables show that their coefficients are significant. The Hausman tests of the orthogonality of the random effects to the regressors show that the random effects models are not rejected in the specification without lagged dependent variables. In the specifications with lagged dependent variables, though, the Hausman statistic always rejects the random effects model (as one may expect, *cf.* our discussion in Section 3.3.2). The table also reports tests on the joint significance of the ALMP variables. If the effects are significant at the 10 percent level, the costs to prevent an additional outflow from employment into unemployment are calculated in Table 35. Positive numbers in Table 35 therefore mean that the ALMP programme in question prevents outflows from employment into unemployment. Negative numbers can be interpreted as evidence for displacement effects.

**Table 27:** Estimation of Outflows from Employment without Lagged Dependent Variables

| Variable | With current ALMP expenditure | | | | Without current ALMP expenditure | | | |
|---|---|---|---|---|---|---|---|---|
| | Fixed Effects | | Random Effects | | Fixed Effects | | Random Effects | |
| | Coeff. | t-value | Coeff. | t-value | Coeff. | t-value | Coeff. | t-value |
| Employment | 2.041 | 3.69 | 1.664 | 3.47 | 1.514 | 2.89 | 1.276 | 2.77 |
| Empl. (t-1) | -2.163 | -3.52 | -2.313 | -3.79 | -1.633 | -2.73 | -1.764 | -3.04 |
| Empl. (t-2) | 1.904 | 2.91 | 1.595 | 2.57 | 1.566 | 2.48 | 1.404 | 2.35 |
| Empl. (t-3) | -0.813 | -1.25 | -1.074* | -1.67 | -0.880 | -1.38 | -1.053* | -1.69 |
| Empl. (t-4) | 0.869 | 1.58 | 0.715 | 1.37 | 0.879* | 1.66 | 0.758 | 1.52 |
| Training | 0.434 | 2.85 | 0.343 | 2.42 | - | - | - | - |
| Training (t-1) | -0.257* | -1.68 | -0.348 | -2.40 | -0.135 | -1.02 | -0.176 | -1.54 |
| Training (t-2) | 0.083 | 0.62 | 0.044 | 0.33 | 0.074 | 0.56 | 0.073 | 0.57 |
| Training (t-3) | 0.095 | 0.67 | 0.043 | 0.31 | 0.024 | 0.18 | 0.010 | 0.08 |
| Training (t-4) | 0.114 | 0.87 | 0.014 | 0.11 | 0.145 | 1.17 | 0.109 | 0.96 |
| Interv. works | -0.217 | -2.40 | -0.142* | -1.70 | - | - | - | - |
| Int.works (t-1) | 0.052 | 0.53 | 0.077 | 0.78 | -0.043 | -0.52 | -0.004 | -0.05 |
| Int.works (t-2) | 0.155 | 1.50 | 0.195* | 1.90 | 0.151 | 1.55 | 0.164* | 1.72 |
| Int.works (t-3) | -0.090 | -0.85 | -0.077 | -0.73 | -0.119 | -1.18 | -0.107 | -1.08 |
| Int.works (t-4) | 0.069 | 0.75 | 0.056 | 0.62 | 0.021 | 0.23 | 0.035 | 0.40 |
| Public works | 0.070 | 0.93 | 0.062 | 0.90 | - | - | - | - |
| Public w. (t-1) | 0.071 | 0.94 | 0.067 | 0.92 | 0.081 | 1.20 | 0.082 | 1.32 |
| Public w. (t-2) | 0.049 | 0.63 | 0.038 | 0.50 | 0.030 | 0.41 | 0.028 | 0.40 |
| Public w. (t-3) | 0.052 | 0.64 | 0.043 | 0.54 | 0.003 | 0.03 | 0.006 | 0.08 |
| Public w. (t-4) | -0.093 | -1.26 | -0.107 | -1.46 | -0.079 | -1.12 | -0.081 | -1.18 |
| Start-up loans | -0.233 | -0.96 | -0.282 | -1.20 | - | - | - | - |
| Start-up l.(t-1) | 0.167 | 0.97 | 0.162 | 0.96 | 0.118 | 0.80 | 0.124 | 0.88 |
| Start-up l.(t-2) | -0.449 | -2.81 | -0.489 | -3.14 | -0.484 | -3.12 | -0.480 | -3.19 |
| Start-up l.(t-3) | -0.009 | -0.06 | -0.061 | -0.39 | 0.009 | 0.06 | 0.013 | 0.09 |
| Start-up l.(t-4) | -0.218 | -1.37 | -0.233 | -1.52 | -0.049 | -0.33 | -0.068 | -0.47 |

**Table 27:** Estimation of Outflows from Employment without Lagged Dependent Variables (ctd.)

| Variable | With current ALMP expenditure | | | | Without current ALMP expenditure | | | |
|---|---|---|---|---|---|---|---|---|
| | Fixed effects | | Random effects | | Fixed effects | | Random effects | |
| | Coeff. | t-value | Coeff. | t-value | Coeff. | t-value | Coeff. | t-value |
| L.to enter. | 0.343 | 2.17 | 0.366 | 2.49 | - | - | - | - |
| L.to enter.(t-1) | 0.129 | 0.89 | 0.140 | 1.03 | 0.170 | 1.21 | 0.230* | 1.78 |
| L.to enter.(t-2) | 0.021 | 0.15 | 0.000 | 0.00 | -0.005 | -0.04 | 0.021 | 0.16 |
| L.to enter.(t-3) | -0.063 | -0.47 | -0.097 | -0.74 | -0.018 | -0.14 | -0.019 | -0.14 |
| L.to enter.(t-4) | -0.203 | -1.49 | -0.216* | -1.66 | -0.132 | -1.03 | -0.127 | -1.02 |
| (fixed time effects omitted) | | | | | | | | |
| Constant | -9.152 | -2.05 | -1.748 | -3.55 | -7.000* | -1.66 | -2.273 | -3.83 |
| $R^2$ overall | 0.271 | | 0.361 | | 0.270 | | 0.330 | |
| $N_i$ | 49 | | 49 | | 49 | | 49 | |
| $\bar{N}$ | 11.41 | | 11.31 | | 12.35 | | 12.23 | |
| F/LM test | 0.000 | | 0.000 | | 0.000 | | 0.000 | |
| Hausman test | - | | 0.999 | | - | | 1.000 | |
| Joint test on training | 0.033 | | 0.120 | | 0.380 | | 0.405 | |
| Joint test on IW | 0.130 | | 0.075 | | 0.602 | | 0.321 | |
| Joint test on PW | 0.364 | | 0.197 | | 0.427 | | 0.348 | |
| Joint test on start-up loans | 0.056 | | 0.004 | | 0.028 | | 0.016 | |
| Joint test on loans to ent. | 0.156 | | 0.050 | | 0.640 | | 0.390 | |

*Notes:* shaded coefficients are significant at the 5 percent level; asterisked coefficients are significant at the 10 percent level;
IW: intervention works; PW: public works; ent.: enterprises;
'$R^2$ overall' (as *Stata* calls it) is the correlation between the actual and the predicted outflows;
the null hypothesis of the F/LM test is the non-existence of voivodship-specific effects; test results are reported in terms of p-values, which means that the null hypothesis is rejected at the 5 percent significance level if the p-value is smaller than 0.05;
the null hypotheses are *non-existence of voivodship-specific effects; equality of random and fixed effects estimates; all training etc. variables equal to zero*;
the time effects are modelled by quarterly dummies.

Sources: *PLFS; Polish Ministry of Labour and Social Policy; own calculations.*

**Table 28**: Estimation of Outflows from Employment with Lagged Dependent Variables

| Variable | With current ALMP expenditure | | | | Without current ALMP expenditure | | | |
|---|---|---|---|---|---|---|---|---|
| | Fixed effects | | Random effects | | Fixed effects | | Random effects | |
| | Coeff. | t-value | Coeff. | t-value | Coeff. | t-value | Coeff. | t-value |
| Outflows from empl. (t-1) | -0.103 | -2.11 | 0.114 | 2.48 | -0.104 | -2.17 | 0.107 | 2.36 |
| Outflows from empl. (t-2) | -0.211 | -4.39 | -0.045 | -0.96 | -0.218 | -4.66 | -0.040 | -0.88 |
| Outflows from empl. (t-3) | -0.055 | -1.14 | 0.088* | 1.87 | -0.063 | -1.33 | 0.109 | 2.39 |
| Outflows from empl. (t-4) | -0.040 | -0.80 | 0.112 | 2.38 | -0.047 | -0.99 | 0.113 | 2.49 |
| Employment | 2.378 | 3.87 | 2.042 | 3.74 | 1.737 | 2.93 | 1.599 | 2.98 |
| Empl. (t-1) | -2.503 | -3.63 | -3.130 | -4.34 | -1.862 | -2.75 | -2.465 | -3.49 |
| Empl. (t-2) | 2.619 | 3.54 | 2.568 | 3.44 | 2.293 | 3.16 | 2.328 | 3.16 |
| Empl. (t-3) | -1.327* | -1.82 | -1.718 | -2.25 | -1.302* | -1.80 | -1.747 | -2.31 |
| Empl. (t-4) | 0.818 | 1.34 | 0.618 | 1.05 | 0.906 | 1.54 | 0.673 | 1.17 |
| Training | 0.411 | 2.67 | 0.339 | 2.28 | - | - | - | - |
| Training (t-1) | -0.180 | -1.16 | -0.321 | -2.09 | -0.068 | -0.51 | -0.156 | -1.34 |
| Training (t-2) | 0.148 | 1.08 | 0.077 | 0.54 | 0.125 | 0.92 | 0.128 | 0.91 |
| Training (t-3) | 0.052 | 0.37 | -0.009 | -0.06 | 0.004 | 0.03 | -0.056 | -0.39 |
| Training (t-4) | 0.161 | 1.24 | 0.006 | 0.05 | 0.179 | 1.45 | 0.096 | 0.82 |
| Interv. works | -0.222 | -2.41 | -0.151* | -1.75 | - | - | - | - |
| Interv. w. (t-1) | 0.039 | 0.39 | 0.093 | 0.89 | -0.050 | -0.58 | 0.030 | 0.37 |
| Interv. w. (t-2) | 0.153 | 1.46 | 0.199* | 1.82 | 0.130 | 1.30 | 0.150 | 1.44 |
| Interv. w. (t-3) | -0.117 | -1.09 | -0.097 | -0.86 | -0.150 | -1.45 | -0.123 | -1.13 |
| Interv. w. (t-4) | 0.107 | 1.12 | 0.082 | 0.83 | 0.062 | 0.67 | 0.060 | 0.63 |
| Public works | 0.063 | 0.83 | 0.053 | 0.75 | - | - | - | - |
| Public w. (t-1) | 0.100 | 1.34 | 0.079 | 1.02 | 0.112* | 1.64 | 0.087 | 1.36 |
| Public w. (t-2) | 0.077 | 0.98 | 0.025 | 0.31 | 0.058 | 0.78 | 0.021 | 0.27 |
| Public w. (t-3) | 0.088 | 1.08 | 0.039 | 0.46 | 0.042 | 0.53 | 0.001 | 0.02 |
| Public w. (t-4) | -0.077 | -1.02 | -0.128* | -1.64 | -0.060 | -0.83 | -0.097 | -1.30 |

**Table 28:** Estimation of Outflows from Employment with Lagged Dependent Variables (ctd)

| Variable | With current ALMP expenditure | | | | Without current ALMP expenditure | | | |
|---|---|---|---|---|---|---|---|---|
| | Fixed effects | | Random effects | | Fixed effects | | Random effects | |
| | Coeff. | t-value | Coeff. | t-value | Coeff. | t-value | Coeff. | t-value |
| Start-up loans | -0.256 | -1.04 | -0.319 | -1.31 | - | - | - | - |
| Start-up l.(t-1) | 0.205 | 1.19 | 0.194 | 1.10 | 0.149 | 1.01 | 0.122 | 0.83 |
| Start-up l.(t-2) | -0.471 | -2.93 | -0.543 | -3.31 | -0.502 | -3.20 | -0.554 | -3.41 |
| Start-up l (t-3) | -0.006 | -0.04 | -0.023 | -0.14 | -0.005 | -0.03 | 0.054 | 0.33 |
| Start-up l.(t-4) | -0.290* | -1.78 | -0.202 | -1.24 | -0.105 | -0.68 | -0.056 | -0.36 |
| L. to enterpr. | 0.376 | 2.41 | 0.357 | 2.35 | - | - | - | - |
| L.to enter.(t-1) | 0.177 | 1.22 | 0.116 | 0.83 | 0.201 | 1.44 | 0.221* | 1.67 |
| L.to enter.(t-2) | 0.072 | 0.52 | 0.004 | 0.03 | 0.067 | 0.50 | 0.029 | 0.21 |
| L.to enter.(t-3) | -0.050 | -0.37 | -0.130 | -0.94 | -0.002 | -0.01 | -0.073 | -0.54 |
| L.to enter.(t-4) | -0.181 | -1.33 | -0.210 | -1.56 | -0.105 | -0.82 | -0.132 | -1.00 |
| (fixed time effects omitted) | | | | | | | | |
| Constant | -9.371* | -1.83 | -1.104 | -2.56 | -8.356 | -1.72 | -1.387 | -3.18 |
| $R^2$ overall | 0.235 | | 0.383 | | 0.221 | | 0.349 | |
| $N_i$ | 47 | | 47 | | 48 | | 48 | |
| $\bar{N}$ | 10.32 | | 9.10 | | 10.94 | | 8.25 | |
| F/LM test | 0.000 | | 0.259 | | 0.000 | | 0.101 | |
| Hausman test | - | | 0.000 | | - | | 0.000 | |

**Table 28:** Estimation of Outflows from Employment with Lagged Dependent Variables (ctd.)

| Variable | With current ALMP expenditure | | Without current ALMP expenditure | |
|---|---|---|---|---|
| | Fixed effects | Random effects | Fixed effects | Random effects |
| Joint test on training | 0.029 | 0.206 | 0.335 | 0.622 |
| Joint test on IW | 0.108 | 0.038 | 0.586 | 0.123 |
| Joint test on PW | 0.088 | 0.183 | 0.161 | 0.325 |
| Joint test on start-up loans | 0.025 | 0.004 | 0.017 | 0.008 |
| Joint test on loans to ent. | 0.084 | 0.076 | 0.556 | 0.415 |

*Notes:* shaded coefficients are significant at the 5 percent level; asterisked coefficients are significant at the 10 percent level;
empl.: employment; IW: intervention works; PW: public works; ent.: enterprises;
'$R^2$ overall' (as *Stata* calls it) is the correlation between the actual and the predicted outflows;
the null hypothesis of the F/LM test is the non-existence of voivodship-specific effects; test results are reported in terms of p-values, which means that the null hypothesis is rejected at the 5 percent significance level if the p-value is smaller than 0.05;
the null hypotheses are *non-existence of voivodship-specific effects; equality of random and fixed effects estimates; all training etc. variables equal to zero*;
the time effects are modelled by quarterly dummies.

Sources: *PLFS; Polish Ministry of Labour and Social Policy; own calculations.*

**Table 29**: Estimated Costs in Euro to Keep a Person Employed through ALMPs

| ALMP programme | Without lagged dependent variables | | | |
|---|---|---|---|---|
| | With current ALMP expenditure | | Without current ALMP expenditure | |
| | Fixed effects | Random effects | Fixed effects | Random effects |
| Training | -91 | **(-444)** | - | - |
| Intervention works | (1388) | **-392*** | - | - |
| Public works | - | - | - | - |
| Start-up loans | 57* | **47** | 105 | **104** |
| Loans to enterprises | - | **-221** | - | - |
| | With lagged dependent variables | | | |
| Training | **-101** | - | - | - |
| Intervention works | **1460** | -249 | - | -257 |
| Public works | **-238*** | - | - | - |
| Start-up loans | **73** | 35 | **132** | 70 |
| Loans to enterprises | **-152*** | -227* | - | - |

*Notes:* Numbers with an asterisk are only significant at the 10 percent level. Numbers in brackets are just about not significant at the 10 percent level; numbers without brackets and asterisks are significant at the 5 percent level; if a number is negative, it might be interpreted as evidence in favour of displacement effects;
the bold numbers indicate the preferred models (fixed or random effects) as indicated by the Hausman test;
we generally prefer the models without current ALMP expenditure (4[th] and 5[th] columns) because they are less likely to be affected by endogeneity bias.

Sources: *PLFS; Polish Ministry of Labour and Social Policy; own calculations.*

There is only evidence for displacement effects if current ALMP expenditure is included in the set of regressors. In these specifications, we find displacement effects for training and loans to enterprises. In the specification without lagged dependent variables, there is also weakly significant evidence for displacement effects in intervention works. But the sign of the effect changes when lagged dependent variables are included. In this case, there is also weakly significant evidence for displacement effects in public works. For training, it seems that an additional € 100 spent on the programmes leads one more worker being displaced. If we just consider the rough size of the estimate and compare it with the estimates of the training effect on outflows from unemployment, we come to the conclusion that training just turns over the unemployment pool. However, this interpretation should not be taken too seriously, as we see that the displacement effect disappears completely if we strike out *current training expenditure* from our model. It is in fact quite probable that ALMP expenditures increase when more people lose their jobs. In this case, current ALMP expenditure is an endogenous variable and its coefficient is likely to be severely upward biased (*i.e.* the estimated cost in Table 29 is downward biased). This point applies to training as well as to public works and loans to enterprises. It is nevertheless interesting to observe that we have some weak evidence on displacement effects in loans for enterprises. As we have seen in our discussion of Section 2.4, these loans are tied to the precondition that the firm receiving the loan has not reduced its employment for the last 12 months. If there are displacement effects, then firms have found a way to circumvent the spirit of this programme by sacking some of their labour force a little later. Yet it should be stressed again that an alternative explanation for the finding of displacement effects is that the statistical results merely reflect endogeneity bias. This view is substantiated by the fact that no displacement effects can be discerned from the estimates without current ALMP expenditures.

We can draw firmer conclusions on *start-up loans* as programmes that can prevent unemployment from occurring in the first place. Why start-up loans should prevent outflows from employment may seem peculiar. An explanation can be that most people receiving loans quit their old jobs as employees and more or less directly become self-employed. As our data are collected quarterly, the period between job switches must be under 3 months to make this hypothesis consistent with the estimation results. Our estimates without current expenditure suggest that start-up loans are a rather cheap way to keep people off the dole. The estimated costs per person kept in employment range between € 100 and € 130. The estimated costs in the other (not preferred) specifications are even lower.

In sum, we do not interpret the results from this section as evidence in favour of displacement effects. The estimates which suggest such effects seem to be biased due to the endogeneity of ALMP expenditures. Instead, we have found that start-up loans can prevent people from becoming unemployed. The estimated costs to keep a person in employment through start-up loans lie between € 100 and € 130, which is very low. However, self-employment is only an option for the more capable amongst the unemployed and can therefore only be applied successfully on a small scale.

## 3.6 Conclusions from the Macroeconometric Analysis

In Chapter 3 we have analysed the Polish active labour market programmes from a macroeconomic point of view. We estimated the effects of training programmes on the outflows from unemployment and the effects of all ALMP programmes on the outflows from employment. The variety of specifications we presented has been revealing. In contrast to other studies on Poland, we have shown that it can make a difference to the estimates whether current ALMP expenditure is excluded from the set of regressors to reduce the endogeneity problem, whether lagged dependent variables are included to take account of the dynamics, and whether fixed or random effects models are estimated.

The empirical evidence from both the time-series as well as the panel data gives some tentative support to the view that public training programmes can be used to reduce unemployment. In the specifications where significant effects of training programmes can be detected, the average cost to reduce unemployment by one person in Poland through training programmes lies between € 200 and € 500. That these costs are comparatively low in relation to the estimates for the Czech and Slovak Republic (between € 1,000 and € 3,000) speaks in favour of the Polish training programmes. Our regional analysis has shown that the costs to reduce unemployment through training are higher in the *industrial* voivodships (between € 500 and € 900), than in the *agricultural* ones (around € 100). No effects of training could be detected in the *modern* voivodships.

It also has to be stressed that positive training effects can only be found when using register data. All model specifications that use Polish labour force survey (PLFS) data suggest that training has no effect on the outflows from unemployment. One explanation of the sensitivity of the estimates with respect to the data set can be the imprecision with which outflows from unemployment are measured in some voivodships in the PLFS. Another explanation can be the different definitions of unemployment in the two data sets. The register unemployment data may include less long-term unemployed people than the PLFS data, because they might drop off the register after unemployment benefits run out. Our estimates of the coefficients on the *unemployment stock* in the matching functions are consistent with this hypothesis, which leads to the conclusion that training works better for the more able amongst the unemployed (as positive training effects are only found with the register data). This is unsurprising as training requires the ability to acquire new knowledge.

To test whether ALMP programmes have any displacement effects, or whether they can prevent unemployment to occur in the first place, we have estimated the effects of the programmes on the outflows from employment into unemployment. We have found no convincing evidence on displacement effects. However, start-up loans seem to be able to keep down the number of people who join the dole queue. Nevertheless, those people who dare to take out a loan in order to run their own business are only a small group and so the small costs estimated to keep a person in employment through start-up loans (between € 100 and € 130) should not be interpreted as safe evidence that an expansion of start-up loans would be successful. In addition, more empirical evidence would be required on start-up loans, especially on the type and length of self-employment, before any firm statements should be made.

# 4 Microeconometric ALMP Evaluation: Methodological Issues and Previous Work

Macroeconometric approaches to ALMP evaluation are fairly recent. Microeconometric evaluations have a slightly longer tradition, especially in the United States, where evaluation has mostly focused on the earnings effect of training programmes (Riddell, 1991; Leigh, 1995, Chapter 3). Studies on transition countries, on the other hand, have mostly concentrated on re-employment effects of ALMPs, as we will see below. The reason for this difference in focus lies in the distinct labour market situations in the United States on the one hand, and in the transition economies on the other. Whereas the incidence of long-term unemployment is fairly low in the U.S. (around 10 percent in total unemployment), it is one of the major problems in the labour markets in transition (around 30 to 40 percent in total unemployment, *cf.* Section 2.2). As a consequence, active labour market policies in transition countries have been designed to address the long-term unemployment problem and we will evaluate Polish ALMPs on this criterion in our microeconometric analysis.

Although micro- as macroeconometric studies face similar difficulties in addressing the endogeneity of the ALMP variables, the availability of a large number of observations makes it easier to address the endogeneity problem in microeconometric studies. In the microeconometric context, the endogeneity problem arises from the fact that ALMP participants are a selected group and are thus not directly comparable to the non-participants in general. The endogeneity problem is thus a sample selection problem.

In Sections 4.1 to 4.5 we present a general discussion of how the selection problem that permeates the evaluation literature can be addressed. Section 4.1 introduces the reader to the nature of the selection problem and shows why randomised social experiments can in theory solve this problem. The practical issues of using experimental versus non-experimental data are discussed in Section 4.2. We only have non-experimental data for Poland. Sections 4.3 and 4.4 therefore present two rather distinct ways to tackle the sample selection problem in this context. One is the statistical matching[6] approach that has been developed in the statistical literature. The other is traditional econometric model building. Both approaches have been applied in the previous literature on transition economies, which is surveyed in Section 4.6. The two approaches will subsequently be applied for Poland in Chapter 5.

---

[6] This has nothing to do with the matching function of the previous chapter.

## 4.1 The Sample Selection Problem and the Theoretical Case for an Experiment

The fundamental problem of estimating causal effects of labour market programmes is that the outcome variable for an individual is never observed in both states of the world: treatment (participation in the ALMP programme) and non-treatment (non-participation). To illustrate this point, let the outcome of a training programme one tries to evaluate be the re-employment opportunity of an unemployed person. For an unemployed person who has participated in a training programme, the causal effect of that participation is the difference in his or her re-employment opportunity with training to his or her re-employment opportunity without training. Of course, his or her re-employment opportunity without training is counterfactual and therefore unobservable. Similarly, for a person who has not participated in a training course, the outcome had the person participated is counterfactual. For this reason, the causal effect of a programme can never be observed. In this sense, the problem of estimating the causal effects of labour market programmes is a missing data problem (Rosenbaum and Rubin, 1983).

More formally, we can define the treatment effect for person $i$ as:

$$\tau_i = Y_{i1} - Y_{i0}$$

where $i$ is an index running over the individuals in the population. $Y_{i1}$ is the hypothetical value of the outcome variable (say unemployed or not) when person $i$ gets treatment (*e.g.* a training course), and $Y_{i0}$ is the hypothetical value of the outcome variable when the same person does not receive treatment. Each person has in theory both a $Y_{i1}$ and a $Y_{i0}$. However, for programme participants only $Y_{i1}$ is observable, and $Y_{i0}$ is counterfactual. On the other hand, for non-participants only $Y_{i0}$ is observable, and $Y_{i1}$ is counterfactual.

To make microeconometric models tractable, one generally assumes that the treatment effect $\tau_i$ for each person is independent of the treatment of other units. This is termed the *assumption* of a *stable unit-treatment value* (SUTVA, Rubin, 1980) and guarantees that average treatment effect can be estimated independently of the size and composition of the treatment population. Indeed, if the treatment population is comparatively small, externalities (*cf.* our introduction to Chapter 3) that might violate the *stable unit-treatment value assumption* are less likely to occur.

Under the SUTVA, the average, or expected, treatment effect in the population can simply be written

$$\begin{aligned} \tau &= E(\tau_i) \\ &= E(Y_{i1}) - E(Y_{i0}) \end{aligned}$$

which can be expressed in terms of conditional expectations (Dehejia and Wahba, 1995a):

$$\begin{aligned}\tau &= \left[E(Y_{i1}|T_i=1)\Pr(T_i=1)+E(Y_{i1}|T_i=0)\Pr(T_i=0)\right]\\ &\quad-\left[E(Y_{i0}|T_i=0)\Pr(T_i=0)+E(Y_{i0}|T_i=1)\Pr(T_i=1)\right]\end{aligned}$$

where $T_i$ indicates whether a person has actually received treatment $(T_i=1)$ or not $(T_i=0)$. $E(Y_{i1}|T_i=1)$ describes the expected value of the outcome variable with treatment for the subpopulation of those people who actually were subject to treatment. $E(Y_{i0}|T_i=1)$, on the other hand, describes the expected value of the hypothetical outcome without treatment for the subpopulation of those people who actually were subject to treatment. Clearly, $E(Y_{i1}|T_i=0)$ and $E(Y_{i0}|T_i=1)$ are counterfactual. What we observe in reality are the expected values $E(Y_{i1}|T_i=1)$ and $E(Y_{i0}|T_i=0)$. We may therefore form the following estimate of $\tau$:

$$\begin{aligned}&\hat{\tau}=\overline{Y}_{i1|T_i=1}-\overline{Y}_{i0|T_i=0}\quad \textit{with}\\ &E(\hat{\tau})=E(Y_{i1}|T_i=1)-E(Y_{i0}|T_i=0).\end{aligned}$$

$\hat{\tau}$ is an unbiased estimate of $\tau$ if

$$\begin{aligned}&E(Y_{i1}|T_i=1)=E(Y_{i1}|T_i=0)\quad \textit{and}\\ &E(Y_{i0}|T_i=0)=E(Y_{i0}|T_i=1).\end{aligned}\qquad [4.\ 1]$$

This is because in this case

$$\begin{aligned}\tau &= E(Y_{i1}|T_i=1)\left[\Pr(T_i=1)+\Pr(T_i=0)\right]-E(Y_{i0}|T_i=0)\left[\Pr(T_i=1)+\Pr(T_i=0)\right]\\ &= E(Y_{i1}|T_i=1)-E(Y_{i0}|T_i=0)=E(\hat{\tau})\\ \Leftrightarrow&\quad E(\hat{\tau})=\tau.\end{aligned}$$

Clearly, if actual assignment to treatment $(T_i=1)$ is random across the population, the conditions [4. 1] are fulfilled. More formally, random assignment of treatment across the population means that

$$\Pr(T_i=1|\mathbf{z}=\mathbf{z}_i)=\Pr(T_i=1|\mathbf{z}=\mathbf{z}_j)\quad \forall \mathbf{z}_i,\mathbf{z}_j$$

where $\mathbf{z}$ denotes a vector of individual characteristics or attributes (as they are called in the statistical literature). Hence, if assignment to treatment is completely random, we would not expect any differences between $E(Y_{i1}|T_i=1)$ and $E(Y_{i1}|T_i=0)$ on the one hand, and $E(Y_{i0}|T_i=0)$ and $E(Y_{i0}|T_i=1)$ on the other.

Therefore, treatment assignment becomes ignorable (Rubin, 1974) such that $\hat{\tau}$ is an unbiased estimate of $\tau$.

There is therefore a strong theoretical case for carrying out social experiments, in which treatment (ALMP participation) is randomly assigned. At least in theory, experiments assure that an unbiased estimate of $\tau$ can be obtained.

It is important to note that in many cases, one does not dispose of experimental data. In Europe, to our knowledge only the UK and the Nordic countries have ever carried out randomised experiments. However, Romania will probably start a social experiment soon in co-operation with the World Bank. In Poland, assignment to treatment, *i.e.* active labour market programmes, does not occur randomly, but through the choice of labour office officials. The people proposed for an ALMP programme also have the choice whether they want to participate or not. The selection process of treatment assignment is thus rather involved. Data from such non-randomised situations are called *non-experimental* or *observational* data. The practical issues of using experimental versus non-experimental data will be discussed in the following section.

## 4.2 What Can We Do with Non-Experimental Data?

In a stylised way, the evaluation community can be divided into two schools. One school believes that the only valid method to evaluate social programmes is by way of randomised social experiments. The other group argues that proper evaluations can be carried out using non-experimental data with appropriate econometric methods. The debate between these two views is both theoretical and empirical. On the theoretical level, various arguments are made on the representative character of experimental studies. On the empirical level, results of experimental and non-experimental studies are compared with each other. Here, the experimental studies are usually taken as the benchmark, or the 'correct' estimates. It is then attempted to reproduce the results from the experiment with non-experimental methods.

In the Polish case, we have no choice between using experimental or non-experimental data. We are forced to do something with the non-experimental data at hand. However, it is important to discuss the pros and cons of non-experimental evaluation in order to put our results into perspective. The claim that not much can be said without an experiment of course launches a heavy attack on any non-experimental evaluation as the one that will follow in Chapter 5. We therefore feel the need to lay the arguments against as well as in favour of our non-experimental approach open.

**Arguments that Speak in Favour of Experimental Data**

The most fundamental theoretical argument in favour of carrying out social experiments has already been mentioned in Section 4.1: by assigning people randomly to the programmes to be evaluated, one can at least in theory guarantee that treatment assignment is ignorable. If treatment is not assigned randomly but through real-world mechanisms like applicants being chosen by labour office officials according to some interpretable guidelines, any attempt to pick appropriate comparison persons from the pool of the non-treated has to rely on some sort of good guess whatever the selection mechanism into treatment might have been. This good guess might be carefully wrought out. Guidelines for labour office officials selecting programme participants can be studied. Labour office officials can be interviewed on their actual practices of participant selection. On the basis of this information, econometric techniques can be used to estimate a model of programme selection. Such models can even identify selection mechanisms that were not conceived of by policy makers by controlling for a wide range of observed variables. This estimate of the programme selection equation may then be used to correct for sample selection in one way or another.

However, one can argue that even the most carefully specified procedure to correct for sample selection has to contain an element of arbitrariness. It will have to be arbitrary because in no case will the actual selection mechanism be known. This is not only true for the personal characteristics which govern the selection process. It is also true for the way (functional form) in which these characteristics or attributes drive the programme participation. *Item*, the evaluator in practice will have to do with the variables he or she can observe in his or her data set. Many characteristics important for participation in a programme are likely to be unobservable for the researcher, though. This is true first, because traits like motivation cannot be correctly measured in practice. Second, many data sets that are used for evaluations have been designed for other purposes, so that at lot of useful variables that could have been measured are not collected.

In econometric terms, the problems just outlined mean that the evaluator trying to work with non-experimental data will have no idea on the correct functional form and face heavy problems of missing variables. As a result, one has to expect biased estimates even when estimating the selection equation used to correct for selection bias. Furthermore, most methods developed in the literature to correct for sample selection (Heckman, 1976; 1978; 1979) rest on heroic and untestable assumptions about the distributions of unobserved covariates. That some sort of assumption has to be invoked, though, adds another layer of arbitrariness to the non-experimental methods. Although some tests have been developed to choose between alternative non-experimental estimators (Heckman and Hotz, 1989), the low power of these tests makes them an insufficient tool to reduce the variability of results obtained from non-experimental methods (Burtless, 1993; 1995).

Experimental methods, argue their proponents, circumvent all these troubles. In particular, random assignment is able to remove any correlation between treatment status and other characteristics no matter whether those characteristics are observable or not (Burtless and Orr, 1986; Burtless, 1993; 1995). A further advantage of experiments mentioned in the literature is that they can be used to evaluate new programmes that have not been implemented so far. They can thus provide good guidance to policy makers which type of programmes should be used on a larger scale and which ones should never be implemented in the first place. Further, one may argue that the workings of experiments and the results obtained are easy to understand for policy markers (and the general public). According to Burtless (1993; 1995), a statement on an experiment would read something like: 'in comparisons to the non-participants, the programme participants had a so and so much higher chance to find a job in which they would earn so and so many dollars more money.' By contrast, any conclusions on non-experimental studies would get lost in discussions between scientists on the appropriate statistical method to correct for sample selection. The results may often conflict with each other, because there is no agreed-upon procedure of how to correct for sample selection. As a consequence, the academic community is hardly able to communicate any firm results to the bemused politicians when focusing on non-experimental research only.

The arguments of the 'experiments-only' school are thus simple, yet extremely powerful. The existence of problems concerning selection bias in non-experimental studies is undeniable. There is, however, no consensus on the importance of these problems and hence the quality of the non-experimental techniques to control for sample selection. To provide empirical evidence on this issue, Ashenfelder and Card (1985) have estimated the effects of training programmes under the U.S. Job Training Partnership Act (see description below) on earnings. Their results show that the estimated effect of training varies significantly for men depending on which models for training participation and earnings are used. The estimated training effect even changes sign across the specifications. One of the first studies that compare experimental with non-experimental techniques is the one by LaLonde (1986). He uses experimental data from the U.S. National Supported Work Demonstration (NSW) programme and non-experimental data from the Panel Study of Income Dynamics (PSID) as well as the Current Population Survey-Social Security Adminsitration File (CPS-SSA). The non-experimental methods he uses are differences-in-differences (described in Section 4.5 below), ordinary regression adjustment, and Heckman's (1978) two step estimator. LaLonde's (1986) finding is that the non-experimental estimators on earnings are not able to reproduce the results from the experimental data.

### Arguments that Speak Against Experimental Data

The fundamental criticism of randomised experiments is that social experiments are not comparable to experiments in the natural sciences, because the experiment itself can alter human behaviour, but cannot the reactions of, say, chemical substances (a point which is related to the Lucas, 1976, critique). Indeed, the arguments in favour of experiments have treated randomisation as an abstract concept. Nothing so far has been said on the incentives of the treatment and control groups in such an experiment. To get a better understanding of the criticisms of randomised experiments, we will present an example of a typical experiment in the United States.

Randomisation within the Job Training Partnership Act

*The Job Training Partnership Act of the United States is a federal legislative document which governs a multitude of training programmes to decrease the dependence of disadvantaged persons on social assistance by increasing their human capital and thus their employment and earnings potential. Some of these programmes have been assigned randomly under the National JTPA Study between 1986 and 1989. Initially, the programme designers selected a stratified random sample of 73 out of over 600 service delivery areas (SDAs) and asked them whether they would be interested to take part in the experiment. However, the SDAs could not be forced to participate in an experiment, and it emerged that not a single SDA out of the 73 was willing to join. In the end, most SDAs had to be 'bribed' to participate. The average payment received by a participating SDA was $170,000 (Hotz, 1992). It finally took two years to convince 16 SDAs to take part (although the National JTPA Study allowed up to 20 to join the experiment). SDAs were surveyed why they did not want to carry out randomised experiments. It turned out that more than half of them had ethical reservations and also feared hostile public opinion, because services were to be denied to the control group. What is also interesting is that a quarter of the 228 SDAs surveyed feared that they would have to lower their performance standards, because of the large number of applicants that had to be assessed before randomisation.*

*The initial implementation plan proposed to the SDAs was the following: applicants for the programme should be screened whether they were eligible for services. Then 50 percent of the eligible applicants were to be randomised out of treatment and assigned control status. Those people were to be denied any services from the SDAs for 30 months. In particular, the controls should not receive any information of possible alternative training programmes in order to increase the chances that they really stay untrained. The applicants assigned treatment status were to be assessed to decide on the type of programme they should join. The options were classroom training, on-the-job training, and job search assistance.*

*It turned out, though, that this plan encountered resistance from the SDAs. Random assignment between the eligibility check and the assessment would have changed the normal institutional workings of the SDAs. As a consequence, randomisation was introduced not before but after the assessment process, which meant that a larger number of people had to be assessed. SDAs were further worried about their capability to meet their performance standards when 50 percent of the eligible applicants were randomised out. They also saw ethical problems with denying help to the controls for more than two years. Therefore, only one third to one fifth of the eligible applicants were randomised into the control pool, the service denial period was reduced to 18 months, and the controls received information on alternative ways to receive training at the time of control assignment (Hotz, 1992).*

This example gives a good impression on what problems might arise in reality with randomised experiments. For descriptions of other social experiments, see Björklund (1989), or Burtless (1995). In Europe, similar problems were encountered in an Norwegian experiment for the evaluation of training measures in 1991: Torp, Raaum, Hernaes, and Goldstein (1993) report that programme administrators strategically withdrew programme applications to obtain some influence on who would be eligible for random assignment in the first place.

In statistical terms, the difficulty of finding labour offices that are willing to participate in the experiment may change the population for which the inference made from the experiment is valid. Some people might be deterred from application for a programme by knowing they might have to go through the recruitment procedure for nothing. Moreover, the barriers to eligibility might be lowered, because more people need to be assessed to obtain a given number of treatments under randomisation. Although the effects of the programmes on the participating population might be estimated without bias, the population for which this estimate would be valid might not be the one policy makers are interested in. Heckman and Smith (1993; 1996) call this *randomisation bias.*

Heckman and Smith (1996) further provide evidence that many controls do manage to receive treatment otherwise. The authors report that 32 percent of the JTPA controls received some sort of training within the first 18 months after random assignment. In addition, only between 48 and 65 percent of the persons assigned to treatment actually received it. The bias that results from controls obtaining treatment as well is termed *substitution bias.*

The problem of substitution bias is not trivial. In fact, it undermines the very nature of the randomised experiment: if we were just to compare those of the treatment group who were actually treated with those of the controls who were not treated, we would again be in a non-experimental world, because these two groups are not randomly selected.

Heckman and Smith (1993) therefore disagree with Burtless (1993) in that results from experiments would be easier to communicate to audiences outside the academic world. Indeed, their arguments suggest that results obtained from experimental data can be subject to similar controversy as those obtained from non-experimental data. As in many experimental studies the scientific community did at first not gain access to the data, the criticisms of experimental evaluations by Heckman and Smith (1993) have only come up recently.

Another argument against experiments is that they are costly both in terms of money and time. An illustrative example is the National JTPA Study, where huge sums had to be offered to the SDAs to make them join the experiment. Eventually, it took two years until the experiment could start. What is more, outcomes could only be observed when the programme participants had finished their courses. One the other hand, if appropriate data are regularly collected on ongoing non-experimental programmes, evaluation can start immediately. This argument in favour of non-experimental studies is especially important in the context of transition, where institutional changes occur frequently such that policy advice is required on the spot.

On the ethical side, the denial of services to the control group is the most frequently made argument against experiments. Burtless and Orr (1986), however, point out that when a new programme is to be introduced, the controls should have the option to receive any services they could have received had they not participated in the experiment. This way, the controls cannot be worse off. Further, Burtless (1995) points out that in medicine the introduction of a new drug very often requires experiments by law and that the ethical situation is the same there as with social experiments. Burtless and Orr (1986) also suggest compensatory payments for participants in the experiment. However, such payments can have economic effects that influence the behaviour of the controls. For evaluation purposes, it would therefore be better to do without compensatory payments. In this case, ethical problems can be severe in the context of ongoing programmes, when suddenly some people who feel entitled to an established service are denied it. On the other hand, one might have fewer ethical reservations with experiments on new programmes.

In sum, there are both arguments in favour and against experiments. Clearly, as we have seen from the example of the National JTPA Study of the United States, the conceived advantages of experiments can get significantly lost if too many compromises have to be made during the implementation of the experiment. Both in the United States and in Norway, the administrations did not like the idea of randomisation and either rejected it completely or worked against it. Nevertheless, we believe that experiments, if properly implemented, are the most compelling way to evaluate labour market programmes. On the other hand, the critique of non-experimental methods has made researchers focus more closely on the quality of various methods to control for sample selection. This has clearly led to improvements in the way non-experimental research is conducted today. Heckman, Ichimura, and Todd (1997) point out that a careful selection of the comparison group is essential for the reproducibility of experimental estimates by non-experimental techniques. In particular, the authors find that the geographic mismatch between LaLonde's (1986) treatment and comparison groups and the different data sources from which the two groups were drawn were decisive for the sensitivity of the estimation results with respect to the method to control for sample selectivity.

In an empirical study on the same data as used by LaLonde (1986), Dehejia and Wahba (1995a; 1995b) and Heckman, Ichimura, and Smith (1997) are able to reproduce the experimental results by a non-experimental method which selects a comparison group amongst the non-participants on the basis of an estimate of the programme participation probability. The ideas behind the so-called matching approach which has been successfully applied by these authors will be presented in the following section.

## 4.3 The Statistical Matching Approach to the Selection Problem in Non-Experimental Studies

It is the purpose of the statistical matching method to obtain unbiased estimates of $\tau$ when working with non-experimental data. Statistical matching means to explicitly select (match) one or more control observations to each treatment observation such that both persons are as similar as possible in terms of observed characteristics. Of course, in the non-experimental context, assumption [4. 1] on page 108 obviously cannot be assumed to hold when treatment assignment is not random. However, treatment assignment may be random given a set of covariates (Rubin, 1977). More formally, this reads

$$\Pr(T_i = 1|\mathbf{z} = \mathbf{z}_i) = \Pr(T_i = 1|\mathbf{z} = \mathbf{z}_j) \quad \forall \mathbf{z}_i = \mathbf{z}_j. \qquad [4.\ 2]$$

If assumption [4. 2] is fulfilled we have

$$\begin{aligned} &E(Y_{i1}|T_i = 1, \mathbf{z}) = E(Y_{i1}|T_i = 0, \mathbf{z}) \quad \textit{and} \\ &E(Y_{i0}|T_i = 0, \mathbf{z}) = E(Y_{i0}|T_i = 1, \mathbf{z}). \end{aligned} \qquad [4.\ 3]$$

Using the law of iterated expectations we can write the treatment effect as

$$\begin{aligned} \tau &= E_{\mathbf{z}}\{E(\tau_i|\mathbf{z})\} \\ &= E_{\mathbf{z}}\{E(Y_{i1}|\mathbf{z}) - E(Y_{i0}|\mathbf{z})\} \\ &= E_{\mathbf{z}}\left\{\begin{matrix} [E(Y_{i1}|T_i = 1, \mathbf{z})\Pr(T_i = 1|\mathbf{z}) + E(Y_{i1}|T_i = 0, \mathbf{z})\Pr(T_i = 0|\mathbf{z})] \\ -[E(Y_{i0}|T_i = 0, \mathbf{z})\Pr(T_i = 0|\mathbf{z}) + E(Y_{i0}|T_i = 1, \mathbf{z})\Pr(T_i = 1|\mathbf{z})] \end{matrix}\right\}. \end{aligned}$$

Under assumption [4. 3] we can write $\tau$ as

$$\tau = E_{\mathbf{z}}\left\{E(\tau_i|\mathbf{z})\right\}$$
$$= E_{\mathbf{z}}\begin{Bmatrix} E(Y_{i1}|T_i=1,\mathbf{z})\left[\Pr(T_i=1|\mathbf{z})+\Pr(T_i=0|\mathbf{z})\right] \\ -E(Y_{i0}|T_i=0,\mathbf{z})\left[\Pr(T_i=1|\mathbf{z})+\Pr(T_i=0|\mathbf{z})\right]\end{Bmatrix}$$
$$= E_{\mathbf{z}}\left\{E(Y_{i1}|T_i=1,\mathbf{z})-E(Y_{i0}|T_i=0,\mathbf{z})\right\}.$$

Thus one can form an unbiased estimate for $\tau$. The practical question, though, is how to condition on $\mathbf{z}$. The standard procedure in the literature is to match one person without treatment to each person with treatment on the basis of the observed characteristics $\mathbf{z}$. This way, the *average treatment effect of the treated* is estimated:

$$\hat{\tau}|_{T=1} = \overline{Y}_{i1|T=1,\mathbf{z}} - \overline{Y}_{i0|T=0,\mathbf{z}} \quad \textit{with} \qquad [4.\ 4]$$
$$E\left(\hat{\tau}|_{T=1}\right) = \tau|_{T=1} = E_{\mathbf{z}|T=1}\left\{E(Y_{i1}|T_i=1,\mathbf{z})-E(Y_{i0}|T_i=0,\mathbf{z})\right\}.$$

Although the *average treatment effect of the treated* in randomised experiments is equal to that of the non-treated, this is generally not the case in observational studies. One can also calculate the average effect for the non-treated, if one has enough treated observations to match. However, this is uncommon (Deheja and Wahba, 1995b).

The problem that arises in practice is that exact conditioning on a vector of covariates $\mathbf{z}$ (*e.g.* age education, previous employment history) is not feasible because of the high number of possible combinations of characteristics. Therefore, Rosenbaum and Rubin (1983) have shown that the dimensionality of the matching problem can be reduced to one by matching not on $\mathbf{z}$, but on

$$\Pr(T=1|\mathbf{z})$$

*i.e.* the probability of receiving treatment conditional on $\mathbf{z}$. In case the programme participation probability is equal for two individuals, these two people can be regarded as taking part in a 'sub-experiment': if one of these two people has participated in a programme and the other one not, there is no *a priori* reason that the distributions of the outcome variables ($Y_1$, $Y_0$) should differ between the treatment and comparison persons. In other words, the probability to receive treatment *balances* the distributions of the outcomes ($Y_1$, $Y_0$) for treatment and comparison persons. It is therefore called a *balancing score* (Rosenbaum and Rubin, 1983). The principle of matching is to find for each treatment person a comparison person with equal balancing score. This way one simulates 'sub-experiments' for each treatment person. The difference in the average outcome between the treatment and matched comparison samples is therefore an unbiased estimate of the treatment effect. We can therefore rewrite [4. 4] as

$$\tau|_{T=1} = E_{\mathbf{z}|T=1}\left\{E\left(Y_{i1}|T_i=1,\Pr(T_i=1|\mathbf{z})\right)-E\left(Y_{i0}|T_i=0,\Pr(T_i=1|\mathbf{z})\right)\right\}. \qquad [4.\ 4^*]$$

As $\Pr(T=1|\mathbf{z})$ is unknown, it has to be replaced by an estimate. The empirical power of matching to reduce selection bias therefore relies crucially on the quality of that estimate as well as the existence of comparison persons that have equal balancing scores to the treatment persons.

The matching approach is in essence a model-free method of evaluation that stands in the statistical tradition. The traditional approach of econometricians is to first build an economic model of the outcome variable of interest and then specify on the basis of this model a relationship that can be estimated empirically. This procedure will be described in the following section.

## 4.4 Evaluation of ALMPs by Way of Duration Models

In addition to estimating the causal effect of a programme, the traditional econometric approach builds a whole model of the outcome variable. Programme participation is then only one of many determinants of the outcome, and may be implemented by way of a dummy variable, which takes on the value *one* if participation has occurred and *zero* if not. Critics of this approach may quite rightly argue that the additional assumptions that have to be invoked to estimate a model of the outcome variable are a potential source of misspecification that are unnecessary when the only issue of interest is the effect of the programme. However, econometric models have several advantages, too. By attempting to explain the outcome variable completely, one can also receive valuable information on other factors that determine the outcome. In addition, Ham and LaLonde (1996) point out that econometric models might be necessary even in experimental settings to control for the different occurrence in historical (calendar) time of treatment and comparison unemployment spells. The standard statistical matching approach does not usually take this issue into account. Hujer, Maurer, and Wellner (1997b) have therefore combined matching methods with econometric duration analysis.

In this study, we will apart from applying the matching approach evaluate active labour market programmes in the context of unemployment duration models. Section 4.4.1 briefly outlines the economic theory behind these models. A selection of widely-used empirical duration models is then presented in Section 4.4.2. This section also introduces the model used in the empirical analysis of Chapter 5. In Section 4.4.3, we show how the causal effect of a programme can be identified within the duration model framework and how we may test for sample selectivity. Whereas the methodology presented in Section 4.4.3 is the one subsequently applied in Chapter 5, we give an overview of alternative methods to identify causal effects in Section 4.5.

### 4.4.1 Theoretical Background: Job Search Theory

The theoretical underpinning of the duration models that will be presented below is the theory of job search. Neoclassical labour market theory assumes that any unemployed worker looking for a job can and will take one up immediately. The assumptions in the neoclassical model are that information is perfect and complete, which means that the unemployed worker knows any job vacancy that is on offer in the economy. The fact that many workers are unemployed for a significant amount of time can therefore not be explained by standard neoclassical theory.

Job search theoretic models of the labour market are able to explain the duration of unemployment by allowing for *uncertainty* concerning job offers. Individual unemployment spells can then be described by stochastic processes (see Lippman and McCall, 1976; McKenna, 1985; Mortensen, 1986, for more formal, and Wurzel, 1993, for intuitive surveys). In the following, we describe a very basic search theoretic model. We also touch on possible extensions concentrating on the results that are relevant for our empirical implementation that will be presented in the following chapter.

One of the standard search models as presented, for example, in Lippman and McCall (1979) or McKenna (1985) assumes that the unemployed individual sequentially receives job offers. These job offers are exclusively characterised by the wage offered. The wage is drawn from some known wage distribution. Search is only possible in the state of unemployment. There are no other labour force states than employment and unemployment. Moreover, should the unemployed worker accept a job offer, he or she will stick with that job and wage for the indefinite future. The time horizon is infinite and there are no budget or wealth constraints. In this setting, the unemployed person has to decide each period whether to continue search in the hope to be offered a higher wage or whether to stop. If the person stops searching, the net present value of this decision will be the discounted future income stream from the offered wage. During search, the person receives unemployment benefits, but has to incur search costs. In each period, the person will only stop searching if the discounted future income stream from the offered wage exceeds the net present value of searching.

It can be shown that the unemployed person will have an optimal stopping rule such that he or she will stop searching and accept a job if the offered wage exceeds a certain limit, which is called the reservation wage (Mortensen, 1986). In this standard model, the reservation wage is constant over time, but varies with the job offer distribution, the job offer arrival rate, unemployment benefits, and search costs. Hence, one has not only got a theory which can explain why unemployment may last for a significant period of time, but one can also hypothesise why certain individuals have longer unemployment spells than others. A straightforward reduced-form empirical formulation of this model therefore models the exit probability in each time period as a function of unemployment benefits and variables influencing search costs and earnings potential.

Exit into non-participation in the labour force has also been integrated into the standard search-theoretic framework (see Wurzel, 1993, for a summary). If non-participation is modelled as an additional labour force state, which delivers utility in the form of leisure, there can be situations in which both the value of accepting a job and the value of search are below the value of leisure. This occurs, for example, if the distribution of job offers is very unfavourable to the unemployed person, and non-participation has a very high pay-off, *e.g.*, in terms of early retirement schemes. The variables affecting the exit from unemployment into non-participation would be the same as those affecting exit into employment. This is because the three labour force states are alternatives from which one must be chosen at each point in time under a given set of fundamental conditions.

Our discussion of ALMPs in Poland in Section 2.4 suggests two main channels through which active labour market programmes might impact on the duration of unemployment. First, the regulation that the benefit entitlement period is renewed after intervention or public works may raise unemployment durations by increasing the value of future search. Hence one can expect longer unemployment durations which would be mirrored in a lower probability to take up a new job as well as to leave the labour force. Second, the ALMP programme may have effects on the offered wage distribution. These can work in many ways. If the ALMP programme raises the human capital of the participant person, then the wage offer distribution can be expected to shift towards the right. The effect of a higher expected value of the offered wage is unclear, as it will increase a persons reservation wage (Lippman and McCall, 1976). Hence, although it is widely stated in policy documents that ALMPs are supposed to improve the human capital of the participants, it is interesting to note that the standard job search model does not clearly predict whether increases in human capital lengthen or shorten unemployment spells. However, the situation in Poland as well as in most other labour markets is that many unemployed people hardly receive any job offers. If ALMPs also increase the job offer arrival rate, the duration of unemployment will most likely be reduced because the availability of a job offer is the main constraint for many people to leave unemployment. As a consequence, one may expect that if ALMPs improve job opportunities, this will also lead to a reduction in the average duration of unemployment.

In sum, it has to be stressed that it is not only potential *human capital effects* of ALMP programmes which have a likely impact on unemployment durations, but also the *institutional framework* in which ALMPs work. In particular, interactions between ALMP participation and entitlement to unemployment benefits might have negative incentive effects. Before we discuss the identification of ALMP effects within econometric models in Sections 4.4.3, we will give an overview of widely applied empirical duration models in the following section.

### 4.4.2 Empirical Duration Models

Duration models have been frequently used in the analysis of unemployment benefits, but there are also a number of recent applications on active labour market programmes. Mostly, reduced-form models of the re-employment probability are estimated. Some attempts have been made, though, to estimate structural models which model the offered wage and the reservation wage distributions jointly. Lancaster (1985) and Schmidt and Winkelmann (1993) present structural models for Britain and western Germany, respectively. However, as these models require data on reservation wages or job offers, they are very seldom implemented. As neither reservation wages nor job offers are not available to us, we only discuss reduced-form approaches in the following.

Here, a variety of models has been developed. If only exit into one category (employment) is specified, one speaks of hazard rate models, if more than one exit category is possible (*e.g.* employment and non-participation), one speaks of competing risks models. Hazard rate models were originally developed in the biometric literature to estimate the life duration of human beings or animals. Hence the terms *hazard* rate and *survivor* function (see below). In our context, the hazard rate is defined on the probability to leave unemployment during *process time* interval $[t, t+dt[$ conditional on having been unemployed up to *process time* $t$. *Process time* differs from *calendar time* in that *process time* starts counting at the beginning of each person's unemployment spell. More formally, the limit $(dt \rightarrow 0)$ of the conditional exit probability is called the hazard rate and can be written in continuous time as follows:

$$h(t) = \lim_{dt \rightarrow 0} \frac{\Pr(t \leq D_t < t + dt | D_t \geq t)}{dt}.$$

The hazard rate depends both on the supply side (the reservation wage) and the demand side (the offered wage). The hazard rate for each point in process time $t$, $h(t)$, gives a complete description of the distribution of unemployment duration $D_t$ with density function $f(t)$ and distribution function $F(t)$. The function $1-F(t)$ is called the survivor function as it states the probability of still remaining in the original state at process time $t$.

The relationships between the hazard $h(t)$, the survivor function $1-F(t)$, and the density function $f(t)$ are given by (see, *e.g.*, Lancaster, 1990):

$$h(t) = \frac{f(t)}{1-F(t)}$$

$$1-F(t) = e^{-\int_0^t h(s)ds}$$

$$f(t) = h(t)e^{-\int_0^t h(s)ds}.$$

When exits into more than one state are allowed (competing risks), we have a hazard rate for transition into each state. The hazard rate for leaving unemployment is then the sum of the exit state-specific hazards. In the example of two exit states, we have

$$h(t) = h_1(t) + h_2(t) = \frac{f(t)}{1 - F(t)}$$

where $j = 1{,}2$ denotes the two exit states. The survivor and density functions for the distribution of unemployment duration are as above with the overall hazard rate $h(t)$ in the integral.

Assuming independence between the observations, the sample likelihood function for a sample of $N_i$ individuals for a competing risks model can be written

$$L = \prod_{i=1}^{N_i} \prod_{j=1}^{J} \left[h_j(t_i)\right]^{\delta_{ij}} \times \left[1 - F(t_i)\right]$$

where $\delta_{ij}$ is a dummy variable indicator which takes on value *one* if exit occurred into state $j$ at process time $t_i$, and *zero* otherwise. $t_i$ denotes time person $i$ is known to have been unemployed.

If person $i$ exits into state $j$ at time $t_i$, his or her contribution to the likelihood function is the state-specific hazard rate $h_j(t_i)$ and the survivor function $F(t_i)$. If no exit occurs, the observation is censored. For censored observations, one only knows that they have 'survived' in unemployment for a period of length $t_i$. Hence, their contribution to the likelihood is only the survivor function $F(t_i)$ at $t_i$.

So far, time has been treated as continuous. However, we mostly measure time only in discrete intervals of significant length, say in months. Therefore, it seems more appropriate to model time in discrete intervals and estimate discrete hazard rate models. As Hamerle and Tutz (1989) note, a large number of equal spell lengths (ties) can lead to inconsistent estimates in continuous-time hazard rate models, which generally assume that ties only occur with a probability of zero.

In discrete time, the survivor function at time $t_i$ can be expressed as the product of one less the hazard rate at process time periods 1 to $(t_i - 1)$. We can hence write the likelihood function of a discrete-time competing risks model as (Hamerle and Tutz, 1989, Chapter 6)

$$L = \prod_{i=1}^{N_i} \prod_{j=1}^{J} \left[h_j(t_i)\right]^{\delta_{ij}} \times \prod_{s=1}^{t_i - 1} \left[1 - \sum_{j=1}^{J} h_j(s)\right].$$

### The Weibull Model

Various methods in parameterising the hazard rate have been applied in the empirical literature. A very popular specification especially in earlier studies has been the Weibull model (see Lancaster, 1979; Narendranathan, Nickell, and Stern, 1985; Steiner, 1987; 1990; Puhani, 1996; and Winter-Ebmer, 1996, for applications). The standard Weibull model is a single risk (exit state) model with hazard rate

$$h(t) = \alpha t^{\alpha-1}\left(e^{\beta'\mathbf{x}}\right)^{\alpha}$$

where $\mathbf{x}$ is a vector of observed characteristics. Salient features of the standard Weibull model are the proportional hazard rate assumption (see below in this paragraph), no time-varying parameters, and the parametric distribution of the baseline hazard. The baseline hazard $\alpha t^{\alpha-1}$ describes the development of the hazard rate over process time for every person. The Weibull model is implemented in econometric software packages like *Stata* and *LIMDEP* and can thus be applied straightforwardly. The proportional hazard rate assumption implies that the exogenous variables shift the baseline hazard rates of different individuals parallel to each other. This means that the effect of the covariates $\mathbf{x}$ is constant over process time. In the standard Weibull model, the covariates are assumed not to change their value over process time. Petersen (1986a; 1986b), though, shows how time-varying covariates can be treated in the Weibull and other models. The Weibull model with time-varying covariates is implemented in *LIMDEP*.

The specific parametric specification of the baseline hazard allows the hazard rate to fall or to rise with process time, or to stay constant. The latter case applies if $\alpha = 1$. For $\alpha < 1$, we have negative duration dependence (*i.e.* the hazard rate falls with process time, *e.g.* due to depreciating human capital), and for $\alpha > 1$ positive duration dependence (*i.e.* the hazard rate rises with process time, *e.g.* through falling reservation wages). As the hazard rate in the Weibull model is either monotonically de- or increasing, it is not possible that the hazard rate both rises and falls over process time.

**The Cox Model**

This rather restrictive assumption on the baseline hazard is avoided by Cox's (1972; 1975) proposal to estimate the parameters of a continuous-time proportional hazard model without the baseline hazard. Cox (1972) specifies the hazard rate as

$$h(t) = h_0 e^{\beta'\mathbf{x}}$$

where $h_0$ is the unknown baseline hazard. Cox (1972; 1975) proposes to estimate the parameters $\beta$ of the model by maximising the so-called partial likelihood

$$L = \prod_{i=1}^{N_c}\left[e^{\beta'\mathbf{x}_i} \Big/ \sum_{r=1}^{N_r} e^{\beta'\mathbf{x}_r}\right]$$

where $N_c$ is the number of completed (*i.e.* not right-censored) spells, and $N_r$ is the number of spells ongoing at process time $t_i$ of individual $i$. In other words, $N_r$ is the size of the risk set.

As the baseline hazard is ignored here, the likelihood is a partial likelihood. However, Cox (1975) shows that the partial likelihood may be treated like an ordinary likelihood function for the purposes of estimating the $\beta$ coefficients. The baseline hazard rate may then be obtained by non-parametric methods, such as the Kaplan-Meier (1958) estimator. The Cox model has been applied in the analysis of unemployment duration, for example, by Steiner (1987) on Austria, Hunt (1995) on western Germany or Vodopivec (1995) on Slovenia. Recently, the Cox proportional hazard-rate model has frequently been estimated by general maximum likelihood, where the baseline hazard is estimated non-parametrically and jointly with the shift parameters $\beta$. Applications can be found in Moffitt (1985), Katz and Meyer (1990), Meyer (1990), and Hujer, Maurer, and Wellner (1997a; 1997b). The partial likelihood Cox model with time-varying covariates is implemented in econometric software packages like *Stata, LIMDEP* or *SPSS*. The general maximum likelihood version, however, has to be programmed by the researcher.

**The Logit Model**

A similar model that estimates the baseline hazard rate non-parametrically, but works in discrete time, has been applied in Nickell (1979); Ham and Rea (1987); Narendranathan and Stewart (1993); Steiner and Kraus (1995); Ham, Svejnar, and Terrell (1996); Wolff (1996); and Leiprecht (1997); Micklewright and Nagy (1997); and Steiner (1993; 1994; 1997). In the logit model, the hazard rate for discrete time $t$ is specified as

$$h(t) = \frac{e^{\beta'\mathbf{x}+\alpha\mathbf{p}_t}}{1+e^{\beta'\mathbf{x}+\alpha\mathbf{p}_t}}.$$

The logit specification of the hazard rate does not impose the proportional hazard rate assumption. The great advantage of this model is its flexibility. Estimation is very simple, as it amounts to estimating a logit model in the single exit state case, and a multinomial logit model in the competing risks case. Before the logit model can be applied, however, the data have to be structured such that each month represents one observation, and the dependent variable equals, for example, *one* in the month a transition into employment occurs, and *zero* otherwise. The (multinomial) logit model is the most widely available one in econometric software packages amongst the models just outlined (one can use *Stata, LIMDEP, SPSS, SAS, Micro TSP, RATS, Microfit, EViews* and *GAUSS Quantal Response Applications*). Time-varying covariates can easily be implemented. The vector $\mathbf{p}$, for example, consists of time-varying dummy variables defined on process time intervals, and therefore describes a non-parametrically estimated baseline hazard rate.

As the logit model will be employed in this study, we will elaborate on it in Chapter 5 below. In the following section, we discuss how the causal effect of a programme can be estimated within a duration model framework.

### 4.4.3 A Reduced-Form Approach for Identification of a Causal Effect in an Econometric Model

As outlined in Section 4.1, the identification problem for causal effects arises from the fact that programme participants and non-participants may differ in other aspects besides treatment. The matching approach presented in Section 4.3 attempts to solve this problem by selecting for each member of the treatment group one person of the non-treatment group who is as similar as possible to the treatment group member in terms of observed characteristics. Likewise, regression-type methods control for differences in observed characteristics by including them as regressors in an econometric model of the outcome variable.

Consider the following structural specification:

$$\begin{aligned} Y^*_{ijt} &= \beta_j{}'\mathbf{x}_{it} + \tau_j T_{it} + u_{it} \\ T^*_{it} &= \gamma'\mathbf{z}_{it} + v_{it} \end{aligned} \qquad [4.\ 5]$$

where $Y^*_{ijt}$ is the latent index which defines the outcome variable of interest for person $i$ at process time $t$. The outcome variable is the probability of leaving unemployment for a different labour force state $j$, where in our case $j$ can stand for employment or non–participation. This is to say, $Y^*_{ijt}$ defines the state-specific hazard rate. $T^*_{it}$ is the latent index which drives the transition from unemployment into training at process time $t$ for person $i$.

Estimating the outcome equation in model [4. 5] alone, one has to expect inconsistent estimates of the treatment effect $\tau$. The fact that the error term $u$ is not likely to be orthogonal to the regressor $T$ can be illustrated by substituting for $T$ in model [4. 5]:

$$Y^*_{ijt} = \beta_j{}'\mathbf{x}_{it} + \tau_j f[\gamma'\mathbf{z}_{it} + v_{it}] + u_{it}$$

where $T_{it} = f[T^*_{it}]$ such that $T_{it} = 0$ or $T_{it} = 1$.

It is the endogeneity of treatment $T$ which causes selection bias. Selection bias can arise through a correlation between $\mathbf{z}$ and $u$ (*selection on observables*), or through a correlation between $v$ and $u$ (*selection on unobservables*) (Heckman and Hotz, 1989).

As to *selection on observables*, the problem leading to inconsistency is that due to the correlation between $\mathbf{z}$ and $u$, the expected value of $u$ conditional on $\mathbf{x}$ and $T$ is not zero. In particular, the expected value of $u$ conditional on $\mathbf{x}$ and $\mathbf{z}$ is not equal to zero. More formally (Heckman and Hotz, 1989):

$$E(u_{it}|T_{it},\mathbf{x}_{it}) \neq 0 \text{ and}$$

$$E(u_{it}|T_{it},\mathbf{x}_{it},\mathbf{z}_{it}) = E(u_{it}|\mathbf{x}_{it},\mathbf{z}_{it}) \neq 0.$$

The equality of the two conditional expectations with and without conditioning on $T$ follows from the fact that we assume for the moment that there is no correlation between $v$ and $u$, *i.e.* there is no *selection on unobservables.* We can therefore write the conditional expectation of $Y^*$ as:

$$E(Y^*_{ijt}|T_{it},\mathbf{x}_{it},\mathbf{z}_{it}) = \beta_j\text{'}\mathbf{x}_{it} + \tau_j T_{it} + E(u_{it}|\mathbf{x}_{it},\mathbf{z}_{it}).$$

By making an assumption on the functional form of $E(u|\mathbf{x},\mathbf{z})$, we can include it in the estimation of $Y^*$ to obtain a consistent estimate of the treatment effect $\tau$ (Heckman and Hotz, 1989). Estimators of this sort are called *control function estimators* and have been suggested by Heckman and Robb (1985). In our study, we will impose a linear specification for the control function $E(u|\mathbf{x},\mathbf{z})$. The *linear control function estimator* is thus obtained by adding all $\mathbf{z}$ variables to the set of regressors of our model of $Y^*$. Hence we can estimate

$$Y^*_{ijt} = \beta_j\text{'}\begin{bmatrix}\mathbf{x}_{it}\\ \mathbf{z}_{it}\end{bmatrix} + \tau_j T_{it} + \xi_{it}.$$

Note that the $\beta$-vector in the last equation is different from the $\beta$-vectors above. We only use the same symbol to economise on notation.

In the case of *selection on observables*, we can therefore control for sample selection by including the $\mathbf{z}$ variables amongst the set of regressors of the outcome equation. In many cases, the $\mathbf{z}$ variables will be included in $\mathbf{x}$ anyway, as all observed variables influencing ALMP participation are also likely to influence the outcome variable directly (Pannenberg, 1996; Fitzenberger and Prey, 1998).

However, there might also be *selection on unobservables, i.e.*, $u$ might be correlated with $v$. This is equivalent to saying that some of the $\mathbf{z}$ variables are unobservable. In this case, the *linear control function estimator* would be inconsistent as $\xi$ would be correlated with the treatment variable $T$ through $v$. However, this is only possible if $\xi$ is different from zero. $\xi$ would be zero if the $\mathbf{x}$ and $\mathbf{z}$ variables provide a complete description of the hazard rate, so that all the individual heterogeneity can be explained by these variables. As the existence of any remaining unobserved individual heterogeneity, *i.e.* whether $\xi$ is differs from zero, can be tested, one can use a test on unobserved individual heterogeneity as a test for *selection on unobservables.* If no unobserved individual heterogeneity is found, then one can reject selection on unobservables. In the presence of unobserved individual heterogeneity, selection on unobservables cannot be rejected, which means that estimates may be biased, although they need not necessarily be biased. Details on the test for unobserved individual heterogeneity which will be applied in this study are described in Chapter 5, Section 5.3.2, below.

## 4.5 Other Methods to Identify Causal Effects

### Structural Approaches

Prominent alternatives to the *linear control function estimator* outlined in Section 4.4.3 are structural approaches in the tradition of Heckman (1976; 1978; 1979). Heckman (1976; 1978; 1979) shows that the sample selection problem can be expressed as a missing variable problem. The missing variable is an auxiliary construct obtained from the estimation of the programme participation equation and an assumption on the joint distribution of the error terms of the outcome and participation equations. Heckman (1976; 1978; 1979) thus proposes a two-step method to estimate models with selection bias. The two-step method in our context amounts to estimating the control function $E(u|\mathbf{x},\mathbf{z})$ in the first step and then include this estimate in the outcome equation in the second step. Of course, the two equations can also be estimated jointly.

Although this structural approach looks appealing from a conceptual point of view, it is unclear whether it has much empirical benefit. The empirical identification of the structural model depends crucially on the implementation of meaningful exclusion restrictions. That is to say, one needs some $\mathbf{z}$ variables in the participation equation that are not contained in the $\mathbf{x}$ variables of the outcome equation. These variables only impact on programme participation, but not directly on unemployment duration. Of course, the structural model can in theory still be estimated in the absence of exclusion restrictions through identification by functional form (Fitzenberger and Prey, 1995; 1996; 1997). However, identification of the model then rests entirely on the assumption on the joint distribution of $v$ and $u$. Such assumptions are generally made on grounds of mathematical tractability instead of economic reasoning. Therefore, they are mostly arbitrary from an economic point of view. As a consequence, the very nature of the structural model evaporates, because the structural model without exclusion restrictions is only identified by purely mathematical rather than economic assumptions.

What is more, Monte Carlo Studies have shown that if the estimated control function is highly collinear with the $\mathbf{x}$ variables of the outcome equation, structural estimation methods will be very inefficient even when there are exclusion restrictions (Nawata, 1993; 1994; Leung and Yu, 1996). For a short survey of these and other Monte Carlo studies, see Puhani (1997b).

**Instrumental Variables**

Instrumental variable estimation (IV) amounts to substituting the treatment variable for a variable (the instrument) that is highly correlated with treatment $T$, but not correlated with $u$ (Heckman, 1997). Empirical applications as those of Hujer, Maurer, and Wellner (1997b) and Staat (1997) take the predicted probability of treatment (*i.e.* a function of $\hat{T}^*$) as instruments. An important point in the context of instrumental variable estimation is the quality of the instruments. Although the studies of Hujer, Maurer, and Wellner (1997a) and Staat (1997) provide careful discussions of the choice of instruments, in many data sets no variables are available which can effectively act as instrumental variables. Even if some variables are found which might in theory act as instruments, the empirical quality of the instruments still has to be assessed. In particular, if the correlation between the instrument and the variable to be instrumented is very low, the IV estimator will be highly inefficient (see, for example, Greene, 1997, Chapter 6). Angrist and Krueger (1991; 1995) and Angrist and Imbens (1995) estimate the effect of schooling on earnings by the IV method. In their particular situation, an institutional feature of the U.S. schooling system provides a credible instrument, namely the fact that compulsory school attendance is one year lower for pupils born in the first quarter of a year. As there is no *a priori* reason to believe that the quarter of a year a person is born in has a direct effect on earnings, it can be used as an instrument for years of schooling. Similarly, Angrist, Imbens, and Rubin (1996) use the Vietnam draft lottery as an instrument for participation in the Vietnam war. As the lottery is random, there is no *a priori* reason to believe that the result of the lottery has a direct impact on mortality (the outcome variable). Yet the lottery is strongly correlated with participation in the war. It can therefore act as an instrument. In the just mentioned papers that use IV estimation, the authors dispose of something that is plausibly exogenous, as it is random (see Heckman, 1995, for a discussion of randomisation as an instrumental variable). However, it is unclear what could plausibly serve as an instrument in the context of programme evaluation when there is no experiment.

**Difference-in-Differences**

The last type of popular estimator we present here is the difference-in-differences approach. Its attractiveness lies in the fact that it can control for both observed and unobserved heterogeneity between treatment and comparison groups as long as that heterogeneity is constant over time. Furthermore, in its simplest form, it can be implemented very easily through mean comparisons of the outcome variable. The idea is not to compare the simple difference in the outcomes for participants and non-participants, but the difference in the outcomes after treatment with the difference in the outcomes before treatment. More formally, the difference-in-differences estimator can be written

$$\hat{\tau} = \left(\overline{Y}_{1t} - \overline{Y}_{0t-1}\right)_{|T=1} - \left(\overline{Y}_{0t} - \overline{Y}_{0t-1}\right)_{|T=0}$$

where in period $t-1$ nobody has been treated yet, whereas in period $t$, the treatment group has received treatment (see, for example, Moffitt, 1991). This estimator is unbiased if and only if there is no difference between the before and after treatment differences in the non-treatment outcomes between the treatment and comparison groups, *i.e.* it has to be true that

$$E\left(Y_{0it} \middle| T_i = 1\right) - E\left(Y_{0it} \middle| T_i = 0\right) = E\left(Y_{0it-1} \middle| T_i = 1\right) - E\left(Y_{0it-1} \middle| T_i = 0\right). \qquad [4.\ 6]$$

This assumption of the difference-in-differences estimator also underlies the pre-programme test suggested by Heckman and Hotz (1989). The pre-programme test checks whether the treatment and comparison groups differ from each other before treatment (*i.e.* whether $E\left(Y_{0it-1} \middle| T_i = 1\right) - E\left(Y_{0it-1} \middle| T_i = 0\right) = 0$). This can be done, for example, by including a pre-treatment dummy in a panel estimation of the outcome variable which equals *one* if the person will receive treatment in the future (Fitzenberger and Prey, 1995; 1996; 1997; 1998; Pannenberg, 1996; Hübler, 1997) and *zero* otherwise. If the coefficient on the pre-treatment dummy is significantly different from zero, then there is some unobserved individual heterogeneity between the treatment and comparison groups and simple post-treatment comparison is not appropriate. However, post-treatment comparison is still appropriate if one invokes assumption [4. 6], *i.e.* one has to assume that the unobserved individual heterogeneity is constant over time. One can thus control for unobserved individual heterogeneity when doing non-parametric inference on matched samples if one is willing to interpret the non-parametric estimator as a difference-in-differences estimator (Heckman, Ichimura, and Todd, 1997).

In Section 5.2.3 of Chapter 5, we will carry out a test in the spirit of the Heckman and Hotz (1989) pre-programme test. In the duration model approach, however, this method cannot be applied due to the way we structure our unemployment spells (*cf.* Section 5.3.1 of Chapter 5). The concepts described in this section have been applied in one form or another in the empirical literature on transition economies, which we now turn to.

## 4.6 Literature Survey of Empirical Studies on Transition Economies

For the interested reader, we present previous microeconometric evidence on the effects of ALMPs in transition economies in this section. The reader who just wants to get a quick overview is referred to Table 34 on page 160, which provides a summary of the studies surveyed in the following. Section 4.6.4 on page 142 draws our conclusions from the previous studies on eastern Germany, Hungary, and Poland, which are reviewed in Sections 4.6.1, 4.6.2, and 4.6.3, respectively.

To our knowledge, there exits no microeconometric evaluation of Czech ALMPs so far.

There are various ways to distinguish the empirical analyses. First, one can distinguish by country. The fact that delivery mechanisms and institutional settings vary across countries is likely to have an impact on the effectiveness of ALMPs. Further, one can distinguish between the outcome variable. Whereas most North-American papers deal with wage effects of ALMP programmes, re-employment probabilities are the most important outcome in the European context of high unemployment. The treatment of the selection problem, which has been discussed in Sections 4.3 to 4.5, is another important difference between the existing analyses. As most of the microeconometric evaluation literature on transition economies has been written on ALMPs in eastern Germany, eastern Germany is the only economy in transition where a significant scientific debate on the effects of ALMP programmes has been developed. As this debate to a large extent revolves around the appropriate method to correct for sample selectivity, each study on eastern Germany will be introduced by the approach taken on this issue.

### 4.6.1 Evidence on Eastern Germany

#### Lechner (1995; 1996a; 1996b)

Lechner's evaluations of training programmes in eastern Germany are the first papers which apply the *statistical matching* approach (see Section 4.3) to German data. The 1995; 1996a; and 1996b papers are distinguished by the type of training they investigate. The 1995 paper analyses off-the-job training which can be both publicly (*Fortbildungs- und Umschulungsmaßnahmen, FuU*) or privately financed. A clearer distinction is drawn in the 1996a and 1996b studies, which estimate the effects of publicly-financed and enterprise-related training (only 8 percent of which is publicly-financed), respectively. The number of training participants is 122 in the 1995, 103 in the 1996a, and 185 in the 1996b paper.

All papers estimate the effects of the specified training programmes on *employment* and *earnings* on the basis of the German Socio-Economic Panel (GSEOP) for the period 1990 to 1994. No significant effects of the training programmes on employment can be detected in any of the studies. There are also no effects on earnings except for enterprise-related training where former training participants earn around € 200 more than non-participants. In all three papers, Lechner also distinguishes between different subperiods defined on the calendar time when training took place. In all cases, his results are robust.

#### Fitzenberger and Prey (1995; 1996; 1997; 1998)

Fitzenberger and Prey (1995; 1996; 1997) are the first to evaluate east German training programmes in the tradition of Heckman (1976; 1978; 1979) by building a *simultaneous model* of sample attrition, training participation, labour force status, and wages (see our discussion in Section 4.5). The 1997 article is the publication of the 1995 discussion paper. Unlike in the 1996 paper, no wage effects are estimated in the 1995 / 1997 analysis. The 1996 discussion paper can be seen as a more up to date version of the 1995 / 1997 article, as essentially the same estimation method is used on a longer observation period (east German Labour Market Monitor 1990 to 1994 instead of 1990 to 1992). In the 1998 article, Fitzenberger and Prey apply the statistical matching approach similarly to Lechner (1995; 1996a; 1996b), but on the Labour Market Monitor (LMM) data. The 1998 comparative study on estimation techniques has been motivated by the fact that Fitzenberger and Prey (1995; 1995; 1997) in contrast to Lechner (1995; 1996a; 1996b) find positive employment and wage effects for some training programmes (see below for details).

Fitzenberger and Prey (1996) distinguish between on-the-job and off-the-job training, as well as training with and without public income maintenance (*Fortbildungs- und Umschulungs-maßnahmen, FuU*). By also estimating the equations separately for men and women, the authors obtain eight subgroups for their analysis. The number of treatment observations in these subgroups ranges between 50 and 1,000 persons. The estimation results hardly differ for men and women. Positive employment effects are found for off-the-job training with income maintenance. On the other hand, positive effects on wages can only be detected for training without income maintenance. For on-the-job training with (without) income maintenance, the authors even find negative effects on employment for men (women). The positive wage effects lie around half a deutschmark per hour, which amounts to around € 40 per month for a full-time employee.

All models in the 1996 paper are random effects probits, except the wage equation, which is specified by a tobit model. In principle, the joint error term structure is modelled as a multivariate normal distribution. However, to make the model tractable, the cross-time and cross-equation correlations of the error term component apart from the random effect have been restricted to zero. In order to test whether this type of set up is able to correct for sample selectivity, Fitzenberger and Prey include Heckman and Hotz (1989)-type pre-programme dummies (*cf.* Section 4.5). It is shown that these dummies are significant in a variety of cases, which shows that the training participation equation is not a sufficient means to correct for sample selection in the authors' model. Furthermore, specification tests reported by the authors show that random effects probits are preferable to ordinary probit models thus pointing to the significance of unobserved individual heterogeneity.

In the 1998 paper, Fitzenberger and Prey also report positive effects for training with income maintenance estimated by using difference-in-differences on matched samples (*cf.* Section 5.2.3 below). However, the authors point out that their statistical matching approach has not been very successful in finding appropriate comparison groups. Therefore, the matching results have to be interpreted with care. Furthermore, in a comparison with a parametric model similar to the one of the 1996 study, Fitzenberger and Prey find that the precision of the estimate is lower when using the statistical matching technique than when estimating an econometric model. Fitzenberger and Prey's results are thus consistent with the ones of Lechner (1995; 1996a; 1996b) in that statistically significant results are not easy to obtain using matched samples due to the smaller number of comparison observations than in traditional econometric studies.

**Pannenberg (1995; 1996)**

Pannenberg uses the *linear control function estimator* (*cf.* Section 4.4.3) to address the sample selectivity problem, although he does not use that term explicitly. In both the 1995 and the 1996 studies, the author estimates the effect of off-the-job training measures (*Fortbildungs- und Umschulungsmaßnahmen, FuU*) in western and eastern Germany on the basis of the German Socio-Economic Panel (GSOEP). In the 1995 study, the author uses a logit unemployment duration model (*cf.* Section 4.4.2) with one exit state, *viz. employment* of any sort (full-time, part-time, or temporary employment). Pannenberg's west German data set consists of 715 unemployment spells of which 26 come out of off-the-job training. For eastern Germany, there are 721 spells with 76 coming from off-the-job training.

Pannenberg's result for western Germany during the period 1985 to 1991 is that training improves the individual's re-employment chances irrespective of whether he or she receives a training allowance or not. For eastern Germany during the period 1990 to 1992, he does not find positive effects, though.

In contrast to his 1995 analysis, Pannenberg specifies unemployment duration to have an extreme value distribution with Gamma-distributed unobserved individual heterogeneity in the 1996 paper. This way in combination with the inclusion of a Heckman and Hotz (1989)-type pre-programme dummy variable, the author tests for sample selectivity. There is evidence for unobserved individual heterogeneity and the pre-programme dummy is significant. Another difference to the 1995 study is the observation period, which is 1990 to 1994 for eastern Germany. The data are again from the GSOEP-East. Pannenberg now finds positive effects of training on re-employment. The estimation results are based on the spells of 1,075 persons, 90 of whom have participated in publicly-financed training.

Both the 1995 and the 1996 analyses also investigate the earnings effects of training participation in eastern Germany. Positive impacts are found in both studies. The effects seem extremely high, namely between 30 (1995 study) and 90 (!, 1996 study) percent higher gross monthly earnings. The reason for these implausibly large estimates is probably the inability of the few exogenous variables in the model to adequately control for sample selectivity.

**Hübler (1997)**

In the light of the equivocal results of the just reviewed research on eastern Germany, which has applied various methods to control for sample selectivity, Hübler carries out a *sensitivity analysis with respect to the estimation method.* To this end, Hübler instruments programme participation by the estimated participation probability, uses linear control functions, and in his preferred specification he estimates random effects panel probit models of the labour force state on matched samples. As to the statistical matching approach, Hübler proceeds in an iterative way: for each non-participant, a distance measure from the average participant is calculated in terms of the estimated participation probability. Then a pre-specified share of the comparison group with the closest distance to the treatment group is selected. The outcome model is estimated with this selected comparison group until the Heckman and Hotz (1989) pre-programme variable is insignificant. As long as the pre-programme dummy is significant, the comparison group is diminished further on the basis of the distance criterion. As in Fitzenberger and Prey (1995; 1996; 1997; 1998), Hübler's tests for random effects show that unobserved individual heterogeneity is present. Hübler further finds that a careful treatment of sample selectivity is important. It is shown that the estimated effects of the active labour market programmes are quantitatively very sensitive to the treatment of selection bias. In some cases, even a qualitative sensitiveness can be found in that the sign of the effect changes.

Hübler estimates the employment effects of - amongst others - public works (*Arbeitsbeschaffungsmaßnahmen, ABM*, which also include subsidised jobs) and publicly-financed training programmes (*Fortbildungs- und Umschulungsmaßnahmen, FuU*) in eastern Germany on the basis of the east German Labour Market Monitor (LMM) between 1990 and 1994. Sample sizes are not reported in the article. In general, the author concludes that no clearly positive effects can be detected for either active labour market programme. For training, Hübler finds a negative effect for men one year after the programme, that turns to a positive effect two years after the programme. In the case of women, there is also a negative employment effect of training one year after the programme, but this becomes insignificant at the 5 percent level a further year later. Public works programmes are found to have significantly negative effects on the employment opportunities of men, but no effects on women's employment chances.

**Steiner and Kraus (1995); Kraus, Puhani, and Steiner (1997; 1998)**

Kraus, Puhani, and Steiner's approach can be seen as an *extension to the linear control function estimator* (*cf.* Section 4.4.3). In the 1997 and 1998 papers, the authors test for sample selection bias by testing for the existence of unobserved individual heterogeneity in both the ALMP participation and the outcome models. The authors show that, in dependence on the heterogeneity components, an upper bound for the correlation of the error terms in both models can be determined. In both papers the upper bounds are found to be sufficiently low to assume that sample selection does not influence the results obtained. The participation and outcome models are estimated as multinomial logit duration models with unobserved individual heterogeneity (*cf.* Section 4.4.2 above and Section 5.3.1 below). The distribution of the heterogeneity component is estimated non-parametrically as suggested by Heckman and Singer (1994).

Kraus, Puhani, and Steiner (1997) and (1998) investigate the effect of publicly-financed training (*Fortbildungs- und Umschulungsmaßnahmen, FuU*) and public works (*Arbeitsbeschaffungs-maßnahmen, ABM*, which also include subsidised jobs) programmes on the chances of the programme participants to find stable employment, respectively. The authors use the east German Labour Market Monitor (LMM) 1990-1994 as their data base. In both papers, Kraus, Puhani, and Steiner distinguish between two subperiods, *viz.* from the beginning of 1990 to the end of 1991 on the one hand, and from the beginning of 1992 till the end of 1994 on the other. The first period marks the set-up phase of the active labour market programmes, whereas the programmes were firmly established during the second period. Separate estimates for men and women are provided. The authors also include a dummy variable to allow for differences in on-the-job and off-the-job training. The number of treatment observations ranges between 110 and 600 per subgroup.

For the first period, negative employment effects of training are found, but the effects generally become positive in the second period for both genders. An exception are men in on-the-job training, for whom the training effect is still negative. More positive effects of off-the-job than on-the-job training have already been reported by Fitzenberger and Prey (1996).

As to public works, the authors find negative impacts on the re-employment chances for both periods and genders. In a previous paper on public works, Steiner and Kraus (1995) have analysed the effect of public works on individual employment opportunities on the basis of the LMM between the beginning of 1990 and the end of 1992. Their results are slightly different from those of Kraus, Puhani, and Steiner (1998) in that public works programmes do not have a negative effect on job prospects for men in the 1995 study. However, there are some methodological differences to the Kraus, Puhani, and Steiner (1998) paper. Kraus and Steiner (1995) do not distinguish between exit into stable and unstable employment in their duration model. Further, Kraus and Steiner's (1995) analysis of the effects of public works is based on the selection of specific reference persons, not on the mean of all programme participants as in their later paper (Kraus, Puhani, and Steiner, 1998).

**Staat (1997)**

Staat corrects for sample selectivity by *instrumental variable* estimation (*cf.* our discussion in Section 4.5). Staat uses data from the German Socio-Economic Panel

(GSOEP) to estimate wage and employment effects of training programmes for both western and eastern Germany. The coverage period is 1983 to 1993 for western and 1991 to 1993 for eastern Germany, respectively. The number of sampled training participants is slightly over 300 for both parts of Germany. Staat estimates duration in unemployment by ordered probit models, based on a suggestion of Han and Hausman (1990). The advantages of the Han and Hausman (1990) approach, which has not been presented in our discussion of duration models above, are that this method is appropriate for discrete-time data, estimates the baseline hazard non-parametrically, and is not negatively effected by ties. Hence, it has many of the properties of the (multinomial) logit approach to the estimation of duration data suggested by Nickell (1979).

For eastern Germany, no effects can be found neither on the duration in unemployment nor on the level of hourly wages. Things look a little bit more positive for western Germany. As Staat uses interaction dummies, the estimated effects differ between socio-economic groups. For women in western Germany, the reduction of the unemployment period through training is estimated to be between five and eight months. For men, no effect is found. In general, workers without occupational qualification can expect the largest benefits from training. Their time in unemployment is reduced by between 10 and 21(!) months according to Staat's estimates. Also, young workers under 25 years of age benefit through a reduction of their unemployment spells by around seven months. However, all these estimated effects do not include the time spent in training. Indeed, Staat points out that the reduction in the unemployment duration is in the large majority of cases not larger than the duration spent in training. Therefore, the positive effects found for western Germany net out to around zero if one adds the training period to the time spent in unemployment. The results for eastern Germany suggest that the time east Germans spent in training is a net loss for them. They seem to be back in the same situation where they started after leaving the training programme.

Staat also investigates whether training has an effect on the stability of the employment relationships found after the programme. For eastern Germany, the employment period of former trainees of all age groups except those between 45 and 54 years of age as well as the employment period of female former trainees is shorter than the one for workers who have found a job without training. Taken together with the insignificance of the training programme variables in the estimation of re-employment probabilities, the evidence suggests that trainees in eastern Germany are worse off than non-trainees. For western Germany, on the other hand, positive effects on employment stability are found for former trainees without occupational qualifications. If this is seen in combination with the shorter unemployment spells for trainees from this occupational group, it follows that - at least in western Germany - training may be used to assist groups with difficulties in the labour market.

As to the effects of training on wages, Staat finds no effects except for west German women, for whom hourly wages are significantly higher after training.

Indeed, Staat's estimate suggests that women with training earn more than twice as much as women without training. This estimate seems extremely high and therefore Staat like Pannenberg (1995; 1996) only interprets the sign of the estimate.

### 4.6.2 Evidence on Hungary

#### O'Leary (1997b)

O'Leary estimates the effects of training and public works (*public service employment*) programmes on the re-employment probability as well as on monthly earnings in Hungary for the period 1992 to 1993. His data are from a panel survey organised by the International Labour Office (ILO) in three Hungarian counties, *viz.* Borsod-Abaúj-Zeplén, Hajdú-Bihar, and Somogy. O'Leary's sample consists of 445 training participants, 429 participants in public works, and a comparatively small pool of 604 unemployed comparison persons. The author estimates the effects of the programmes by simple mean comparisons, mean comparisons based on matched samples, as well as by regression analysis. O'Leary finds small positive effects of training in terms of employability and earnings power, although the latter are not significant. Simple mean comparisons suggest that the re-employment rate of trainees is a significant 19 percentage points higher than the one of the naive comparison group. When adjusting for sample selection, this number shrinks to 1.2 percentage points when using matched pairs and 6.3 percentage points when using regression adjustment. However, only the regression adjusted estimate is significant, and that only at the 10 percent level. The effects on earnings are positive, but not significant irrespective of the estimation method employed. Estimates vary between € 4.5 (HUF 500) and € 18 per month.

For public works, the estimated effects are negative. Irrespective of the estimation method employed, the re-employment rate of public works participants is estimated to be around 16 percentage points lower than of persons who have been ordinarily unemployed. The earnings effect is also negative, but insignificant in the matched-sample and regression estimates. O'Leary therefore concludes that public works should be better seen as a means of income transfer with the purpose of keeping up work ethics. However, O'Leary stresses that the re-integration of ALMP participants into regular jobs is hampered by the generosity of the unemployment benefit system. Similarly to Polish works programmes, the eligibility period for unemployment benefits may be reset to the full length after completion of an ALMP programme in Hungary. Hence, interactions between active and passive policies can arise letting beneficiaries circulate between the two support systems.

A positive finding on both Hungarian ALMP programmes, though, comes from O'Leary's subgroup analysis of the programme effects. The subgroups are categorised according to age, education, occupation, work experience, and county of residence. The author finds that both training and public works are most effective for those groups most disadvantaged in the labour market. These are older workers, persons with a low level of education and the unskilled. Comparing these groups with those who are most likely to get into an ALMP programme, O'Leary finds that the efficiency of training programmes could be improved by supporting more males, older persons, persons with a lower level of education, and low skills. For public works, efficiency can be improved by targeting more females and older people.

### 4.6.3 Evidence on Poland

#### Puhani and Steiner (1996; 1997); Puhani (1996)

Puhani and Steiner (1997), which is an abridged and revised version of the 1996 paper, estimate the effect of training, intervention works, and public works programmes on the individual labour force state. This is done by multinomial logit regression of the labour force state as of August 1994. Puhani (1996) estimates the re-employment probabilities for the unemployed on the basis of Weibull duration models with and without unobserved individual heterogeneity. Here only the effect of training programmes is modelled. In all papers, sample selection is implicitly controlled for by the linear control function estimator. Both Puhani's and Puhani and Steiner's estimates suggest that there are no positive effects of any of the programmes under investigation. Puhani and Steiner even find negative effects of works programmes on the employability of the participants. The authors therefore argue that these programmes might stigmatise the participants. The data set used in both Puhani's and Puhani and Steiner's papers is the Polish Labour Force Survey of August 1994 together with its Supplement on the Evaluation of Labour Market Policies. The number of treatment observations per programme ranges between 200 and 500 people. The survey asks some retrospective questions back to January 1990. However, unlike in the survey we use in this study, no information on the exact timing of training and unemployment spells is given. Therefore, the results on Poland so far have to remain tentative.

**Table 30**: Microeconometric Programme Evaluations for Transition Economies

| Study | Data | Method to correct for sample selectivity | Main findings |
|---|---|---|---|
| | | *Studies on Eastern Germany* | |
| Lechner (1995; 1996a; 1996b) | German Socio-Economic Panel (GSOEP) 1990-1994;<br>between 100 and 200 treatment observations per subgroup | Matching | No effects of public training programmes on employment nor earnings;<br>positive effects of enterprise-related training on earnings |
| Fitzenberger and Prey (1995; 1997) | Labour Market Monitor 1990-1992;<br>around 300 treatment observations per subgroup | Structural approach; joint parametric estimation of participation and outcome equations;<br>difference-in-difference interpretation in relation to Heckman and Hotz (1989) pre-programme dummy | Positive effects of off-the-job training on employment;<br>negative effects of on-the-job training on employment |

**Table 30:** Microeconometric Programme Evaluations for Transition Economies (ctd.)

| Study | Data | Method to correct for sample selectivity | Main findings |
|---|---|---|---|
| Fitzenberger and Prey (1996) | Labour Market Monitor 1990-1994<br><br>between 50 and 1000 treatment observations per subgroup | Structural approach; joint parametric estimation of participation and outcome equations;<br><br>difference-in-difference interpretation in relation to Heckman and Hotz (1989) pre-programme dummy | Positive employment effects of off-the-job training with income maintenance; negative effects of on-the-job training with (without) income maintenance for men (women); no employment effects of training without income maintenance for men as well as training off-the-job without income maintenance and training on-the-job with income maintenance for women<br><br>positive wage effects of off-the-job training; no wage effects of on-the-job training |
| Fitzenberger and Prey (1998) | Labour Market Monitor 1990-1994<br><br>number of treatment observations not given | Matching; linear control function estimator;<br><br>difference-in-difference interpretation in relation to Heckman and Hotz (1989) pre-programme dummy | Positive effects of training with income maintenance on employment;<br><br>no effects of training with income maintenance on employment;<br><br>poor quality of matched samples |

**Table 30:** Microeconometric Programme Evaluations for Transition Economies (ctd.)

| Study | Data | Method to correct for sample selectivity | Main findings |
|---|---|---|---|
| Pannenberg (1995) | German Socio-Economic Panel (GSOEP) 1990-1992<br>76 treatment observations | Linear control function estimator | No positive effects of training on employment;<br>Positive effects of training on earnings |
| Pannenberg (1996) | German Socio-Economic Panel (GSOEP) 1990-1994<br>90 treatment observations | Linear control function estimator | Positive effects of training on employment and earnings |
| Hübler (1997) | Labour Market Monitor 1990-1994<br>number of treatment observations not given | Matching combined with linear control function estimator | No clearly defined positive effects of training on employment; some evidence for positive effects for men and negative effects for women;<br>negative effects of public works on employment for men |

**Table 30:** Microeconometric Programme Evaluations for Transition Economies (ctd.)

| Study | Data | Method to correct for sample selectivity | Main findings |
|---|---|---|---|
| Steiner and Kraus (1995) | Labour Market Monitor 1990-1992<br>around 300 treatment observations per subgroup | Linear control function estimator | Negative effects of public works on employment for women; no significant positive effects of public works on employment for men |
| Kraus, Puhani, and Steiner (1997) | Labour Market Monitor 1990-1994<br>between 200 and 600 treatment observations per subgroup | Linear control function estimator plus test based on heterogeneity components | Positive effects of training on employment for women; positive employment effects of off-the-job training, but negative effects of on-the-job training for men |
| Kraus, Puhani, and Steiner (1998) | Labour Market Monitor 1990-1994<br>between 110 and 254 treatment observations per subgroup | Linear control function estimator plus test based on heterogeneity components | Negative effects of public works on employment |
| Staat (1997) | German Socio-Economic Panel (GSOEP) 1991-1993<br>around 300 treatment observations | Instrumental variable estimator | No effects of training on employment nor wages |

**Table 30:** Microeconometric Programme Evaluations for Transition Economies (ctd.)

| Study | Data | Method to correct for sample selectivity | Main findings |
|---|---|---|---|
| | | *Study on Hungary* | |
| O'Leary (1997b) | ILO survey for 3 Hungarian counties 1992-1993<br>Between 400 and 500 treatment observations per subgroup | Matching; linear control function estimator | Positive effects of training on employment;<br>negative effects of public works on employment;<br>no effects of training nor public works on earnings |
| | | *Studies on Poland* | |
| Puhani and Steiner (1996; 1997) | Polish Labour Force Survey 1990-1994<br>Between 200 and 500 treatment observations per subgroup | Linear control function estimator | No effects of training on employment;<br>negative effects of intervention and public works on employment |
| Puhani (1996) | Polish Labour Force Survey 1990-1994<br>Between 60 and 90 treatment observations per subgroup | Linear control function estimator | No effects of training on employment |

### 4.6.4 Conclusions from Previous Work on Transition Economies

The research which has been carried out so far on transition economies might at first sight not be able to provide a clear picture on the effectiveness of ALMPs. However, the studies not only vary in respect of whether they find any effects of ALMPs, but also in the estimation procedures which they apply. Taking these into account, some tentative conclusions can be drawn from previous research on eastern Germany. The studies which have found no effects of training on employment generally apply either the matching approach (Lechner, 1995; 1996a; 1996b; Fitzenberger and Prey, 1998) or the instrumental variable estimator (Staat, 1997). Given the small number of observations on ALMP participants, one has to expect large standard errors for estimates using matched samples, so that obtaining statistically significant programme effects is difficult. Furthermore, it is well known that the instrumental variable estimator is not very efficient, especially if the instrument is not highly correlated with actual ALMP participation.

Studies which use econometric modelling techniques, on the other hand, mostly find positive effects of training programmes in eastern Germany (Fitzenberger and Prey, 1995; 1996; 1997; Pannenberg, 1996; Kraus, Puhani, and Steiner, 1997). However, there are exceptions. Hübler (1997) reports a negative employment effect of training for women. Fitzenberger and Prey (1996) estimate positive employment effects only for off-the-job training with income maintenance. Kraus, Puhani, and Steiner (1997) agree with Fitzenberger and Prey (1996) in that, for men, they also only find positive employment effects of off-the-job training. In addition, the authors point out that training has had negative effects in the first phase of transition (1990-1992) when the institutional structure of public training still had to be build up, which is in line with Pannenberg's (1995) results.

To conclude on the evidence on training in eastern Germany, there is some support for positive employment effects, yet more work needs to be done to obtain statistically safer results. Training has in general been found more effective than public works (Hübler, 1997; Steiner and Kraus, 1995; Kraus, Puhani, and Steiner, 1997; 1998). The result of the relative low effectiveness of public works not only applies to eastern Germany, but also to Hungary (O'Leary, 1997b), and Poland (Puhani and Steiner, 1996; 1997; Puhani, 1996). O'Leary (1997b) estimates positive effects for training in Hungary, but negative ones for public works. Puhani and Steiner (1996; 1997) and Puhani (1996) find no effect for training in Poland, but negative effects of works programmes (Puhani and Steiner, 1996; 1997).

The quality of the data used for evaluation purposes is a general problem in all the studies, because the questionnaires have mostly not been designed for the evaluation of ALMPs. However, the problem has been particularly severe for Poland, as the timing of unemployment and ALMP participation could not be identified from the Polish Labour Force Survey Supplement of August 1994, which has for long been the only available data source with which microeconometric ALMP evaluation could be attempted. We have therefore proposed to ascertain retrospective monthly calendar information on employment, unemployment, and ALMP programme participation in the August 1996 Supplement to the Polish Labour Force Survey (Steiner, Puhani, and Kwiatkowski, 1995). Such data is now available and, to our knowledge, the following chapter presents the first microeconometric evaluation of the re-employment effects of ALMP programmes in Poland that use this data.

# 5 Microeconometric ALMP Evaluation: Empirical Analysis for Poland

In this chapter, we estimate the effects of training, intervention, and public works programmes on the re-employment chances of the unemployed. As unemployment is *the* indicator of being disadvantaged in the Polish labour market, we will exclusively focus on re-employment effects and not consider any possible effects on wages. The Supplement on Active Labour Market Policies to the Polish Labour Force Survey of August 1996 so far provides the best data source in Poland for the purpose of programme evaluation. Section 5.1 describes this data source as well as our methodology to create unemployment spells from it. The empirical evaluations of Polish ALMPs are then presented in Sections 5.2 and 5.3. Following the literature surveyed in Section 4.6, the two estimation methods used will be mean comparisons on the basis of matched samples on the one hand (*cf.* Lechner, 1995; 1996a; 1996b; O'Leary, 1997b; and Fitzenberger and Prey, 1998), and duration model analysis on the other (*cf.* Pannenberg, 1995; 1996; Puhani, 1996; Kraus, Puhani, and Steiner, 1997; 1998; and Staat, 1997).

## 5.1 Data

The best currently available data source which allows an evaluation of ALMPs on the individual level in Poland is the Polish Labour Force Survey (PLFS) together with its Supplement on Active Labour Market Policies of August 1996. There has already been a supplementary survey on ALMPs in August 1994, yet the information on the timing and duration of ALMPs is very sparse there and not compatible with the August 1996 survey (*cf.* Puhani and Steiner, 1996; 1997; Puhani, 1996; Kwiatkowski, Kubiak, and Kucharski, 1997). Therefore, we only use data from the August 1996 survey. The main part of the PLFS, which has been shortly described in Section 3.4, has information on socio-economic variables like age, gender, education, occupation, and industry at the time of interview or the last time of employment. Unlike the 1994 survey, the August 1996 supplement gives *retrospective monthly calendar information on a person's labour force state* from January 1992 to August 1996. This information is asked for in the following way:

**Figure 9:** Retrospective Information on the Labour Force State in the Polish Labour Force Survey Supplement of August 1996

| In which months of the year 1992 (1993/4/5/6) were you | 01 | 02 | 03 | 04 | 05 | 06 | 07 | 08 | 09 | 10 | 11 | 12 |
|---|---|---|---|---|---|---|---|---|---|---|---|---|
| Working for money | x | | | | | | | | | | x | x |
| Registered as unemployed | | x | x | x | x | | | | x | x | | |
| Participating in your last public training course | | | | | | x | x | x | | | | |
| Participating in intervention works | | | | | | | | | | | | |
| Participating in public works | | | | | | | | | | | | |

*Note:* In this example, the person has been employed (working for money), unemployed, and in a training programme in 1992. The person has obviously not participated in any intervention or public works programmes in 1992.

Source: *Polish Labour Force Survey August 1996 Supplement Questionnaire; available from the Central Statistical Office (GUS) of Poland.*

It is thus possible to observe the labour market history of each individual between January 1992 and August 1996. Employment, registered unemployment, and ALMP participation spells can hence be retrieved. However, whereas all intervention and public works spells between 1992 and 1996 can be identified from the survey, only the last publicly-financed training course is asked for. Therefore, we do not know whether somebody has been in public training more than once.

In case a person ticks more than one labour force state, we classify the person to be in the state mentioned in a lower line of Figure 9. To give an example, if somebody reports to be employed and to be in an intervention works programme, we classify that person to be in an intervention works programme. This makes sense, as an employee in an intervention works programme cannot be treated as regularly employed for our purposes. A problem arises when somebody states that he or she is both employed and unemployed. In this case, we classify that person to be unemployed on the assumption that he or she is working for less than half the minimum wage, which is officially allowed in Poland whilst being registered as unemployed and receiving benefits (Kwiatkowski, 1995b; Góra and Schmidt, 1997). Unfortunately, we do not have any further information on the type of employment to check whether that person broke the rules and was in fact regularly employed. It is also quite likely that many persons who report both employment and unemployment as labour force states for a month have in fact been in both of these states during that month. By classifying those people as unemployed we also identify short unemployment spells which last less than a month. As it occurs in less than one percent of the cases that a person reports to be both employed and unemployed, these people do not seem to embody a major problem for the empirical analysis.

The focus of this evaluation is on people who join an active labour market programme out of the state of unemployment, because the main purpose of ALMPs is to reduce the re-employability of the unemployed. Therefore, persons who receive treatment (participate in a programme) without a preceding unemployment spell are not included in the sample. As a consequence, all persons that have never been registered as unemployed cannot act as valid comparison persons and are therefore also excluded from the sample. When creating unemployment spells, the state of being in an ALMP programme is also treated as unemployment. To take the example of Figure 9, if a person becomes unemployed in February 1992, gets into a publicly-financed training scheme in June 1992, then becomes unemployed again after the scheme in September 1992 only to find a job in November 1992, we treat the whole period from February 1992 up to October 1992 as one unemployment spell. Figure 10 gives a graphical presentation.

**Figure 10:** The Definition of the Unemployment Spell Corresponding to Figure 9

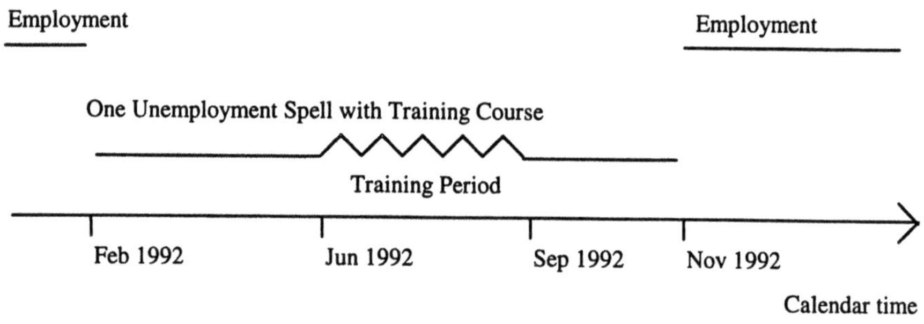


The only labour force states which terminate an unemployment spell are employment and non-participation in the labour market. A person is classified as not participating in the labour market if he or she is not in any of the labour force states mentioned in Figure 9.

Table 35 presents the number of the ALMP participants and comparison spells in our sample. As some persons experience more than one spell during the observation period, we report the number of persons and the number of spells separately. Left-censored observations do not allow modelling of process time (Blossfeld and Rohwer, 1995, Chapter 2). As the statistical treatment of left-censored observations is generally not straightforward (Hamerle, 1991), we follow the standard approach in the empirical literature and do not include these observations in the sample. The loss of observations through excluding left-censored spells lies between 20 and 30 percent. Right-censored observations will be included in the statistical analyses of the following two sections. However, because one does not know the time when the spell ends nor the state into which exit occurs, the information content of right-censored spells is much smaller than the one of completed spells.

The share of right-censored spells varies between 19 percent for men in training and 71 for women in public works. The small number of observations for women in public works makes a serious statistical analysis impossible. Nevertheless, we will also carry out an evaluation for this group in the hope that at least some tentative evidence can be obtained. Unfortunately, the number of completed spells for men in public works is also very small.

However, a very important and positive characteristic of the sample, especially for the matching approach, is the large number of comparison spells. The larger the pool of comparison spells, the more likely it is to find good matches for the treatment spells. Depending on the programme, we have 26 to 78 times as many comparison as treatment persons (not considering women in public works with 286 times as many comparison as treatment persons). The corresponding figures are lower in other studies which use the matching approach where treatment and comparison persons are drawn from the same data source. Lechner (1995; 1996a) has around 10 times more comparison than treatment persons. In Lechner (1996b), O'Leary (1997b), and Hujer, Maurer, and Wellner (1997b) these ratios are around 4, 1.3, and 3.2, respectively. Our sample thus provides very good *a priori* conditions for applying the matching approach, which will be presented in the following section.

**Table 31**: Selection of the ALMP Participants Samples

| Selection criterion | Men | Women | Total |
|---|---|---|---|
| *Training* | | | |
| Former or Current Participants | 97 | 151 | 248 |
| Age between 16 and 65 | 97 | 150 | 247 |
| Persons / spells where unemployment precedes ALMP | 67 / 67 | 115 / 115 | 182 / 182 |
| **Persons / spells not left censored** | **52 / 52** | **88 / 88** | **140 / 140** |
| Not right-censored | 42 / 42 | 52 / 52 | 94 / 94 |
| *Intervention Works* | | | |
| Former or Current Participants | 313 | 269 | 582 |
| Age between 16 and 65 | 313 | 268 | 581 |
| Persons / spells where unemployment precedes ALMP | 267 / 269 | 217 / 219 | 484 / 488 |
| **Persons / spells not left censored** | **193 / 193** | **154 / 155** | **347 / 348** |
| Not right-censored | 74 / 74 | 68 / 68 | 142 / 142 |
| *Public Works* | | | |
| Former or Current Participants | 82 | 26 | 108 |
| Age between 16 and 65 | 82 | 26 | 108 |
| Persons / spells where unemployment precedes ALMP | 70 / 72 | 20 / 20 | 90 / 92 |
| **Persons / spells not left censored** | **49 / 50** | **14 / 14** (!) | **63 / 64** |
| Not right-censored | 18 / 18 (!) | 4 / 4 (!) | 22 / 22 |
| *Non-participants (comparisons)* | | | |
| Unemployed persons / spells aged between 16 and 65 | 3684 / 4727 | 4169 / 5068 | 7853 / 9795 |
| **Unemployed persons / spells not left censored** | **3160 / 3922** | **3422 / 4010** | **6582 / 7932** |
| Not right-censored | 2165 / 2612 | 2041/ 2301 | 4206 / 4913 |

*Note*: The bold lines refer to the sample for the empirical analyses below; non-participants have not participated in any ALMP programme.

Source: *Polish Labour Force Survey; own calculations.*

## 5.2 Empirical Evaluation of ALMPs by Way of the Statistical Matching Approach

Although the general principles behind the matching approach have already been outlined in Section 4.3, we discuss the specific implementation for our Polish data in the subsequent Section 5.2.1. The matching method is then applied in Section 5.2.2, and evaluation results are presented in Section 5.2.3.

### 5.2.1 Methodological Issues

Equation [4. 4*] of Section 4.3 has shown that the treatment effect for the treated can be written

$$\tau|_{T=1} = E_{\mathbf{z}|T=1}\left\{E\left(Y_1 \middle| T=1, \Pr\left(T=1|\mathbf{z}\right)\right) - E\left(Y_0 \middle| T=0, \Pr\left(T=1|\mathbf{z}\right)\right)\right\}.$$

To build an estimator of $\tau|_{T=1}$ by matching on the programme participation probability $\Pr(T=1|\mathbf{z})$, the first step is to estimate this probability, which is unknown. To this end, a probit equation for participation in each programme will be estimated by maximum likelihood (similarly, Lechner, 1995; 1996a; 1996b estimates probit, Dehejia and Wahba, 1995a; 1995b; and Heckman, Ichimura, and Todd, 1997 estimate logit models). The probit model is specified as follows (see, *e.g.*, Maddala, 1983; Chapter 2):

$$\begin{aligned} &T_i^* = \gamma' \mathbf{z}_i + v_i \qquad && v_i \sim N(0;1) \\ &T_i = 1 \quad \text{if} \quad T_i^* > 0 && \\ &T_i = 0 \quad \text{if} \quad T_i^* \le 0 && \end{aligned}$$

where $T^*$ is the latent index which drives the programme participation probability. The estimated programme participation probability for person $i$ is then

$$\hat{\Pr}\left(T_i = 1|\mathbf{z}_i\right) = \Phi\left(\hat{\gamma}' \mathbf{z}_i\right)$$

where $\Phi(\cdot)$ denotes the cumulative distribution function of the normal distribution.

Having obtained an estimate of the programme participation probability $\Pr(T=1|\mathbf{z})$, one can match to each treatment person a comparison person with the same estimated participation probability $\Phi(\hat{\gamma}'\mathbf{z})$, which acts as the *balancing score*.

Often, it is not possible to find a comparison person with exactly the same estimated balancing score $\Phi(\hat{\gamma}'\mathbf{z})$. In this case, one can define the *nearest neighbour* to the treatment person as that comparison person who has the closest estimated balancing score $\Phi(\hat{\gamma}'\mathbf{z})$. A related method has been applied by Lechner

(1995; 1996a; 1996b) who uses $\hat{\gamma}'\mathbf{z}$ as the balancing score. The index $\hat{\gamma}'\mathbf{z}$ is also a balancing score as $\Phi(\cdot)$ is a monotonous function:

$$\Pr(T=1|\gamma'\mathbf{z}) = \Pr(T=1|\Phi(\gamma'\mathbf{z})).$$

The difference to matching on $\Phi(\hat{\gamma}'\mathbf{z})$ is that when $\Phi(\hat{\gamma}'\mathbf{z})$ is close to zero or one, relatively large differences in $\mathbf{z}$ between treatment and control groups can have asymmetric effects on $\Phi(\hat{\gamma}'\mathbf{z})$ and lead to different matches. For example, given a treatment person with probability $\Phi(\hat{\gamma}'\mathbf{z})$ close to one, a comparison person with a much higher index $\hat{\gamma}'\mathbf{z}$ may be closer to the treatment person in terms of $\Phi(\hat{\gamma}'\mathbf{z})$ than a different comparison person with only a slightly lower index $\hat{\gamma}'\mathbf{z}$. In this case, it may be preferable to match the treated person with the second comparison person, as he or she is closer to the treatment person in terms of $\mathbf{z}$. We will therefore follow Lechner's (1995; 1996a; 1996b) approach and match on $\hat{\gamma}'\mathbf{z}$.

However, we will only use the estimate $\hat{\gamma}'\mathbf{z}$ from the probit model as a *partial* balancing score. The reason is that in order to improve the comparability of treatment and matched comparison persons, we want to match *exactly* on a set of variables, which means we want some variables to take on identical values for treatment and comparison persons. These variables are the *labour force state* before the beginning of the unemployment spell and, most importantly, the *time in unemployment until somebody gets into an ALMP programme*, which is defined as

$$\begin{aligned} m_T &= \textit{calendar time when ALMP started} \\ &\quad - \textit{calendar time when unemployment started} \end{aligned}$$

In the example of Figure 9 on page 145, $m_T$ is equal to 4 months. In our sample, $m_T$ ranges between 1 to 52 months, whereas the median durations $m_T$ are around 6 months for training and 12 months for intervention and public works programmes.

We choose to condition on $m_T$ exactly, because it is only defined for treatment persons and can therefore not be included in the cross-sectional probit estimation for programme participation. However, when matching a comparison to a treatment person, we require the comparison person to have been unemployed more than $m_T$ months. This way we ensure that the comparison person is also comparable to the treatment person in terms of process time in unemployment until the treatment person joined the ALMP programme. If this requirement is fulfilled, we match on the estimated *partial balancing score* $\hat{\gamma}'\mathbf{z}$. The *total balancing score* is $(\hat{\gamma}'\mathbf{z}, m_T, E_{1,}, E_3, E_6)$. The variables $E_1$ to $E_6$ and the matching algorithm in detail are described in the following.

***The Matching Algorithm***

*Step 1: For (formerly) unemployed people, a probit model for ALMP participation is estimated. The estimated index* $\hat{\gamma}'\mathbf{z}$ *from this probit model is in the following used as the partial balancing score.*

*Step 2: The observations are split into two pools, a treatment (ALMP participant;* $T = 1$*) and a comparison (non-participant;* $T = 0$*) pool.*

*Step 3: The person from the treatment pool with the lowest partial balancing score is taken and removed from the treatment pool. The number of months* $m_T$ *this treatment person has been unemployed until he or she started the ALMP programme is noted. Furthermore, it is noted whether 1, 3, and 6 months before the start of the unemployment spell in which the ALMP programme took place, the treatment person has been in employment or not (*$E_1 = 1/0, E_3 = 1/0, E_6 = 1/0$*).*

*Step 4: All persons are removed from the comparison pool who have not been unemployed for more than* $m_T$ *months and have not been in the same labour force states (*$E_1$*,* $E_2$*, and* $E_6$*) as the treatment person 1, 3 and 6 months before the start of their unemployment spell.*

*Step 5: If after Step 4 no-one is left in the comparison pool, Step 4 is undone and then repeated again but without the condition that the labour force status 6 months before unemployment (*$E_6$*) is equal to the one of the treatment person. If still no one is left in the comparison pool after the application of this modified Step 4, the condition that the labour force states 3 and 1 months before unemployment (*$E_3$ *and* $E_1$*) equal those of the treatment person are also dropped one by one. The condition on the number of months in unemployment before treatment* $m_T$ *is never dropped as this is not necessary with our specific sample.*

*Step 6: For the treatment person, those persons from the comparison pool selected under Steps 4 and 5 are found who have the partial balancing score with the smallest difference* $\left(\hat{\gamma}'\mathbf{z}_{T=1} - \hat{\gamma}'\mathbf{z}_{T=0}\right)^2$ *to the partial balancing score of the treatment person. If the number of comparison persons selected this way exceeds one, one person is randomly drawn from the selected comparison persons. This person is then taken as the matched comparison person and removed from the comparison pool.*

*Step 7: The removals from the comparison pool undertaken under Steps 4 and 5 are undone.*

*Step 8: Steps 3 to 7 are repeated until the treatment pool is empty. Then all treatment observations have exactly one partner from the comparison pool matched to them.*

The quality of the programme effect estimate rests both on the quality of the programme participation estimate and the ability to find comparison persons with equal participation probabilities as the treatment persons. In order to ensure that the best possible estimate of the programme participation probability $\Pr(T=1|\mathbf{z})$ is obtained, the probit model should include all observed variables $\mathbf{z}$ that one may think to influence programme participation. Indeed, probit estimates are inconsistent if any relevant variables are omitted from estimation, even if the omitted variables are uncorrelated with the error term $\nu$ (Greene, 1997; Chapter 19). The estimates of the partial balancing score and the matched samples will be described in the following section.

### 5.2.2 Estimation of the Partial Balancing Score and Matching Results

As mentioned in the description of Polish ALMPs in Section 2.4, there are slight differences in the aims the various ALMPs in Poland are supposed to fulfil. Whereas training programmes are targeted towards the more flexible amongst the unemployed, intervention and especially public works are meant to focus more strongly on the long-term unemployed. However, the factors influencing the ALMP participation probability are likely to be the same for all programmes, in one way or another. A*ge*, *education*, and *occupation* may play important roles and will be included amongst the $\mathbf{z}$ variables. As the transition process has a substantial impact on the industrial structure in Poland, we also include the current or former *industry* a person is working or has worked in. The transition process has also had persistent regional labour market effects (see Section 2.3). We control both for the size of the *place of residence* and the *voivodship* a person lives in. Given that ALMP expenditures are distributed on the voivodship level according to the severity of local labour market problems, it makes sense to include dummy variables for each voivodship amongst the $\mathbf{z}$ variables.

As shown in Sections 2.1 and 2.2, the demand for labour increased in Poland between 1994 and 1996 and the unemployment rate fell correspondingly. In order to obtain consistent estimates of the ALMP effects it is important to make sure that treatment and comparison persons operate in the same macroeconomic environment. A careful consideration of *calendar time* is hence warranted. In the ALMP participation models, we consider the time dimension by including a dummy variable which is equal to one if the beginning of the unemployment spell has been between 1994 and 1996 and zero otherwise. We will also test whether, on average, treatments and matched comparisons operate in difference calendar-time periods.

The previous labour market history of the unemployed is taken into account by three dummy variables ($E_1$, $E_2$, and $E_6$) which control for the *labour force state* 1, 3, and 6 months before the beginning of their unemployment spell (employed or not employed; these are the variables we also try to match exactly on). The number of *previous months in unemployment* since 1992 before the beginning of the unemployment spell is also included to control for effects of the previous labour market history.

**Balancing Score Estimates**

Probit estimation results for the partial balancing score are reported in Table 32, Table 33, and Table 34 for training, intervention, and public works, respectively. The estimated coefficients reflect the different intentions of the various labour market programmes. Young and better educated people are comparatively more likely to join training than intervention or public works programmes. It is also no surprise that public works, which also perform a social policy task, accept more people who have worked as *technicians* or in *simple jobs* in industries like *construction* or *other services* (*e.g.*, cleaning). However, it is rather striking that people who have previously worked in the (mostly public) administration have extremely good chances of getting into either intervention or public works programmes. This result has already been obtained by Puhani and Steiner (1996; 1997) as well as Kwiatkowski, Kubiak, and Kucharski (1997). The fact that one can find no *a priori* reason why former administrators should get a special attention in ALMP programmes (they are not particularly hard hit by unemployment), and the fact that it is *administrators* in the labour offices who decide who gets to join an ALMP programme, raise the question whether network effects account for the high share of administrators in works programmes.

**Table 32**: Probit Estimates of the Partial Balancing Score (Training)

| Variable | Men | | Women | |
|---|---|---|---|---|
| | Coeff. | t-value | Coeff. | t-value |
| Age between (36 and 45) | | | | |
| 16 and 25 | 0.118 | 0.51 | -0.001 | -0.01 |
| 26 and 35 | -0.256 | -1.27 | 0.094 | 0.60 |
| 46 and 55 | 0.090 | 0.42 | -0.136 | -0.64 |
| 56 and 65 | 0.130 | 0.30 | - | - |
| Education (basic vocational) | | | | |
| Higher | 0.882 | 1.93 | **0.672** | 2.16 |
| Post-secondary | **0.803** | 2.10 | **0.575** | 2.37 |
| Secondary vocational | 0.073 | 0.38 | **0.544** | 3.37 |
| Secondary general | 0.349 | 0.98 | **0.844** | 4.59 |
| Primary or less | -0.075 | -0.36 | -0.076 | -0.34 |
| Occupation (industrial worker) | | | | |
| Manager | 0.208 | 0.55 | -0.594 | -1.20 |
| Professional | -0.490 | -0.82 | 0.131 | 0.39 |
| Technician | -0.172 | -0.54 | -0.004 | -0.02 |
| White collar | -0.056 | -0.17 | 0.062 | 0.27 |
| Personal services | -0.279 | -0.94 | -0.438* | -1.76 |
| Farmer | 0.218 | 0.32 | 0.400 | 0.85 |
| Simple blue-collar | -0.162 | -0.73 | -0.098 | -0.25 |
| Other simple jobs | -0.495* | -1.84 | -0.284 | -1.09 |
| Single | -0.034 | -0.16 | 0.013 | 0.09 |
| Children | -0.295 | -1.19 | 0.103 | 0.57 |
| No information about children | -0.268 | -1.18 | -0.200 | -1.19 |
| Disabled | -0.046 | -0.14 | **0.511** | 2.06 |

**Table 32:** Probit Estimates of the Partial Balancing Score (Training) (ctd.)

| Variable | Men | | Women | |
|---|---|---|---|---|
| | Coeff. | t-value | Coeff. | t-value |
| Industry (mining, manufacturing) | | | | |
| Agriculture, forestry, fishing | -1.047 | -1.55 | -0.610 | -1.35 |
| Electricity, gas, water | 0.015 | 0.03 | 0.382 | 0.66 |
| Construction | -0.223 | -1.10 | 0.172 | 0.51 |
| Trade, repairs | 0.127 | 0.57 | 0.349* | 1.74 |
| Hotels, restaurants | 0.162 | 0.39 | 0.487* | 1.75 |
| Transport, communication | 0.072 | 0.24 | 0.165 | 0.49 |
| Financial intermediation | 1.048* | 1.72 | -0.439 | -0.89 |
| Real estates | - | - | 0.135 | 0.42 |
| Administration | - | - | 0.345 | 1.23 |
| Education | 0.216 | 0.38 | -0.343 | -1.05 |
| Health, social work | 0.843 | 2.20 | -0.447 | -1.31 |
| Other services | -0.025 | -0.07 | 0.072 | 0.26 |
| None, unknown | -0.249 | -0.61 | -0.020 | -0.09 |
| Place of residence (countryside) | | | | |
| 100,000 inhabitants or more | -0.182 | -0.84 | 0.210 | 1.39 |
| 20,000 to 99,999 | -0.073 | -0.36 | 0.073 | 0.46 |
| 19,999 or less | -0.115 | -0.53 | -0.078 | -0.42 |

**Table 32:** Probit Estimates of the Partial Balancing Score (Training) (ctd.)

| Variable | | Men | | Women | |
|---|---|---|---|---|---|
| | | Coeff. | t-value | Coeff. | t-value |
| Employed 1 month before unemployment ($\varepsilon$) | | -0.255 | -1.08 | 0.088 | 0.41 |
| Employed 3 months before unemployment ($\varepsilon$) | | 0.347 | 1.00 | -0.524* | -1.79 |
| Employed 6 months before unemployment ($\varepsilon$) | | 0.249 | 0.92 | 0.342 | 1.49 |
| Previous months in unemployment | | 0.018 | 1.61 | -0.020 | -1.25 |
| Beginning of unemployment spell between 1994 and 1996 | | -0.151 | -1.00 | -0.218 | -1.97 |
| Voivodship (Warsaw) | | | | | |
| (voivodships with insignificant coefficients not reported) | | | | | |
| Bydgoskie | (high U / industrial) | 0.933* | 1.89 | 0.002 | 0.01 |
| Lodzkie | (high U / industrial) | 1.064 | 2.18 | 0.033 | 0.10 |
| Olsztynskie | (high U / other) | 0.765 | 1.49 | 0.569* | 1.80 |
| Slupskie | (high U / modern) | 1.114 | 2.05 | 0.691 | 1.99 |
| Walbrzyskie | (high U / industrial) | 0.951* | 1.86 | 0.572* | 1.64 |
| Constant | | -2.485 | -4.77 | -2.229 | -6.47 |
| Number of observations | | 2,081 | | 3,387 | |
| *ln* likelihood | | -206.25 | | -340.54 | |
| Pseudo-R2 (McFadden) | | 0.152 | | 0.166 | |
| Pseudo-R2 (Veall-Zimmermann) | | 0.235 | | 0.262 | |

*Notes:* shaded (asterisked) coefficients are significant at the 5 (10) percent level;
base categories for dummy variables are given in parentheses; the number of observations lies below the number of treatment plus comparison persons given in Table 31 on page 148, because there are no treatment persons in some categories so that all comparison persons in these categories had to be dropped from the comparison pool; in essence, this means we also match exactly on these categories;
comparison persons have not participated in any ALMP programme;
the classifications of the voivodships according to U (unemployment), and *modern, industrial, agricultural*, and *other* employment structures, correspond to Figure 2 and Figure 3 on page 16.
The pseudo–$R^2$ (Veall–Zimmermann) was found to come closest to the underlying OLS–$R^2$ in a Monte Carlo Study on a binary probit model by Veall and Zimmermann (1996) (where this pseudo–$R^2$ is called $R^2_{\omega}$).

Source: *Polish Labour Force Survey; own calculations.*

**Table 33**: Probit Estimates of the Partial Balancing Score (Intervention Works)

| Variable | Men | | Women | |
|---|---|---|---|---|
| | Coeff. | t-value | Coeff. | t-value |
| Age between (36 and 45) | | | | |
| 16 and 25 | **-0.395** | -2.46 | -0.147 | -0.91 |
| 26 and 35 | -0.068 | -0.57 | -0.006 | -0.04 |
| 46 and 55 | -0.138 | -0.96 | -0.017 | -0.10 |
| 56 and 65 | 0.109 | 0.37 | - | - |
| Education (basic vocational) | | | | |
| Higher | -0.443 | -0.76 | 0.361 | 1.18 |
| Post–secondary | -0.031 | -0.07 | 0.209 | 0.98 |
| Secondary vocational | -0.077 | -0.53 | 0.167 | 1.23 |
| Secondary general | 0.363 | 1.21 | 0.145 | 0.77 |
| Primary or less | **0.243** | 2.43 | **0.323** | 2.44 |
| Occupation (industrial worker) | | | | |
| Professional | -0.567 | -0.88 | **-0.819** | -2.20 |
| Technician | -0.508* | -1.90 | -0.106 | -0.49 |
| White collar | -0.002 | -0.01 | -0.197 | -0.93 |
| Personal services | **-1.284** | -3.76 | -0.279 | -1.27 |
| Farmer | -0.137 | -0.54 | -0.401 | -1.24 |
| Simple blue–collar | **-0.338** | -2.12 | -0.371 | -1.12 |
| Other simple jobs | -0.073 | -0.63 | -0.107 | -0.59 |
| Single | 0.090 | 0.70 | **0.259** | 2.22 |
| Children | 0.148 | 1.08 | -0.108 | -0.70 |
| No information about children | -0.125 | -0.92 | 0.060 | 0.43 |
| Disabled | **-0.988** | -2.68 | -0.265 | -0.92 |

**Table 33:** Probit Estimates of the Partial Balancing Score (Intervention Works) (ctd.)

| Variable | Men | | Women | |
|---|---|---|---|---|
| | Coeff. | t-value | Coeff. | t-value |
| Industry (mining, manufacturing) | | | | |
| Agriculture, forestry, fishing | -0.086 | -0.37 | 0.053 | 0.20 |
| Electricity, gas, water | 0.425 | 1.23 | - | - |
| Construction | 0.311 | 2.45 | 0.218 | 0.66 |
| Trade, repairs | 0.511 | 3.07 | -0.203 | -0.98 |
| Hotels, restaurants | 0.096 | 0.19 | -0.189 | -0.66 |
| Transport, communication | -0.103 | -0.38 | -0.079 | -0.21 |
| Financial intermediation | 1.139 | 2.19 | 0.765 | 2.90 |
| Real estates, renting | 0.770 | 3.04 | 0.686 | 2.51 |
| Administration | 1.818 | 11.00 | 1.419 | 7.41 |
| Education | 0.450 | 1.53 | 0.294 | 1.07 |
| Health, social work | 0.980 | 3.39 | 0.622 | 3.44 |
| Other services | 0.556 | 2.37 | 0.062 | 0.28 |
| None, unknown | -0.227 | -0.71 | -1.172 | -3.33 |
| Place of residence (countryside) | | | | |
| 100,000 inhabitants or more | -0.947 | -5.11 | -0.322 | -2.21 |
| 20,000 to 99,999 | -0.563 | -4.30 | 0.094 | 0.76 |
| 19,999 or less | -0.140 | -1.19 | 0.075 | 0.58 |

**Table 33:** Probit Estimates of the Partial Balancing Score (Intervention Works) (ctd.)

| Variable | | Men | | Women | |
|---|---|---|---|---|---|
| | | Coeff. | t-value | Coeff. | t-value |
| Employed 1 month before unemployment ($\varepsilon$) | | 0.167 | 1.05 | 0.036 | 0.20 |
| Employed 3 months before unemployment ($\varepsilon$) | | -0.166 | -0.87 | -0.149 | -0.64 |
| Employed 6 months before unemployment ($\varepsilon$) | | -0.154 | -1.07 | -0.169 | -0.96 |
| Previous months in unemployment | | -0.003 | -0.34 | -0.009 | -0.89 |
| Beginning of unemployment spell between 1994 and 1996 | | **-0.475** | -5.15 | **-0.236** | -2.57 |
| Voivodship (Warsaw) | | | | | |
| (voivodships with insignificant coefficients not reported) | | | | | |
| Chelmskie | (high U / agricultural) | 0.230 | 0.48 | **1.058** | 2.73 |
| Czestochowskie | (low U / industrial) | -0.283 | -0.72 | **0.710** | 2.04 |
| Kieleckie | (high U / industrial) | 0.074 | 0.26 | **0.885** | 2.97 |
| Koszalinskie | (high U / modern) | **0.714** | 2.39 | **0.676** | 2.04 |
| Lodzkie | (high U / industrial) | 0.558* | 1.81 | -0.108 | -0.27 |
| Pilskie | (mid U / other) | 0.281 | 0.90 | **0.889** | 2.66 |
| Slupskie | (high U / modern) | 0.476 | 1.56 | **0.712** | 2.17 |
| Wroclawskie | (mid U / industrial) | -1.062* | -1.86 | 0.360 | 1.03 |
| Constant | | **-1.151** | -4.22 | **-1.900** | -6.10 |
| Number of observations | | 4,044 | | 3,751 | |
| *ln* likelihood | | -549.46 | | -495.21 | |
| Pseudo-R2 (McFadden) | | 0.292 | | 0.233 | |
| Pseudo-R2 (Veall-Zimmermann) | | 0.405 | | 0.335 | |

*Notes:* shaded (asterisked) coefficients are significant at the 5 (10) percent level; base categories for dummy variables are given in parentheses; the number of observations lies below the number of treatment plus comparison persons given in Table 31 on page 148, because there are no treatment persons in some categories so that all comparison persons in these categories had to be dropped from the comparison pool; in essence, this means we also match exactly on these categories; comparison persons have not participated in any ALMP programme; the classifications of the voivodships according to U (unemployment), and *modern*, *industrial*, *agricultural*, and *other* employment structures, correspond to Figure 2 and Figure 3 on page 16. The pseudo–$R^2$ (Veall–Zimmermann) was found to come closest to the underlying OLS–$R^2$ in a Monte Carlo Study on a binary probit model by Veall and Zimmermann (1996) (where this pseudo–$R^2$ is called $R^{2}_{M}$).

Source: *Polish Labour Force Survey; own calculations.*

**Table 34:** Probit Estimates of the Partial Balancing Score (Public Works)

| Variable | Men | | Women | |
|---|---|---|---|---|
| | Coeff. | t-value | Coeff. | t-value |
| Age between (36 and 45) | | | | |
| 16 and 25 | -0.613 | -2.13 | -0.576 | -0.87 |
| 26 and 35 | -0.141 | -0.63 | -0.408 | -0.80 |
| 46 and 55 | -0.286 | -1.07 | 0.051 | 0.09 |
| 56 and 65 | -0.571 | -0.95 | - | - |
| Education (basic vocational) | | | | |
| Higher | 0.911 | 0.69 | - | - |
| Secondary vocational | -0.363 | -1.02 | -1.593 | -2.25 |
| Secondary general | - | - | -1.325 | -1.42 |
| Primary or less | -0.091 | -0.50 | -0.582 | -1.18 |
| Occupation (industrial worker) | | | | |
| Professional | -0.112 | -0.09 | - | - |
| Technician | - | - | 1.220* | 1.74 |
| Personal services | - | - | -0.582 | -0.79 |
| Farmer | 0.445 | 0.98 | - | - |
| Simple blue–collar | -0.479 | -1.12 | - | - |
| Other simple jobs | 0.548 | 2.73 | 0.564 | 1.14 |
| Single | 0.020 | 0.08 | 0.098 | 0.18 |
| Children | 0.229 | 0.90 | -0.537 | -1.04 |
| No information about children | -0.108 | -0.43 | 0.031 | 0.05 |
| Disabled | -0.347 | -0.74 | -0.054 | -0.06 |

**Table 34:** Probit Estimates of the Partial Balancing Score (Public Works) (ctd.)

| Variable | Men | | Women | |
|---|---|---|---|---|
| | Coeff. | t-value | Coeff. | t-value |
| Industry (mining, manufacturing) | | | | |
| Agriculture, forestry, fishing | 0.001 | 0.00 | - | - |
| Electricity, gas, water | 0.478 | 0.68 | - | - |
| Construction | 0.543 | 2.16 | - | - |
| Trade, repairs | 0.213 | 0.52 | 0.666 | 1.02 |
| Real estates, renting | 0.481 | 0.81 | - | - |
| Administration | **1.755** | 5.56 | **3.281** | 4.77 |
| Education | 0.692 | 1.63 | - | - |
| Other services | **1.218** | 3.25 | **1.277** | 2.21 |
| None, unknown | 0.645 | 1.32 | - | - |
| Place of residence (countryside) | - | - | - | - |
| 100,000 inhabitants or more | **-0.599** | -2.01 | -0.208 | -0.36 |
| 20,000 to 99,999 | **-0.565** | -2.19 | 0.348 | 0.64 |
| 19,999 or less | -0.340 | -1.38 | 0.504 | 0.91 |
| Employed 1 month before unemployment ($\varepsilon$) | 0.582* | 1.95 | 0.756 | 1.04 |
| Employed 3 months before unemployment ($\varepsilon$) | -0.599* | -1.72 | -1.077 | -0.98 |
| Employed 6 months before unemployment ($\varepsilon$) | -0.106 | -0.38 | 0.431 | 0.48 |
| Previous months in unemployment | 0.008 | 0.58 | 0.002 | 0.06 |
| Beginning of unemployment spell between 1994 and 1996 | -0.194 | -1.10 | 0.199 | 0.47 |

**Table 34:** Probit Estimates of the Partial Balancing Score (Public Works) (ctd.)

| Variable | | Men | | Women | |
|---|---|---|---|---|---|
| | | Coeff. | t-value | Coeff. | t-value |
| Voivodship (Warsaw) | | | | | |
| (voivodships with insignificant coefficients not reported) | | | | | |
| Lodzkie | (high U / industrial) | 0.986* | 1.71 | - | - |
| Olsztynskie | (high U / other) | 1.204 | 2.27 | -0.173 | -0.16 |
| Slupskie | (high U / modern) | 1.032* | 1.84 | 0.594 | 0.73 |
| Constant | | -2.458 | -4.31 | -3.137 | -3.37 |
| Number of observations | | 1,770 | | 791 | |
| *ln* likelihood | | -162.21 | | -36.72 | |
| Pseudo-R2 (McFadden) | | 0.287 | | 0.478 | |
| Pseudo-R2 (Veall-Zimmermann) | | 0.374 | | 0.525 | |

*Notes:* shaded (asterisked) coefficients are significant at the 5 (10) percent level;
base categories for dummy variables are given in parentheses; the number of observations lies below the number of treatment plus comparison persons given in Table 31 on page 148, because there are no treatment persons in some categories so that all comparison persons in these categories had to be dropped from the comparison pool; in essence, this means we also match exactly on these categories;
comparison persons have not participated in any ALMP programme;
the classifications of the voivodships according to U (unemployment), and *modern*, *industrial*, *agricultural*, and *other* employment structures, correspond to Figure 2 and Figure 3 on page 16.
The pseudo–$R^2$ (Veall–Zimmermann) was found to come closest to the underlying OLS–$R^2$ in a Monte Carlo Study on a binary probit model by Veall and Zimmermann (1996) (where this pseudo–$R^2$ is called $R'_{a}$).

Source: *Polish Labour Force Survey; own calculations.*

What is new to this analysis and what has not been carried out in neither Puhani and Steiner (1996; 1997) nor Kwiatkowski, Kubiak, and Kucharski (1997), is a *ceteris paribus* investigation of programme participation on the voivodship level. Although only few of the voivodship dummies are significant, we can identify Lodzkie and Slupskie as the regions where the likelihood of getting into an ALMP programme is amongst the highest, at least for men. No other voivodships appear significant in all three models. In Figure 2 and Figure 3 on page 16, we have given a geographical overview of the types of voivodships classified according to unemployment rates and economic structure, respectively. Figure 1 on page 15 has a map with Polish voivodships and their names. It can be seen that both *industrial* Lodzkie and *modern* Slupskie are high unemployment voivodships. Indeed, nearly all voivodships with significant coefficients in the training and public works participation probits are high unemployment areas. The only statistically significant regions which have low or medium unemployment rates are Czestochowskie, Pilskie, and Wroclawskie in the equation for intervention works. Taken together, the regional analysis of ALMP participation in Poland reveals that mostly people in high unemployment and industrial voivodships are targeted in ALMPs, even if one controls for a large set of socio-economic characteristics, as we have done here.

Based on the estimates of the programme participation probabilities we can form the partial balancing score $\hat{\gamma}'\mathbf{z}$ for each person which can then be used to match one comparison spell to each treatment spell. The absolute frequency distributions of the partial balancing scores are depicted in Figure 11, Figure 12, and Figure 13, for training, intervention, and public works, respectively. As the graphs show, the distributions of the treatment scores always have a higher mean than the ones of the comparison groups, as one might expect. Furthermore, the distributions of the treatments have a much higher variance in relation to their mean than the ones of the comparisons. The figures also reveal that there is a significant number of treatment persons with very low partial balancing scores. This indicates that instrumental variable estimation (*cf.* Section 4.5) is unlikely to be successful with the data at hand, as the correlation between actual and estimated programme participation is very low. The fact that the partial balancing score distributions of the comparison groups almost completely overlap those of the treatment groups is a good precondition for applying the matching approach, though.

Nevertheless, the distributions of the partial balancing scores of the treatment and non-treatment groups do not overlap completely for men in intervention works and women in public works where the two distributions have no common support for very high scores. For very high scores, the absolute frequency of comparisons is, if at all, not much higher than the one of the treatments. This raises the question whether the quality of matching will be sufficient in these cases, an issue that will be taken up again below. All in all, however, the overlap between the two distributions seems rather satisfactory and comparable to other studies which present similar graphs. In Lechner (1996b) and Hujer, Maurer, and Wellner (1997b), the area where the two distributions do not overlap is slightly larger than in our worst case, even. In Heckman, Ichimura, and Todd's (1997) sample, the lack of common support of the two distributions is much more severe than in ours.

**Figure 11:** Distributions of the Partial Balancing Score of Trainees and Non-Participants

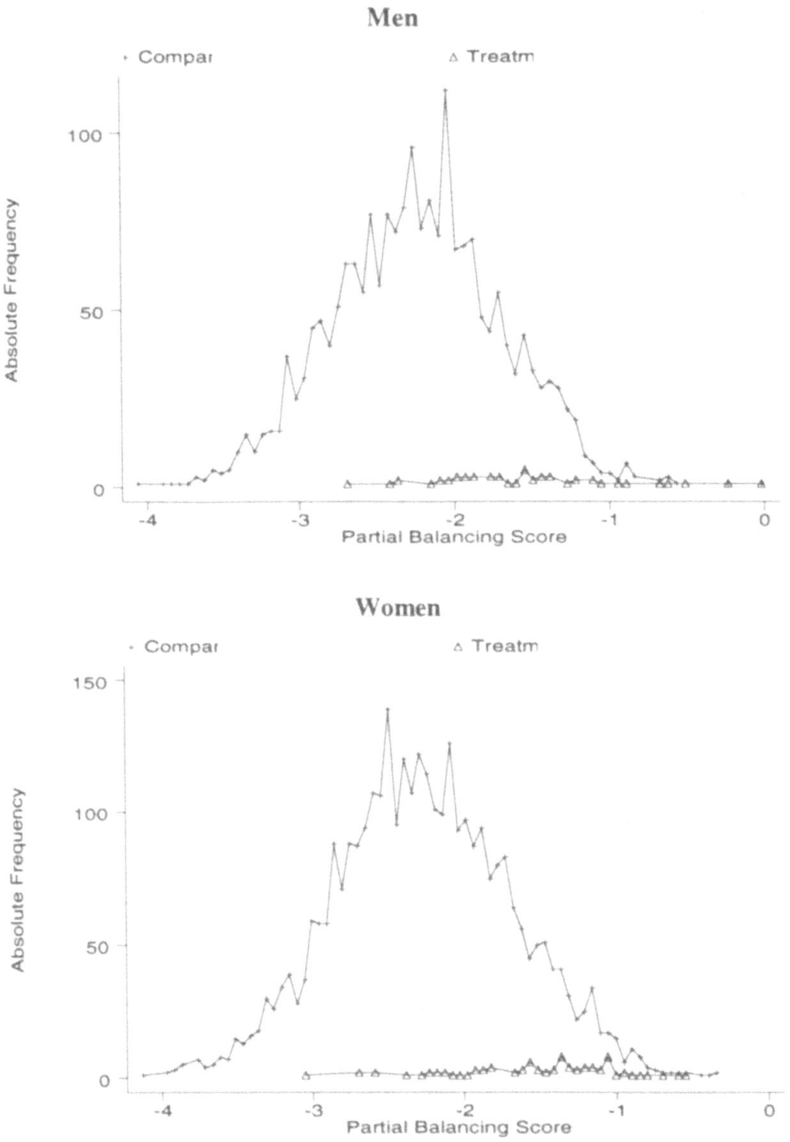


*Notes*: Compar.: non-participants sample; Treatm.: trainees sample.

Source: *Polish Labour Force Survey; own calculations.*

**Figure 12:** Distributions of the Partial Balancing Score of Intervention Works Participants and Non-Participants

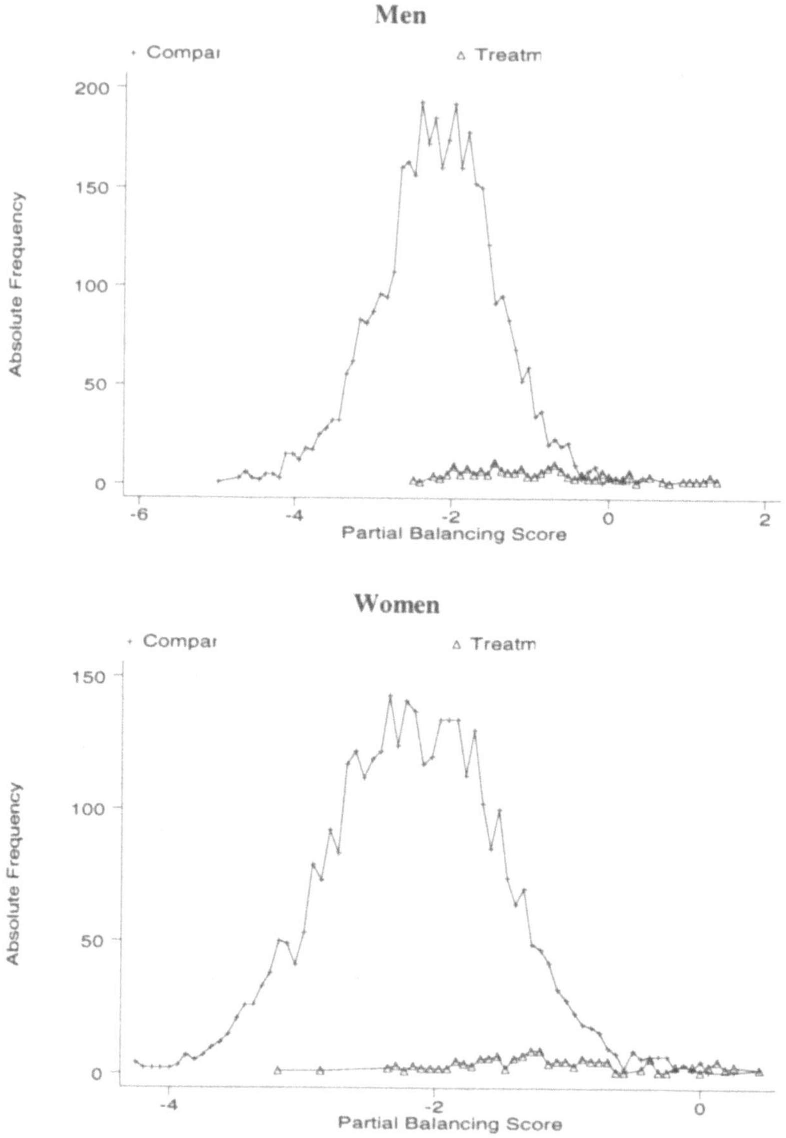


*Notes*: Compar.: non-participants sample; Treatm.: intervention works participants sample.
Source: *Polish Labour Force Survey; own calculations.*

**Figure 13:** Distributions of the Partial Balancing Score of Public Works Participants and Non-Participants

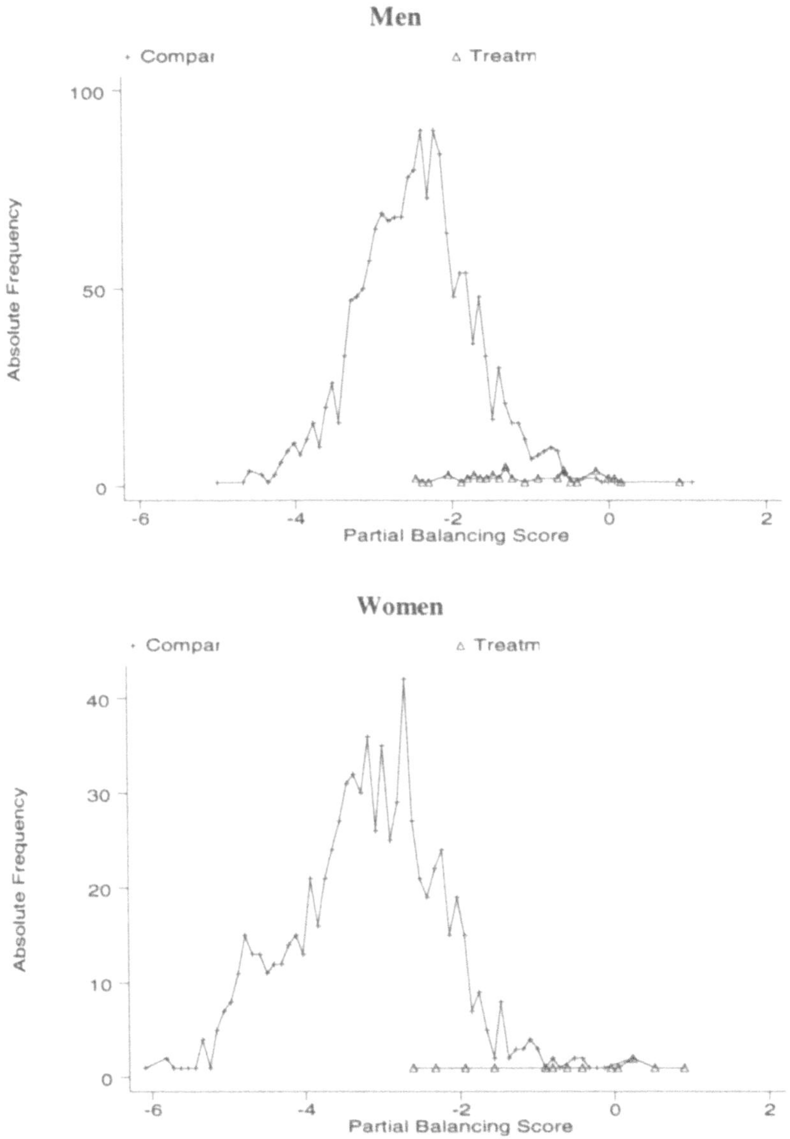


*Notes*: Compar.: non-participants sample; Treatm.: public works participants sample.

Source*: Polish Labour Force Survey; own calculations.*

**Figure 14:** The Partial Balancing Score of Trainees and the Matched Comparison Group

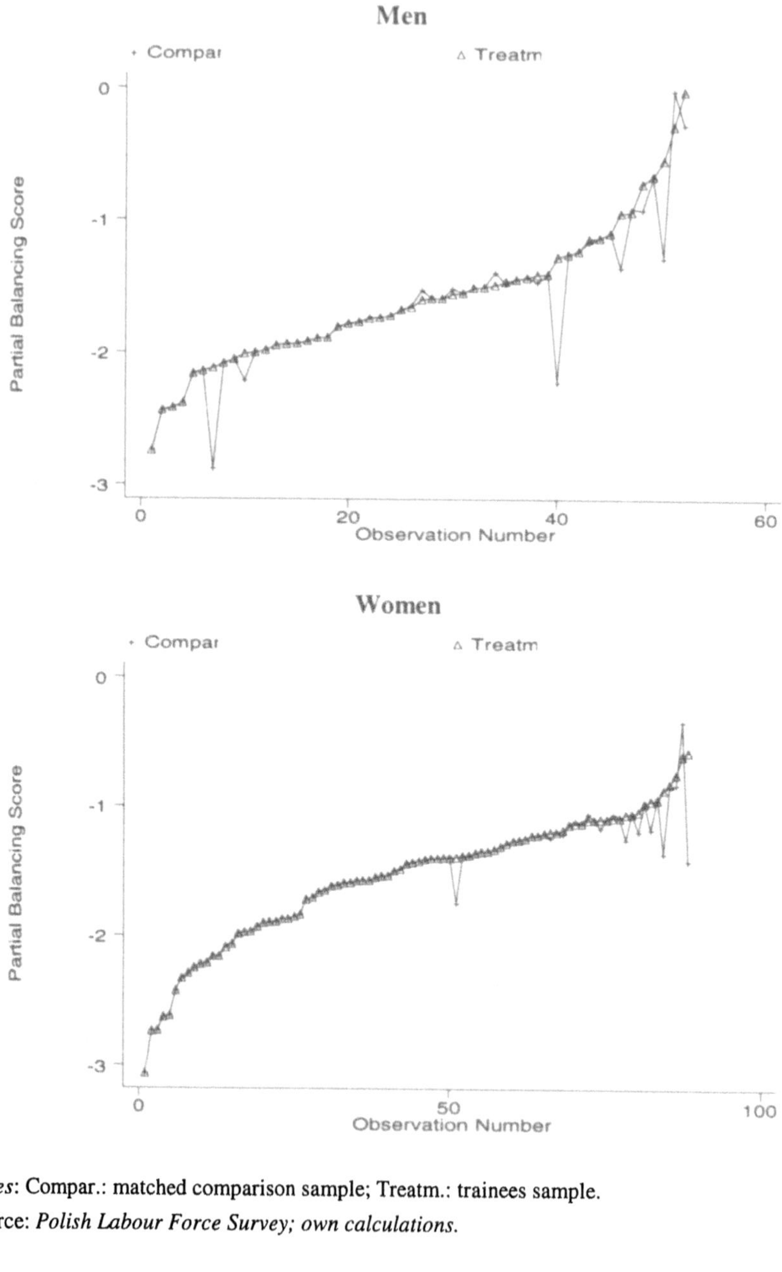


*Notes*: Compar.: matched comparison sample; Treatm.: trainees sample.

Source: *Polish Labour Force Survey; own calculations.*

**Figure 15:** The Partial Balancing Score of Intervention Works Participants and the Matched Comparison Group

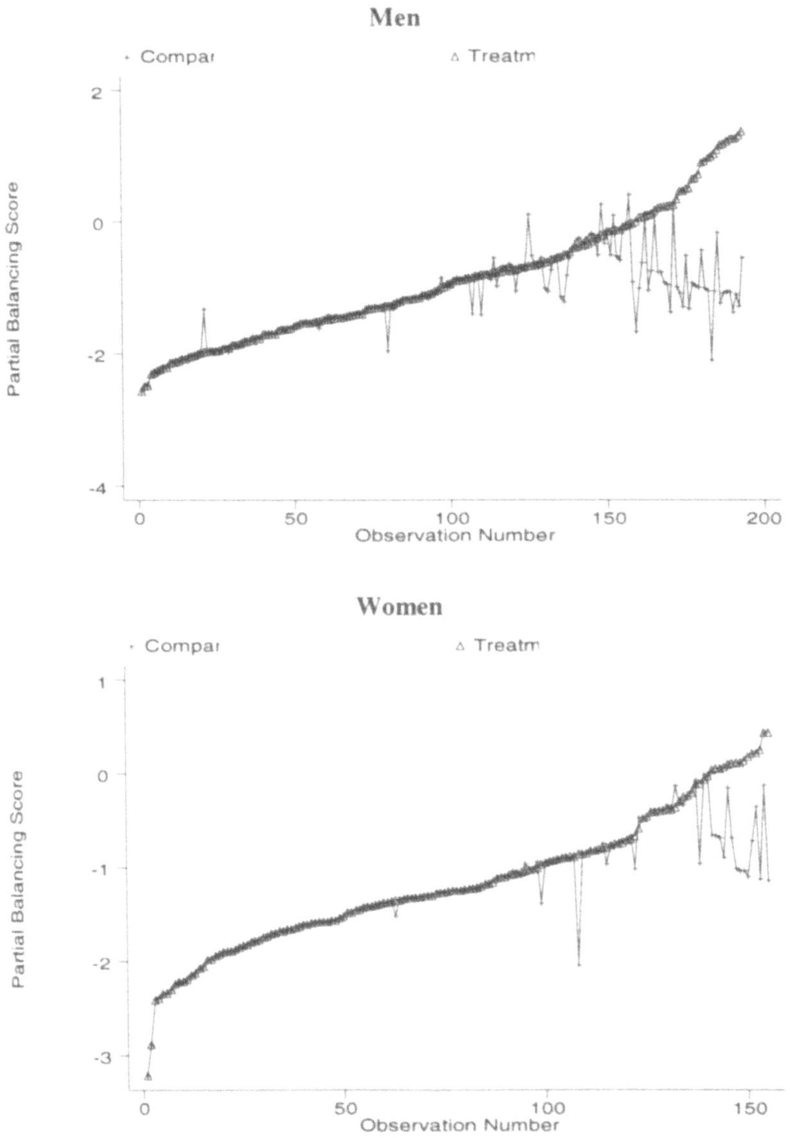


*Notes*: Compar.: matched comparison sample; Treatm.: intervention works participants sample.
Source: *Polish Labour Force Survey; own calculations.*

**Figure 16:** The Partial Balancing Score of Public Works Participants and the Matched Comparison Group

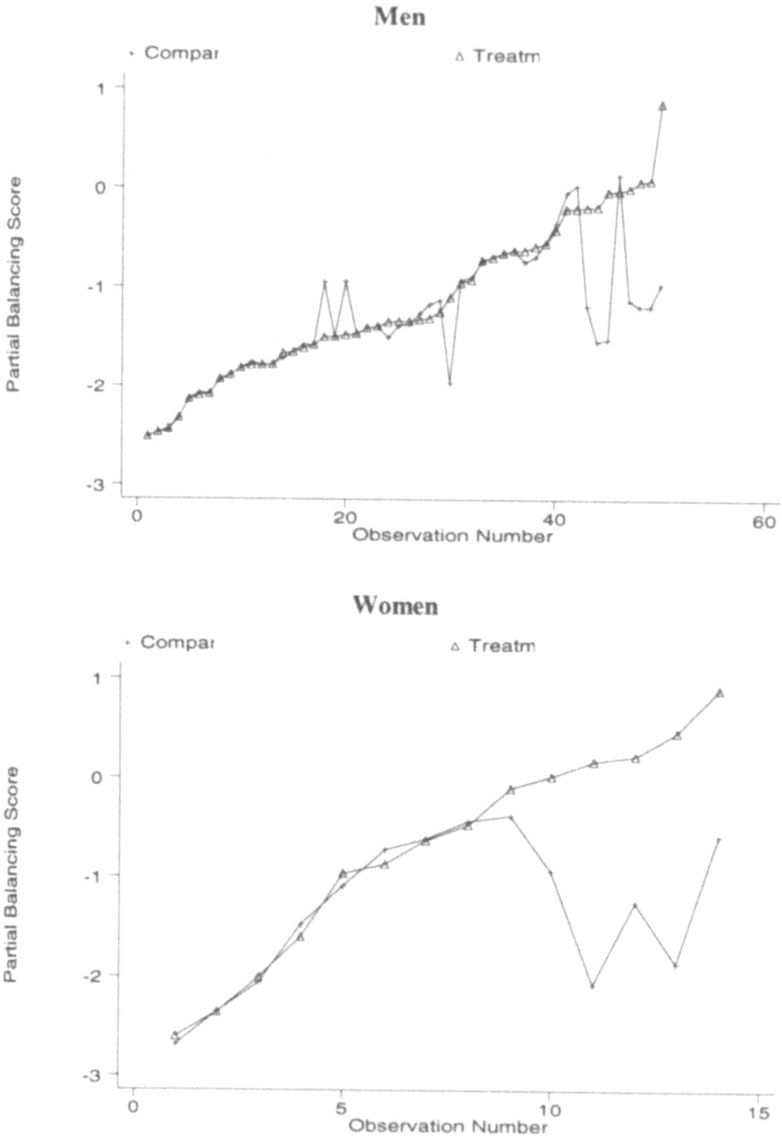


*Notes*: Compar.: matched comparison sample; Treatm.: public works participants sample.
Source: *Polish Labour Force Survey; own calculations..*

**Matching Results**

Figure 14, Figure 15, and Figure 16 above plot the partial balancing scores of treated and matched comparison persons for training, intervention and public works, respectively. It can be seen that in most cases we were able to find a comparison person with exactly the same partial balancing score as the treatment person. Larger differences between the partial balancing scores appear when the treatment person has a comparatively high score. This is unsurprising, because, as we have seen in Figure 11, Figure 12, and Figure 13 above, the number of comparison persons and the overlap of the partial balancing score distributions diminish with the higher the score. Compared to the results of Dehejia and Wahba (1995b), who present a similar graph on U.S. data, the partial balancing scores of our matched comparisons are far more similar to the ones of the treatments.

A better test on the power of the balancing score to equalise the treatment and comparison samples with respect to observed characteristics is to compare the difference in the sample means between treatments and comparisons. This can be done by a simple test on the difference in the means. By the central limit theorem, we can assume that the difference in the means between treatment and comparison group is an asymptotically normally distributed random variable. We can hence build the following confidence interval for the estimated mean difference in a variable $z$ (*e.g.* age):

$$\left(\bar{z}_{|T=1}-\bar{z}_{|T=0}\right)\pm c_\alpha \times \hat{\sigma}\left(\bar{z}_{|T=1}-\bar{z}_{|T=0}\right),$$

where $c_\alpha$ equals 1.96 or 1.645 depending on whether a 95 or 90 percent confidence interval is being built. As $\bar{z}_{|T=1}$ and $\bar{z}_{|T=0}$ are independent, the estimated variance $\hat{\sigma}\left(\bar{z}_{|T=1}-\bar{z}_{|T=0}\right)$ of the difference in the means of $z$ is given by

$$\hat{\sigma}\left(\bar{z}_{|T=1}-\bar{z}_{|T=0}\right)=$$
$$=\sqrt{\frac{1}{\left(N_{T=1}-1\right)N_{T=1}}\sum\nolimits_{\forall i|T=1}\left(z_i-\bar{z}_{|T=1}\right)^2+\frac{1}{\left(N_{T=0}-1\right)N_{T=0}}\sum\nolimits_{\forall i|T=0}\left(z_i-\bar{z}_{|T=0}\right)^2}.$$

The sample means of the treatment, naive (non-treatment) comparison, and matched comparison groups are given in Table 35, Table 36, and Table 37 for training, intervention, and public works participants, respectively. The tables also indicate whether the mean of the naive or matched comparison group differs significantly from the one of the treatment group.

**Table 35:** Sample Means of Trainees and Non-Trainees

| Variable | Men | | | Women | | |
|---|---|---|---|---|---|---|
| | Treatm. | Naive Compar. | Matched Compar. | Treatm. | Naive Compar. | Matched Compar. |
| Age between | | | | | | |
| 16 and 25 | 0.250 | 0.373 | 0.269 | 0.318 | 0.393 | 0.352 |
| 26 and 35 | 0.192 | 0.234 | 0.192 | 0.295 | 0.259 | 0.341 |
| 36 and 45 | 0.346 | 0.255 | 0.308 | 0.295 | 0.253 | 0.239 |
| 46 and 55 | 0.173 | 0.118 | 0.154 | 0.091 | 0.095 | 0.068 |
| 56 and 65 | 0.038 | 0.021 | 0.077 | 0.000 | 0.000 | 0.000 |
| Education | | | | | | |
| Higher | 0.077 | 0.017 | 0.096 | 0.080 | 0.026* | 0.102 |
| Post-secondary | 0.077 | 0.013* | 0.058 | 0.080 | 0.053 | 0.068 |
| Secondary vocational | 0.192 | 0.191 | 0.173 | 0.409 | 0.273 | 0.409 |
| Secondary general | 0.058 | 0.023 | 0.077 | 0.250 | 0.095 | 0.216 |
| Basic vocational | 0.462 | 0.570 | 0.423 | 0.125 | 0.384 | 0.136 |
| Primary or less | 0.135 | 0.186 | 0.173 | 0.057 | 0.170 | 0.068 |
| Occupation | | | | | | |
| Manager | 0.058 | 0.020 | 0.058 | 0.011 | 0.015 | 0.000 |
| Professional | 0.038 | 0.015 | 0.019 | 0.080 | 0.038 | 0.091 |
| Technician | 0.077 | 0.064 | 0.058 | 0.239 | 0.147 | 0.193 |
| White collar | 0.058 | 0.040 | 0.038 | 0.250 | 0.110 | 0.284 |
| Personal services | 0.096 | 0.074 | 0.077 | 0.216 | 0.283 | 0.182 |
| Farmer | 0.019 | 0.077 | 0.000 | 0.034 | 0.077 | 0.057 |
| Industrial worker | 0.462 | 0.432 | 0.615 | 0.102 | 0.144 | 0.125 |
| Simple blue-collar | 0.115 | 0.138 | 0.096 | 0.011 | 0.031* | 0.011 |
| Other simple jobs | 0.077 | 0.139 | 0.038 | 0.057 | 0.155 | 0.057 |
| Single | 0.288 | 0.429 | 0.365 | 0.307 | 0.360 | 0.386 |
| Children | 0.077 | 0.104 | 0.077 | 0.136 | 0.125 | 0.091 |
| No information on children | 0.288 | 0.477 | 0.346 | 0.284 | 0.382 | 0.386 |

**Table 35:** Sample Means of Trainees and Non-Trainees (ctd.)

| Variable | Men | | | Women | | |
|---|---|---|---|---|---|---|
| | T | NC | MC | T | NC | MC |
| Disabled | 0.058 | 0.045 | 0.058 | 0.068 | 0.029 | 0.045 |
| Industry | | | | | | |
| Agriculture, forestry, fishing | 0.019 | **0.108** | 0.000 | 0.034 | **0.091** | 0.045 |
| Mining | 0.000 | **0.010** | 0.000 | 0.000 | **0.004** | 0.000 |
| Manufacturing | 0.365 | 0.303 | 0.385 | 0.182 | 0.239 | 0.148 |
| Electricity, gas, water | 0.019 | 0.019 | 0.019 | 0.011 | 0.004 | 0.034 |
| Construction | 0.135 | 0.195 | 0.115 | 0.034 | 0.018 | 0.034 |
| Trade, repairs | 0.192 | 0.132 | 0.192 | 0.295 | 0.236 | 0.250 |
| Hotels, restaurants | 0.038 | 0.021 | 0.019 | 0.057 | 0.050 | 0.045 |
| Transport, communication | 0.077 | 0.049 | 0.096 | 0.034 | 0.019 | 0.034 |
| Financial intermediation | 0.019 | 0.004 | 0.019 | 0.011 | 0.013 | 0.000 |
| Real estates, renting | 0.000 | 0.000 | 0.000 | 0.045 | 0.020 | 0.011 |
| Administration | 0.000 | 0.000 | 0.000 | 0.068 | 0.021* | 0.125 |
| Education | 0.019 | 0.013 | 0.019 | 0.034 | 0.037 | 0.034 |
| Health, social work | 0.058 | 0.015 | 0.019 | 0.023 | **0.066** | 0.034 |
| Other services | 0.038 | 0.044 | 0.058 | 0.057 | 0.053 | 0.057 |
| None, unknown | 0.019 | **0.088** | 0.058 | 0.114 | 0.128 | 0.148 |
| Place of residence | | | | | | |
| 100,000 inhabitants or more | 0.288 | 0.244 | 0.462* | 0.420 | **0.280** | 0.386 |
| 20,000 to 99,999 | 0.212 | 0.236 | 0.192 | 0.227 | 0.209 | 0.239 |
| 19,999 or less | 0.173 | 0.138 | 0.154 | 0.125 | 0.146 | 0.114 |
| Countryside | 0.327 | 0.381 | 0.192 | 0.227 | **0.365** | 0.261 |

**Table 35:** Sample Means of Trainees and Non-Trainees (ctd.)

| Variable | Men | | | Women | | |
|---|---|---|---|---|---|---|
| | T | NC | MC | T | NC | MC |
| Employed 1 month before unempl. ($\varepsilon$) | 0.731 | 0.625* | 0.731 | 0.432 | 0.510 | 0.432 |
| Employed 3 months before unempl. ($\varepsilon$) | 0.808 | **0.637** | 0.769 | 0.432 | 0.527* | 0.432 |
| Employed 6 months before unempl. ($\varepsilon$) | 0.788 | **0.594** | 0.750 | 0.455 | 0.507 | 0.455 |
| Previous months in unemployment | 2.865 | 2.064 | 1.327 | 0.614 | **1.823** | 0.682 |
| Beg. of unempl. between 1994 and 1996 | 0.615 | 0.687 | 0.558 | 0.500 | **0.671** | 0.489 |
| Beginning of unemployment spell | 27.788 | 26.769 | 26.769 | 25.818 | **32.166** | 25.409 |
| Voivodship | | | | | | |
| (voivodships with insignificant mean differences not reported) | | | | | | |
| Stoleczne Warszawskie (Warsaw) | 0.000 | **0.039** | 0.000 | 0.034 | 0.032 | 0.057 |
| Gdanskie | 0.019 | 0.056* | 0.019 | 0.034 | 0.041 | 0.057 |
| Kieleckie | 0.000 | 0.000 | 0.000 | 0.011 | **0.042** | 0.011 |
| Lubelskie | 0.019 | 0.055* | 0.038 | 0.023 | 0.028 | 0.023 |
| Lomzynskie | 0.019 | 0.021 | 0.000 | 0.000 | **0.010** | 0.011 |
| Lodzkie | 0.173 | **0.067** | 0.288 | 0.068 | 0.047 | 0.057 |
| Slupskie | 0.058 | 0.028 | 0.000* | 0.057 | 0.021 | 0.023 |
| Wroclawskie | 0.058 | 0.053 | 0.038 | 0.011 | **0.035** | 0.000 |
| Number of observations | 52 | 2,029 | 52 | 88 | 3,299 | 88 |

*Notes*: Treatm.: trainee sample; Naive Compar.: non-participants sample; Matched Compar.: matched non-participants sample; shaded (asterisked) means are significantly different from the treatment means at the 5 (10) percent level; the *beginning of unemployment spell* variable is measured in calendar time months, where month 1 is January 1992.

Source: *Polish Labour Force Survey; own calculations.*

**Table 36:** Sample Means of Intervention Works Participants and Non-Participants

| Variable | Men | | | Women | | |
|---|---|---|---|---|---|---|
| | Treatm. | Naive Compar. | Matched Compar. | Treatm. | Naive Compar. | Matched Compar. |
| Age between | | | | | | |
| 16 and 25 | 0.176 | 0.382 | 0.150 | 0.348 | 0.397 | 0.303 |
| 26 and 35 | 0.295 | 0.251 | 0.316 | 0.271 | 0.262 | 0.310 |
| 36 and 45 | 0.363 | 0.242 | 0.342 | 0.271 | 0.246 | 0.290 |
| 46 and 55 | 0.140 | 0.106 | 0.155 | 0.110 | 0.095 | 0.097 |
| 56 and 65 | 0.026 | 0.019 | 0.036 | 0.000 | 0.000 | 0.000 |
| Education | | | | | | |
| Higher | 0.005 | 0.014 | 0.005 | 0.032 | 0.025 | 0.019 |
| Post-secondary | 0.005 | 0.013 | 0.021 | 0.071 | 0.052 | 0.058 |
| Secondary vocational | 0.093 | 0.175 | 0.088 | 0.329 | 0.265* | 0.413 |
| Secondary general | 0.021 | 0.024 | 0.016 | 0.077 | 0.095 | 0.090 |
| Basic vocational | 0.497 | 0.573 | 0.508 | 0.232 | 0.383 | 0.239 |
| Primary or less | 0.378 | 0.203 | 0.363 | 0.258 | 0.180 | 0.181* |
| Occupation | | | | | | |
| Manager | 0.000 | 0.000 | 0.000 | 0.000 | 0.000 | 0.000 |
| Professional | 0.005 | 0.012 | 0.005 | 0.019 | 0.040* | 0.026 |
| Technician | 0.021 | 0.068 | 0.026 | 0.187 | 0.143 | 0.200 |
| White collar | 0.036 | 0.033 | 0.041 | 0.187 | 0.110 | 0.194 |
| Personal services | 0.010 | 0.072 | 0.000 | 0.135 | 0.281 | 0.168 |
| Farmer | 0.073 | 0.122 | 0.098 | 0.052 | 0.083* | 0.045 |
| Industrial Worker | 0.440 | 0.409 | 0.472 | 0.123 | 0.149 | 0.129 |
| Simple blue-collar | 0.073 | 0.132 | 0.119 | 0.013 | 0.033 | 0.000 |
| Other simple jobs | 0.342 | 0.152 | 0.238 | 0.284 | 0.161 | 0.239 |
| Single | 0.352 | 0.457 | 0.321 | 0.419 | 0.359 | 0.400 |
| Children | 0.181 | 0.096 | 0.135 | 0.142 | 0.126 | 0.123 |
| No information on children | 0.363 | 0.515 | 0.363 | 0.394 | 0.390 | 0.335 |
| Disabled | 0.010 | 0.039 | 0.000 | 0.019 | 0.030 | 0.006 |

**Table 36:** Sample Means of Intervention Works Participants and Non-Participants (ctd.)

| Variable | Men | | | Women | | |
|---|---|---|---|---|---|---|
| | T | NC | MC | T | NC | MC |
| Industry | | | | | | |
| Agriculture, forestry, fishing | 0.098 | 0.149 | 0.145 | 0.071 | 0.096 | 0.090 |
| Mining | 0.000 | 0.009 | 0.010 | 0.000 | 0.003 | 0.000 |
| Manufacturing | 0.166 | 0.265 | 0.218 | 0.213 | 0.242 | 0.226 |
| Electricity, gas, water | 0.016 | 0.014 | 0.021 | 0.000 | 0.000 | 0.000 |
| Construction | 0.181 | 0.184 | 0.238 | 0.019 | 0.017 | 0.052 |
| Trade, repairs | 0.088 | 0.118 | 0.109 | 0.090 | 0.230 | 0.090 |
| Hotels, restaurants | 0.005 | 0.015* | 0.000 | 0.019 | 0.051 | 0.026 |
| Transport, communication | 0.021 | 0.046 | 0.021 | 0.013 | 0.018 | 0.019 |
| Financial intermediation | 0.010 | 0.004 | 0.000 | 0.045 | 0.015* | 0.058 |
| Real estates, renting | 0.041 | 0.020 | 0.016 | 0.039 | 0.018 | 0.065 |
| Administration | 0.280 | 0.023 | 0.130 | 0.245 | 0.022 | 0.148 |
| Education | 0.026 | 0.017 | 0.010 | 0.032 | 0.039 | 0.032 |
| Health, social work | 0.026 | 0.012 | 0.031 | 0.161 | 0.065 | 0.155 |
| Other services | 0.031 | 0.034 | 0.041 | 0.045 | 0.053 | 0.032 |
| None, unknown | 0.010 | 0.091 | 0.010 | 0.006 | 0.132 | 0.006 |
| Place of residence | | | | | | |
| 100,000 inhabitants or more | 0.057 | 0.198 | 0.083 | 0.123 | 0.249 | 0.142 |
| 20,000 to 99,999 | 0.119 | 0.226 | 0.119 | 0.252 | 0.215 | 0.239 |
| 19,999 or less | 0.212 | 0.145 | 0.187 | 0.213 | 0.152* | 0.194 |
| Countryside | 0.611 | 0.431 | 0.611 | 0.413 | 0.384 | 0.426 |

**Table 36:** Sample Means of Intervention Works Participants and Non-Participants (ctd.)

| Variable | Men | | | Women | | |
|---|---|---|---|---|---|---|
| | T | NC | MC | T | NC | MC |
| Employed 1 month before unempl. ($\varepsilon$) | 0.741 | **0.631** | 0.746 | 0.452 | 0.511 | 0.458 |
| Employed 3 months before unempl. ($\varepsilon$) | 0.699 | 0.638$^*$ | 0.699 | 0.432 | **0.524** | 0.445 |
| Employed 6 months before unempl. ($\varepsilon$) | 0.627 | 0.595 | 0.632 | 0.406 | **0.501** | 0.419 |
| Previous months in unemployment | 1.772 | 2.331 | 1.503 | 1.155 | **1.920** | 0.690 |
| Beg. of unemployment between 1994 and 1996 | 0.420 | **0.690** | 0.358 | 0.510 | **0.670** | 0.432 |
| Beginning of unemployment spell | 22.223 | **32.975** | 21.466 | 24.942 | **12.976** | 23.123 |
| Voivodship | | | | | | |
| (voivodships with insignificant mean differences not reported) | | | | | | |
| Stoleczne Warszawskie (Warsaw) | 0.026 | 0.023 | 0.016 | 0.013 | 0.029$^*$ | 0.013 |
| Bialostockie | 0.005 | **0.017** | 0.005 | 0.006 | 0.014 | 0.000 |
| Ciechanowskie | 0.010 | 0.018 | 0.005 | 0.006 | **0.020** | 0.013 |
| Czestochowskie | 0.010 | **0.029** | 0.016 | 0.032 | 0.023 | 0.039 |
| Gorzowskie | 0.026 | 0.017 | 0.031 | 0.006 | 0.019$^*$ | 0.006 |
| Katowickie | 0.021 | **0.046** | 0.026 | 0.052 | 0.085$^*$ | 0.058 |
| Kieleckie | 0.057 | 0.038 | 0.067 | 0.097 | **0.038** | 0.065 |
| Koszalinskie | 0.073 | **0.016** | 0.047 | 0.045 | 0.020 | 0.052 |
| Krakowskie | 0.005 | **0.021** | 0.005 | 0.013 | 0.023 | 0.013 |
| Lomzynskie | 0.005 | 0.012 | 0.026$^*$ | 0.013 | 0.009 | 0.000 |
| Lodzkie | 0.041 | 0.037 | 0.067 | 0.013 | **0.042** | 0.013 |
| Nowosadeckie | 0.016 | 0.028 | 0.016 | 0.006 | **0.024** | 0.000 |

**Table 36:** Sample Means of Intervention Works Participants and Non-Participants (ctd.)

| Variable | Men | | | Women | | |
|---|---|---|---|---|---|---|
| | T | NC | MC | T | NC | MC |
| Opolskie | 0.016 | 0.026 | 0.010 | 0.013 | 0.029* | 0.013 |
| Pilskie | 0.057 | 0.017 | 0.031 | 0.045 | 0.017* | 0.052 |
| Siedleckie | 0.005 | 0.016* | 0.005 | 0.000 | 0.000 | 0.000 |
| Slupskie | 0.067 | 0.015 | 0.052 | 0.065 | 0.019 | 0.013 |
| Suwalskie | 0.041 | 0.018* | 0.031 | 0.019 | 0.015 | 0.019 |
| Tarnowskie | 0.005 | 0.019 | 0.016 | 0.013 | 0.018 | 0.032 |
| Wroclawskie | 0.005 | 0.028 | 0.005 | 0.026 | 0.032 | 0.026 |
| Zielonogorskie | 0.010 | 0.017 | 0.026 | 0.006 | 0.019* | 0.000 |
| Number of observations | 193 | 3,851 | 193 | 155 | 3,596 | 155 |

*Notes*: Treatm.: intervention works participants sample; Naive Compar.: non-participants sample; Matched Compar.: matched non-participants sample; shaded (asterisked) means are significantly different from the treatment means at the 5 (10) percent level; the *beginning of unemployment spell* variable is measured in calendar time months, where month 1 is January 1992.

Source: *Polish Labour Force Survey; own calculations.*

**Table 37:** Sample Means of Public Works Participants and Non-Participants

| Variable | Men | | | Women | | |
|---|---|---|---|---|---|---|
| | Treatm. | Naive Compar. | Matched Compar. | Treatm. | Naive Compar. | Matched Compar. |
| Age between | | | | | | |
| 16 and 25 | 0.140 | **0.366** | 0.100 | 0.214 | 0.332 | 0.071 |
| 26 and 35 | 0.300 | 0.248 | 0.260 | 0.143 | 0.270 | 0.214 |
| 36 and 45 | 0.360 | 0.252 | 0.500 | 0.357 | 0.287 | 0.500 |
| 46 and 55 | 0.180 | 0.112 | 0.140 | 0.286 | 0.111 | 0.214 |
| 56 and 65 | 0.020 | 0.023 | 0.000 | 0.000 | 0.000 | 0.000 |
| Education | | | | | | |
| Higher | 0.020 | 0.011 | 0.020 | 0.000 | 0.000 | 0.000 |
| Post-secondary | 0.000 | 0.000 | 0.000 | 0.000 | 0.000 | 0.000 |
| Secondary vocational | 0.040 | **0.124** | 0.020 | 0.214 | 0.260 | 0.357 |
| Secondary general | 0.000 | 0.000 | 0.000 | 0.071 | 0.088 | 0.071 |
| Basic vocational | 0.580 | 0.641 | 0.540 | 0.429 | 0.466 | 0.357 |
| Primary or less | 0.360 | **0.223** | 0.420 | 0.286 | 0.187 | 0.214 |
| Occupation | | | | | | |
| Manager | 0.000 | 0.000 | 0.000 | 0.000 | 0.000 | 0.000 |
| Professional | 0.020 | 0.014 | 0.020 | 0.000 | 0.000 | 0.000 |
| Technician | 0.000 | 0.000 | 0.000 | 0.071 | 0.062 | 0.286 |
| White collar | 0.000 | 0.000 | 0.000 | 0.214 | 0.115 | 0.214 |
| Personal services | 0.000 | 0.000 | 0.000 | 0.071 | **0.380** | 0.214 |
| Farmer | 0.120 | 0.148 | 0.140 | 0.000 | 0.000 | 0.000 |
| Industrial Worker | 0.320 | **0.523** | 0.380 | 0.000 | **0.243** | 0.071 |
| Simple blue–collar | 0.020 | **0.148** | 0.020 | 0.000 | 0.000 | 0.000 |
| Other simple jobs | 0.520 | **0.168** | 0.440 | 0.643 | **0.201** | **0.214** |
| Single | 0.360 | 0.460 | 0.300 | 0.286 | 0.309 | 0.214 |
| Children | 0.200 | 0.102* | 0.120 | 0.214 | 0.153 | 0.071 |
| No information on children | 0.360 | **0.499** | 0.340 | 0.214 | 0.301 | 0.143 |

**Table 37:** Sample Means of Public Works Participants and Non-Participants (ctd.)

| Variable | Men | | | Women | | |
|---|---|---|---|---|---|---|
| | T | NC | MC | T | NC | MC |
| Disabled | 0.020 | 0.041 | 0.020 | 0.071 | 0.032 | 0.071 |
| Industry | | | | | | |
| Agriculture, forestry, fishing | 0.140 | 0.181 | 0.180 | 0.000 | 0.046 | 0.000 |
| Mining | 0.000 | 0.013 | 0.000 | 0.000 | 0.012 | 0.000 |
| Manufacturing | 0.100 | 0.324 | 0.220* | 0.143 | 0.396 | 0.286 |
| Electricity, gas, water | 0.020 | 0.013 | 0.020 | 0.000 | 0.000 | 0.000 |
| Construction | 0.240 | 0.237 | 0.280 | 0.000 | 0.000 | 0.000 |
| Trade, repairs | 0.040 | 0.072 | 0.040 | 0.071 | 0.418 | 0.214 |
| Hotels, restaurants | 0.000 | 0.000 | 0.000 | 0.000 | 0.000 | 0.000 |
| Transport, communication | 0.000 | 0.000 | 0.000 | 0.000 | 0.000 | 0.000 |
| Financial intermediation | 0.000 | 0.000 | 0.000 | 0.000 | 0.000 | 0.000 |
| Real estates, renting | 0.020 | 0.016 | 0.000 | 0.000 | 0.000 | 0.000 |
| Administration | 0.280 | 0.019 | 0.080 | 0.571 | 0.026 | 0.357 |
| Education | 0.060 | 0.023 | 0.040 | 0.000 | 0.000 | 0.000 |
| Health, social work | 0.000 | 0.000 | 0.000 | 0.000 | 0.000 | 0.000 |
| Other services | 0.080 | 0.033 | 0.100 | 0.214 | 0.102 | 0.143 |
| None, unknown | 0.020 | 0.069 | 0.040 | 0.000 | 0.000 | 0.000 |
| Place of residence | | | | | | |
| 100,000 inhabitants or more | 0.080 | 0.191 | 0.140 | 0.143 | 0.290 | 0.214 |
| 20,000 to 99,999 | 0.120 | 0.238 | 0.060 | 0.143 | 0.239 | 0.357 |
| 19,999 or less | 0.160 | 0.144 | 0.120 | 0.214 | 0.144 | 0.357 |
| countryside | 0.640 | 0.428 | 0.680 | 0.500 | 0.327 | 0.071 |

**Table 37:** Sample Means of Public Works Participants and Non-Participants (ctd.)

| Variable | Men | | | Women | | |
|---|---|---|---|---|---|---|
| | T | NC | MC | T | NC | MC |
| Employed 1 month before unempl. ($\varepsilon$) | 0.820 | 0.642 | 0.820 | 0.571 | 0.574 | 0.571 |
| Employed 3 months before unempl. ($\varepsilon$) | 0.720 | 0.643 | 0.720 | 0.571 | 0.606 | 0.571 |
| Employed 6 months before unempl. ($\varepsilon$) | 0.660 | 0.606 | 0.680 | 0.571 | 0.578 | 0.571 |
| Previous months in unemployment | 3.200 | 2.362 | 2.200 | 3.000 | 2.049 | 0.000* |
| Beg. of unemployment between 1994 and 1996 | 0.560 | 0.687* | 0.380* | 0.714 | 0.624 | 0.357 |
| Beginning of unemployment spell | 26.040 | 33.009 | 23.260 | 28.929 | 30.681 | 21.214 |
| Voivodship | | | | | | |
| (voivodships with insignificant mean differences not reported) | | | | | | |
| Stoleczne Warszawskie (Warsaw) | 0.000 | 0.035 | 0.020 | 0.000 | 0.054 | 0.000 |
| Katowickie | 0.040 | 0.072 | 0.040 | 0.071 | 0.234 | 0.286 |
| Lomzynskie | 0.020 | 0.024 | 0.000 | 0.000 | 0.024 | 0.000 |
| Olsztynskie | 0.120 | 0.037* | 0.160 | 0.071 | 0.067 | 0.000 |
| Number of observations | 50 | 1,720 | 50 | 14 | 777 | 14 |

*Notes*: Treatm.: public works participants sample; Naive Compar.: non-participants sample; Matched Compar.: matched non-participants sample; shaded (asterisked) means are significantly different from the treatment means at the 5 (10) percent level; the *beginning of unemployment spell* variable is measured in calendar time months, where month 1 is January 1992.

Source: *Polish Labour Force Survey; own calculations.*

As can be seen from the above tables, the naive (non-treatment) comparison group differs significantly from the treatment group in a large number of variables. However, this is not the case with the matched comparison group. Here, there are only very few variables which have significantly different means in the matched comparison group than in the treatment group. In virtually all cases where there are significant differences at the 5 percent level between treatments and matched comparisons, the means of the matched comparisons have at least been adjusted towards the mean of the treatments, so that matching has improved the comparability of the comparison group. Exceptions are women from the voivodship of Slupskie in Table 36 as well as the dummy variables for living in the *countryside* and the *beginning of unemployment between 1994 and 1996* in Table 37 for women in public works. However, as we have said above, the results for women in public works (Table 37) have to be taken with a grain of salt. With only 14 treatment observations, any statements can be at best tentative and the approximation by the normal distribution is also very unsafe. Results for this specific group are only presented for comparative purposes to the interested reader.

Special attention should be given to the variable *beginning of unemployment spell* in calendar time, which is to be found on the second page of each table above the voivodship dummies. Because the unemployment rate, which will be our outcome variable of interest, is very likely to be influenced by the general macroeconomic environment, it is important to make sure that treatments and comparisons operate during the same calendar time periods. As Table 35, Table 36, and Table 37 show, the unemployment spells of the treatment and *naive* comparison groups occur on average in almost all cases in different historical time periods. In the case of intervention works (Table 36), this difference can be almost a year. However, all of these differences are insignificant between the *matched* comparison and treatment groups. These differences are also of negligible size, maybe with the exception of public works (but recall that the results for women do not allow a serious interpretation).

The final test on the comparability between treatments and matched comparisons will be carried out in the following section, where we compare pre- and post-treatment differences in unemployment rates between ALMP participants and matched non-participants.

### 5.2.3 Non-Parametric Programme Evaluation Based on Matched Samples

Figure 17, Figure 18, and Figure 19 plot the unemployment rates of the treatment and matched comparison groups for training, intervention, and public works, respectively. The time scale in these figures is defined such that time *zero* for each treatment person is the first month in the ALMP programme. By definition, the unemployment rate must be 100 percent for all persons in that month. Also, the unemployment rate one month before treatment (time *minus one*) must be 100 percent, because only persons are included who join ALMPs from unemployment. Hence, all persons must be unemployed one month before treatment starts.

Whereas it is straightforward to define pre- and post-treatment periods for treatment persons as described in the above paragraph, it is *a priori* unclear how one should set the time scale for the comparisons. Indeed, there is by definition no point in time for the comparison persons when they join an ALMP programme. However, recall from Section 5.2.1 that we have matched on the precondition that the comparison person has to have been unemployed more than $m_T$ months, where $m_T$ is defined for the corresponding treatment person as

$$m_T = calendar\ time\ when\ ALMP\ started$$
$$-\ calendar\ time\ when\ unemployment\ started.$$

$m_T$ is thus the number of months it took the unemployed treatment person to get into the ALMP programme. We can thus define time *zero* for the comparison person at his or her $(m_T + 1)^{th}$ month in unemployment. This definition is very useful, as it guarantees that at time *zero*, the treatment and matched comparison persons have a similar recent unemployment history. The treatment effect starts to work for the treated when they join the ALMP programme. It is an obvious choice to compare the comparison person with the treatment person from process time $(m_T + 1)$ onwards and interpret the difference in unemployment rates after process time $(m_T + 1)$ (defined as time *zero* in Figure 17, Figure 18, and Figure 19) as the causal effect of the ALMP programme. Lechner (1995; 1996a; 1996b) and Fitzenberger and Prey (1998) use a similar approach in their papers.

### Pre-Treatment Tests

To check whether treatment and comparison groups are really comparable, we have tested whether the observed characteristics of the matched comparison group are significantly different from the ones of the treatment group (*cf.* Table 35, Table 36, and Table 37). However, we have not compared *pre-treatment outcomes* between treatment and matched comparison persons yet (Heckman and Hotz, 1989). A test on the comparability of treatment and matched comparison groups in terms of the pre-treatment outcome is presented in the following.

Estimated pre- and post-treatment differences in unemployment rates between treatment and matched comparison groups are plotted in Figure 20, Figure 21, and Figure 22. More formally, the estimated difference between the unemployment rates of treatments and comparisons at time $t$ can be written

$$\Delta\hat{UR}_t = \frac{1}{N_{T=1}} \sum\nolimits_{\forall i|T=1,z} Y_{it} - \frac{1}{N_{T=0}} \sum\nolimits_{\forall i|T=0,z} Y_i = \overline{Y}_{t|T=1,z} - \overline{Y}_{t|T=0,z}$$

where $Y_{it}$ is either *zero* (employed) or *one* (unemployed) for person $i$ at time $t$. If somebody is not in the labour force at time $t$ he or she makes no contribution to the unemployment rate at that time. In order to test whether there are any pre-treatment differences in the unemployment rates of treatments and comparisons, we calculate standard errors for $\Delta\hat{UR}_t$

$$\hat{\sigma}\left(\Delta\hat{UR}_t\right) =$$

$$= \sqrt{\frac{1}{\left(N_{T=1}-1\right)N_{T=1}}\sum\nolimits_{\forall i|T=1,\mathbf{z}}\left(Y_{it}-\overline{Y}_{t|T=1,\mathbf{z}}\right)^2+\frac{1}{\left(N_{T=0}-1\right)N_{T=0}}\sum\nolimits_{\forall i|T=0,\mathbf{z}}\left(Y_{it}-\overline{Y}_{t|T=0,\mathbf{z}}\right)^2}$$

Using the central limit theorem, we approximate the distribution of $\Delta\hat{UR}_t$ by the normal distribution and build a 90 percent confidence interval for $\Delta\hat{UR}_t$ which is given by

$$\Delta\hat{UR}_t \pm 1.645 \times \hat{\sigma}\left(\Delta\hat{UR}_t\right).$$

As Figure 20, Figure 21 and Figure 22 below show, the pre-treatment unemployment rates are in no case significantly different from each other (the results for women in public works are only displayed for comparative purposes in Figure 22). We therefore conclude from this evidence together with the results from Table 35, Table 36, and Table 37 that the matching method has worked well in producing an adequate comparison group for the treatment group. Therefore, we interpret the post-treatment differences in unemployment rates of treatment and matched comparison persons as the causal effect of treatment on unemployment. More formally,

$$\hat{\tau}_{t,t>0|T=1} = \Delta\hat{UR}_{t,t>0}$$

is interpreted as the treatment effect on the treated (ALMP participants) $t$ months after the beginning of the ALMP programme.

This approach also accounts for time-invariant unobserved individual heterogeneity if one gives it a difference-in-differences interpretation. Recalling our discussion of Section 4.5, the difference-in-differences interpretation generally requires the assumption that

$$E\left(Y_{0it}\middle|T_i=1\right)-E\left(Y_{0it}\middle|T_i=0\right)=E\left(Y_{0it-1}\middle|T_i=1\right)-E\left(Y_{0it-1}\middle|T_i=0\right). \qquad [4.\ 6]$$

In the matching context, the required assumption is less strong, namely

$$E\left(Y_{0it}\middle|T_i=1,\mathbf{z}\right)-E\left(Y_{0it}\middle|T_i=0,\mathbf{z}\right)=E\left(Y_{0it-1}\middle|T_i=1,\mathbf{z}\right)-E\left(Y_{0it-1}\middle|T_i=0,\mathbf{z}\right) \qquad [4.\ 6^*]$$

(Heckman, Ichimura, and Todd, 1997). The Heckman and Hotz (1989) pre-treatment test checks whether

$$E\left(Y_{0it-1}\middle|T_i = 1, \mathbf{z}\right) - E\left(Y_{0it-1}\middle|T_i = 0, \mathbf{z}\right) = 0.$$

If this is the case, the difference-in-differences estimator is equal to $\hat{\tau}_{t,t>0|T=1} = \Delta\hat{U}R_{t,t>0}$, which means that simple post-treatment unemployment differences between treatments and comparisons can be interpreted as causal programme effects.

**Figure 17:** Unemployment Rates of Trainees and the Matched Comparison Group

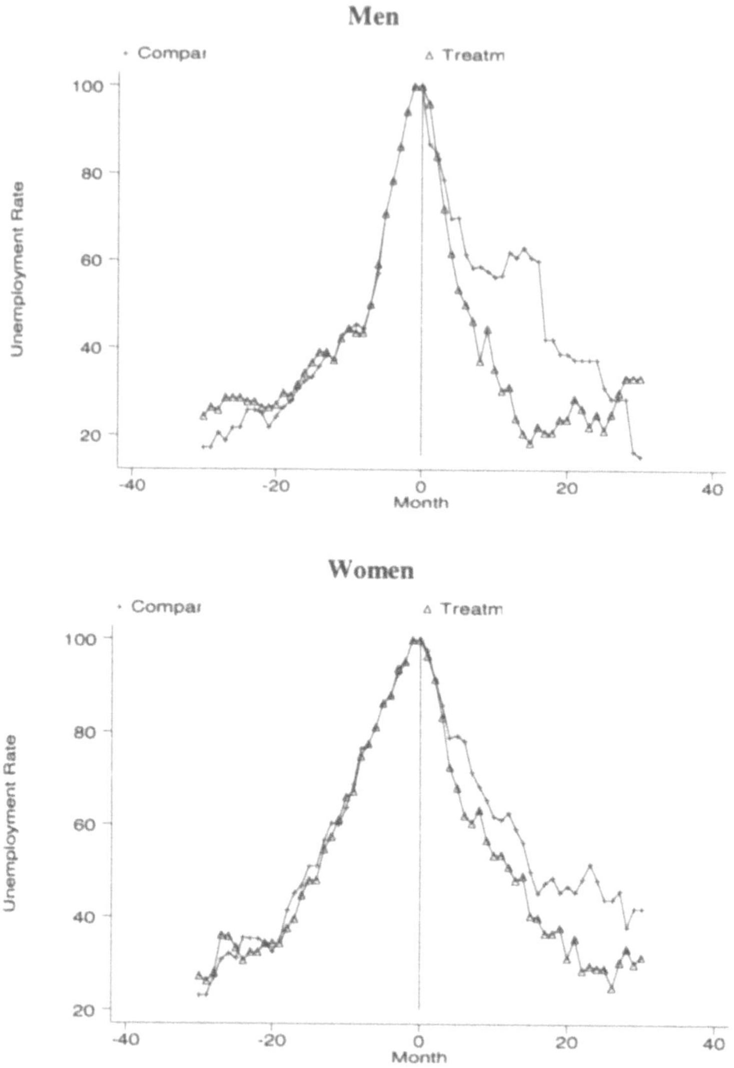


*Notes*: negative (positive) months correspond to the pre- (post-)treatment period; number of observations N (at month t) for men (T: treatment / C: comparison): N(-30) T/C = 33 / 29; N(-15) T/C = 41 / 39; N(0) T/C = 52 / 52; N(15) T/C = 27 / 28; N(30) T/C = 9 / 13; number of observations for women: N(-30) T/C = 22 / 26; N(-15) T/C = 48 / 47; N(0) T/C = 88 / 88; N(15) T/C = 47 / 42; N(30) T/C = 19 / 19.

Source: *Polish Labour Force Survey; own calculations.*

**Figure 18:** Unemployment Rates of Intervention Works Participants and the Matched Comparison Group

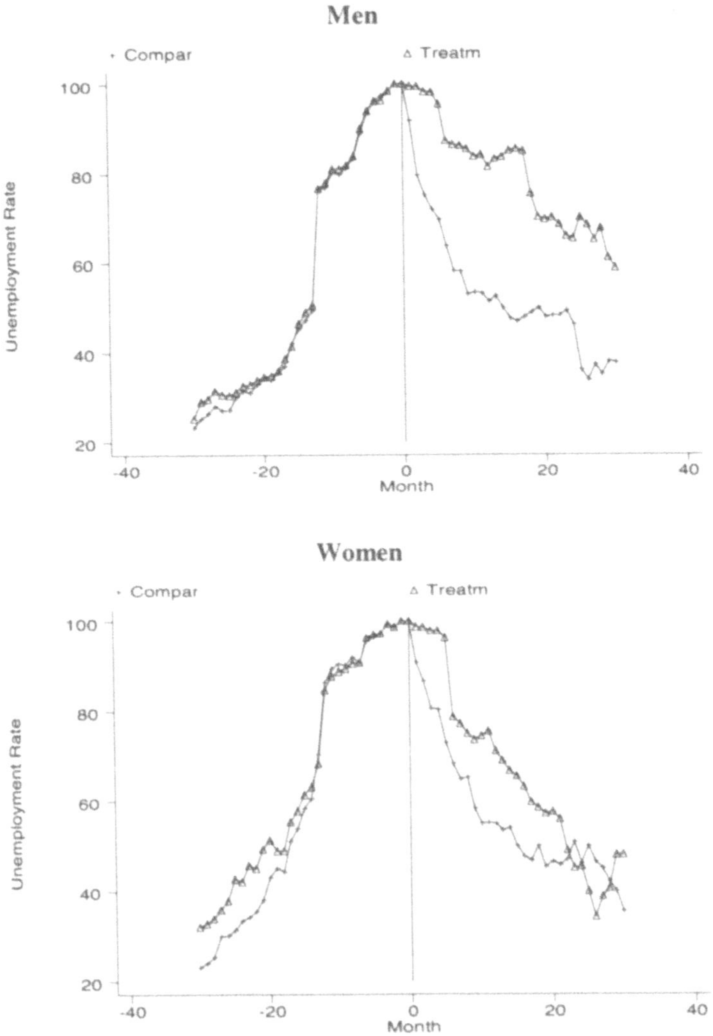


*Notes*: negative (positive) months correspond to the pre- (post-)treatment period; number of observations N (at month t) for men (T: treatment / C: comparison): N(-30) T/C = 91 / 95; N(-15) T/C = 155 / 157; N(0) T/C = 193 / 193; N(15) T/C = 115 / 105; N(30) T/C = 51 / 53; number of observations for women: N(-30) T/C = 53 / 52; N(-15) T/C = 101 / 96; N(0) T/C = 155 / 155; N(15) T/C = 81 / 88; N(30) T/C = 25 / 31.

Source: *Polish Labour Force Survey; own calculations.*

**Figure 19:** Unemployment Rates of Public Works Participants and the Matched Comparison Group

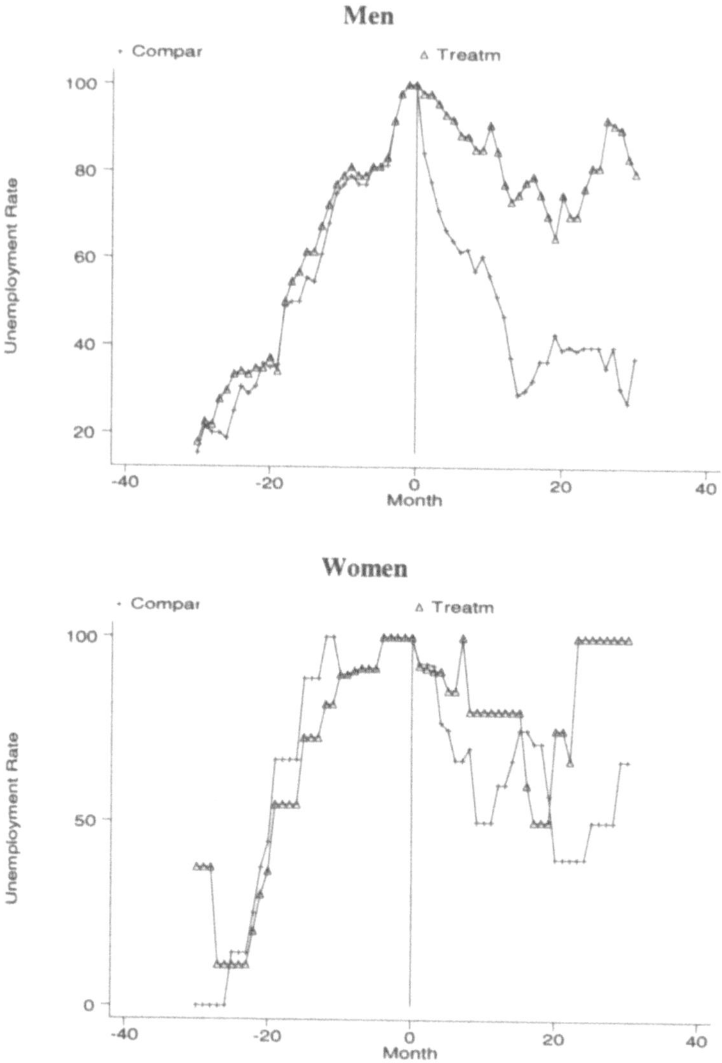


*Notes*: negative (positive) months correspond to the pre- (post-)treatment period; number of observations N (at month t) for men (T: treatment / C: comparison): N(-30) T/C = 28 / 26; N(-15) T/C = 44 / 45; N(0) T/C = 50 / 50; N(15) T/C = 27 / 30; N(30) T/C = 5 / 8; number of observations for women: N(-30) T/C = 8 / 6; N(-15) T/C = 11 / 9; N(0) T/C = 14 / 14; N(15) T/C = 5 / 8; N(30) T/C = 2 / 3.

Source: *Polish Labour Force Survey; own calculations.*

**Figure 20:** Difference in Unemployment Rates between Trainees and the Matched Comparison Group (with 90 Percent Confidence Bands)

Men

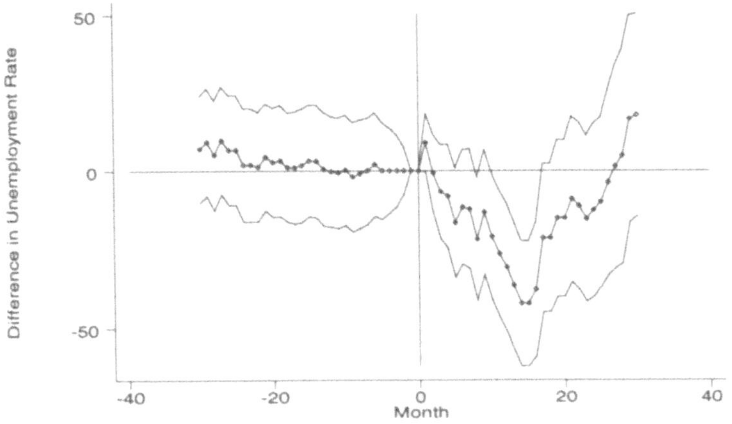


Women

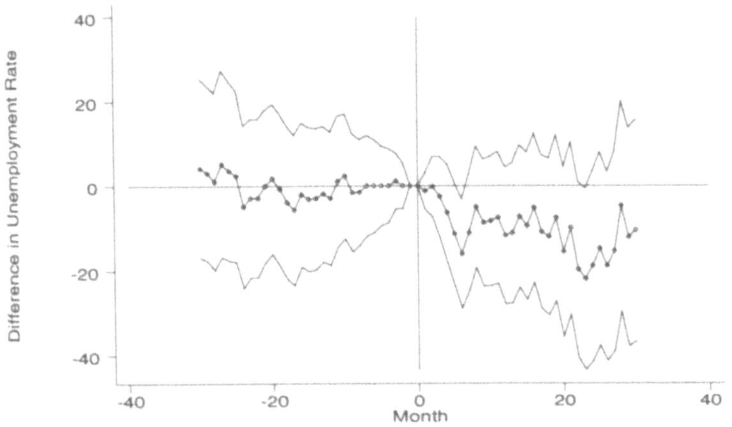


*Notes*: negative (positive) months correspond to the pre- (post-)treatment period; number of observations N (at month t) for men (T: treatment / C: comparison): N(-30) T/C = 33 / 29; N(-15) T/C = 41 / 39; N(0) T/C = 52 / 52; N(15) T/C = 27 / 28; N(30) T/C = 9 / 13; number of observations for women: N(-30) T/C = 22 / 26; N(-15) T/C = 48 / 47; N(0) T/C = 88 / 88; N(15) T/C = 47 / 42; N(30) T/C = 19 / 19.

Source: *Polish Labour Force Survey; own calculations.*

**Figure 21:** Difference in Unemployment Rates between Intervention Works Participants and the Matched Comparison Group (with 90 Percent Confidence Bands)

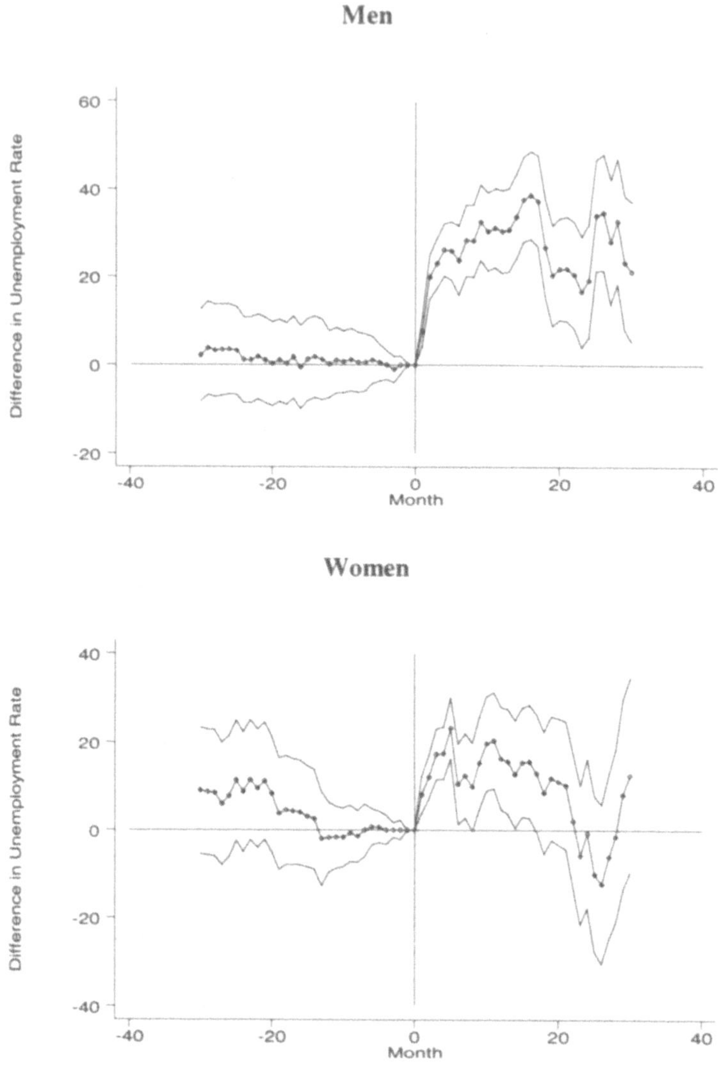


*Notes*: negative (positive) months correspond to the pre- (post-)treatment period;
number of observations N (at month t) for men (T: treatment / C: comparison): N(-30) T/C = 91 / 95; N(-15) T/C = 155 / 157; N(0) T/C = 193 / 193; N(15) T/C = 115 / 105; N(30) T/C = 51 / 53; number of observations for women: N(-30) T/C = 53 / 52; N(-15) T/C = 101 / 96; N(0) T/C = 155 / 155; N(15) T/C = 81 / 88; N(30) T/C = 25 / 31.

Source: *Polish Labour Force Survey; own calculations.*

**Figure 22:** Difference in Unemployment Rates between Public Works Participants and the Matched Comparison Group (with 90 Percent Confidence Bands)

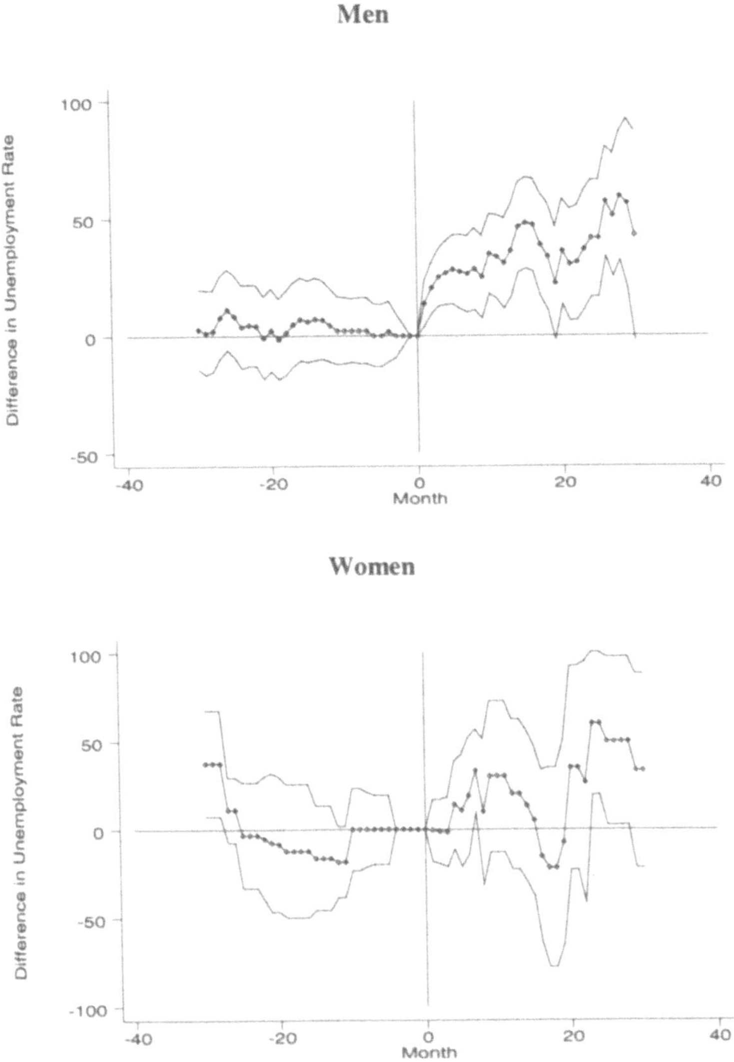


*Notes*: negative (positive) months correspond to the pre- (post-)treatment period; number of observations N (at month t) for men (T: treatment / C: comparison): N(-30) T/C = 28 / 26; N(-15) T/C = 44 / 45; N(0) T/C = 50 / 50; N(15) T/C = 27 / 30; N(30) T/C = 5 / 8; number of observations for women: N(-30) T/C = 8 / 6; N(-15) T/C = 11 / 9; N(0) T/C = 14 / 14; N(15) T/C = 5 / 8; N(30) T/C = 2 / 3.

Source*: Polish Labour Force Survey; own calculations.*

**Evaluation Results**

The point estimates from Figure 20, Figure 21, and Figure 22 above give a rather clear picture on the effects of the ALMP programmes investigated. Whereas the figures show that training programmes improve the re-employment chances of the trainees, intervention and public works programmes seem to have negative effects on employment opportunities. However, not all of these effects are statistically significant. Because the number of observations (and hence the quality of the approximation through the normal distribution) shrinks the further we move away from time *zero*, we will in the following only interpret the results up to the $20^{th}$ month after the beginning of the ALMP programme.

Figure 20 shows that the positive effect of training for men is statistically significant at the 10 percent level for most of the post-treatment time period. This is not so for women, where the positive effect of training is only significant for one month. The point estimates, however, suggest that training reduces the unemployment rate of the female programme participants by about 10 percentage points. For men, the estimate is more erratic over time, but a 10-15 percentage point reduction in unemployment seems to be a conservative average number.

For intervention and public works, the estimated effects are generally significant at the 10 percent level (women in public works are the exception). Men after intervention or public works have unemployment rates about 30 percentage points higher than the comparison group. For women, the unemployment rate after intervention works is about 10 percentage points higher in the first 20 months after the start of the programme. The results for women after public works, which are only presented for comparative purposes and cannot be seriously interpreted, suggest a similar effect as for women in intervention works.

To conclude, we find significantly positive effects of public training programmes (for men) and significantly negative effects of intervention (for both genders) and public works programmes (for men). Although Puhani and Steiner (1996; 1997) already have found negative employment effects for works programmes, significant positive effects of training could not be established neither by Puhani and Steiner (1996; 1997) nor by Puhani (1996). As both Puhani and Steiner (1996; 1997) and Puhani (1996) worked with the August 1994 Supplement to the Polish Labour Force Survey, whose data quality on labour market policies is comparatively poor, one may place more confidence in the results just presented. Compared to the results of Lechner (1995; 1996a; 1996b) and Fitzenberger and Prey (1998), who apply a similar matching approach as the one used here to east German data on training programmes, our conclusions give a more positive picture on public training in Poland. In both Lechner's (1995; 1996a; 1996b) papers and in Fitzenberger and Prey's (1998) study, the effects of training on unemployment are either insignificant (Lechner) or ambiguous due to the poor quality of the matched samples (Fitzenberger and Prey). Although our estimated training effects for women are also insignificant, the point estimates at least suggest positive effects of training on the employability of women. In relation to O'Leary's (1997b) results on Hungary, we have found a larger reduction of unemployment through training in Poland, although the outcome variables are somewhat different in our studies. O'Leary (1997b) estimates a 1.2 percentage point increase in the re-employment rate, we estimate a 10 percentage point reduction in the unemployment rate. As for public works, our estimate for men is closer to the one of O'Leary (1997b). He estimates a 16 percentage point decrease in the re-employment rate, we estimate a 30 percentage point increase in the unemployment rate.

Before we discuss the possible conclusions one may draw from these results, we check whether the evidence just presented is robust with respect to the statistical approach taken. The following section will evaluate training, intervention, and public works programmes by duration models.

## 5.3 Empirical Evaluation of ALMPs by Way of Duration Models

Most previous evaluation studies on transition economies have modelled ALMP effects within parametric models. Some studies have used panel data to estimate the individual labour force state (Fitzenberger and Prey, 1995; 1996; 1997; Hübler, 1997), whereas others have applied duration analysis (Pannenberg, 1995; 1996; Steiner and Kraus, 1995; Kraus, Steiner, and Puhani, 1997; 1998; Puhani, 1996; Staat, 1997). Although both types of approaches are rather similar in that they are parametric models, we choose to estimate duration models, because they allow an explicit accounting for process time (*i.e.* time in unemployment). As ALMPs aim to help the long-term unemployed find employment, it seems an obvious choice to estimate the effects of ALMPs on unemployment duration.

In the following Section 5.3.1 we present the duration model to be estimated as well as the specification of the ALMP effects in this framework. We estimate multinomial logit duration models with unobserved heterogeneity. The unobserved heterogeneity component is estimated as a non-parametric distribution with discrete mass points. The number of mass points will be selected in Section 5.3.2 on the basis of the Akaike Information Criterion. Having chosen the appropriate model, we present our estimation results in Section 5.3.3.

### 5.3.1 Methodological Issues

We estimate a logit-type duration model which was first introduced by Nickell (1979) and has been briefly discussed in Section 4.4.2 above. As argued in Section 4.4.3, sample selection bias due to *selection on observables* can be avoided by including all variables that drive the ALMP programme participation processes in the outcome equation. *Selection on unobservables* is then checked for by testing for the existence of unobserved individual heterogeneity.

More formally, the hazard rate of individual $i$ for exit into state $j$ (*employment* or *non-participation*) in discrete process time $t$ is specified as

$$h_j\left(t \middle| \mathbf{x}_{it}, \mathbf{z}_{it}, \mathbf{T}_{it}, \varepsilon_i\right) = \frac{\exp\left(\beta_j'[\mathbf{x}_{it}, \mathbf{z}_{it}] + \tau_j'\mathbf{T}_{it} + \alpha_j'\mathbf{p}_t + \varepsilon_i\right)}{1 + \sum_{l=1}^{J} \exp\left(\beta_l'[\mathbf{x}_{it}, \mathbf{z}_{it}] + \tau_l'\mathbf{T}_{it} + \alpha_l'\mathbf{p}_t + \varepsilon_i\right)}$$

where the vector $\mathbf{p}$ consists of time-varying dummy variables defined on process time intervals. $\mathbf{p}$ thus defines a non-parametrically estimated baseline hazard rate. As we evaluate three ALMP programmes (training, intervention, and public works), the treatment effects are described as a vector $\tau$. The $\mathbf{z}$ variables are assumed to control for *selection on observables* for all three ALMPs investigated (*cf.* Section 4.4.3).

$\varepsilon$ is the unobserved individual heterogeneity component. We specify $\varepsilon$ to be drawn from a discrete distribution with $\vartheta$ mass points and restrictions

$$E[\varepsilon]=\sum_{l=1}^{\vartheta}\Pr(\varepsilon^{l})\varepsilon^{l}=0, \text{ and } \sum_{l=1}^{\vartheta}\Pr(\varepsilon_i^{l})=1.$$

It is further assumed that $\varepsilon$ is orthogonal to the covariates $\mathbf{x}$, $\mathbf{z}$, $\mathbf{p}$, and $\mathbf{T}$ (*cf.* Steiner, 1997).

An alternative approach would be to specify a parametric distribution for $\varepsilon$. However, Heckman and Singer (1984) show that the choice of parametric distribution for the unobserved heterogeneity component can seriously influence parameter estimates. We therefore follow Heckman and Singer's (1984) suggestion and estimate the distribution of $\varepsilon$ non-parametrically. The number of mass points $\vartheta$ for the distribution of $\varepsilon$ will be chosen on the basis of the Akaike Information Criterion (see, for example, Gourieroux and Monfort, 1989, Chapter 22).

Assuming the individuals in the sample are independent observations, the likelihood function of the competing risks model for the sample is given by

$$L=\prod_{i=1}^{N_i}\sum_{l=1}^{\vartheta}\Pr(\varepsilon_i^{l})\prod_{k=1}^{K_i}\prod_{j=1}^{J}\left[h_j\left(t_{ik}\middle|\mathbf{x}_{itk},\varepsilon_i^{l}\right)\right]^{\delta_{ikj}}\prod_{s=1}^{t_{ik}-1}\left[1-h\left(s\middle|\mathbf{x}_{itk},\varepsilon_i^{l}\right)\right]$$

where $\delta_{ijk}$ equals *one* if the $k^{\text{th}}$ spell of individual $i$ ends in state $j$ at time $t$ and *zero* otherwise. All exogenous variables $\mathbf{x}$, $\mathbf{z}$, $\mathbf{p}$,and $\mathbf{T}$, have been subsumed under the vector $\mathbf{x}$ to simplify notation.

As argued in Section 5.2.3 where ALMP effects were estimated by the statistical matching approach, the causal effect of the ALMP programmes start to work with the beginning of the programme. In the duration model context, we thus set the ALMP participation dummy variables equal to *one* from the first month in ALMPs onwards. Going back to our example person of Figure 9 on page 145, we illustrate the setting of the ALMP participation dummy graphically in Figure 23.

**Figure 23:** The Definition of the ALMP Dummy Variable Corresponding to Figure 9

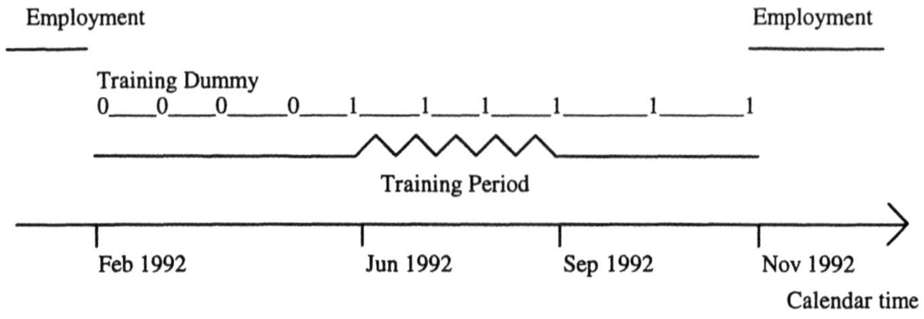


*Notes*: the training period in this example starts in June 1992; from this month onwards, the training dummy variable is set equal to *one*; for the other programmes, the dummy variables are set correspondingly; if a person participates in more than one ALMP programme *of the same type* within one unemployment spell, the ALMP dummy is set equal to one from the first month in the first programme onwards; if a person participates in more than one ALMP programme *of different types* (e.g. training and intervention works) within one unemployment spell, the ALMP dummy of each programme is set equal to *one* from the first month in the corresponding ALMP programme onwards; due to the small number of multiple ALMP participations (cf. notes to Table 39 and Table 40 below), no interaction effects are estimated.

The coefficient on the programme dummies is then interpreted as the causal effect of the programme, as long as there is no unobserved individual heterogeneity in the model (*cf.* Section 4.4.3 above and the following section 5.3.2). If there is evidence for unobserved individual heterogeneity, there might still be some selection bias due to *selection on unobservables* (*cf.* Section 4.4.3 above). In the following section, we test for the existence of unobserved individual heterogeneity.

### 5.3.2 Model Selection

We have estimated competing risks duration models with two exit categories: *employment* and *non-participation* in the labour market. The selection of the spells has been described in Table 31 on page 148. In the male sample, around 46 percent of the spells end in employment, 19 percent in non-participation, and 35 percent are right-censored. For females, these figures are 35, 22, and 43 percent, respectively. Before we discuss the exogenous variables in the following section, we present our choice of heterogeneity components here. All models have been estimated both without unobserved individual heterogeneity ($\varepsilon = 0$) and with unobserved individual heterogeneity, where the number of discrete mass points of the distribution of $\varepsilon$ has been specified as $\vartheta$ = 2, 3, or 4, respectively. As the likelihood ratio test for the existence of unobserved individual heterogeneity is not applicable under the null hypothesis of no heterogeneity, we choose amongst those four models (four for each gender) the one with the highest Akaike Information Criterion (AIC) which is defined as (Gourieroux and Monfort, 1989, Chapter 22; Gritz, 1993):

$$AIC = \ln \textit{likelihood} - \textit{number of estimated parameters}$$

Table 38 displays the natural logarithm of the likelihood and AIC values for various specifications of the unobserved individual heterogeneity component $\varepsilon$.[7]

**Table 38:** Model Choice on the Basis of the Akaike Information Criterion

| Model | Number of Parameters | Men | | Women | |
|---|---|---|---|---|---|
| | | *ln* likelihood | AIC | *ln* likelihood | AIC |
| No heterogeneity | 218 | -11,348.74 | -11,566.74 | -10,778.23 | -10,996.23 |
| 2 mass points ($\vartheta = 2$) | 220 | -11,290.97 | -11,510.97 | -10,739.48 | **-10,959.48** |
| 3 mass points ($\vartheta = 3$) | 222 | -11,273.95 | **-11,495.95** | -10,739.22 | -10,961.22 |
| 4 mass points ($\vartheta = 4$) | 224 | -11,274.06 | -11,498.06 | -10,736.25 | -10,960.25 |

*Notes*: *ln*: natural logarithm; AIC: *Akaike Information Criterion = ln likelihood – number of estimated parameters;* the bold numbers indicate the chosen model; the choice is based on the maximum AIC (Gourieroux and Monfort, 1989, p.348).

Source: *Polish Labour Force Survey; own calculations.*

It is shown that the models with the highest AIC values are the one with three mass points for men and the one with two mass points for women, respectively. There is therefore evidence for the existence of unobserved individual heterogeneity in our models, which means that there might be *selection on unobservables.* This has already been found in most previous studies (Steiner, 1987; Fitzenberger and Prey, 1995; 1996; 1997; 1998; Mühleisen and Zimmermann, 1994; Steiner and Kwiatkowski, 1995; Pannenberg, 1996; Puhani, 1996; Hübler, 1997; Hujer, Maurer, and Wellner, 1997a). However, the coefficients on the ALMP participation variables were not affected neither in size nor statistical significance by allowing for unobserved individual heterogeneity. The estimated ALMP effects, which will be presented in the following section, thus seem to be robust.

---

[7] The models were programmed in *GAUSS*. I thank my colleagues Viktor Steiner and Florian Kraus for letting me use their programme. It takes around 5 days to estimate one multinomial logit model with unobserved individual heterogeneity on a Pentium 133 Mhz computer.

### 5.3.3 Estimation Results

The estimates of our competing risks models for men and women are displayed in Table 39 and Table 40, respectively. The exogenous variables are essentially the same as the ones used for the estimation of the ALMP programme participation equations in Table 32ff. on page 154ff. Exceptions are the time-varying variables *unemployment benefits*, *training*, *intervention works*, *public works*, *calendar time 1994 or after*, *seasonal* dummies, and *process time* dummies.

The *unemployment benefits* variable is set equal to *one* in the months unemployment benefit is received. However, if somebody receives 12 months of unemployment benefit, which is the rule by law, and gets a job in the 13$^{th}$ month, the dependent variable of the model indicates *exit into employment* in the 12$^{th}$ month. The data has to be structured this way to make the effects of unemployment benefits identifiable. If one chose to indicate the transition into employment in the 13$^{th}$ month, when the person is already employed, then the coefficient on *unemployment benefits* could not be estimated, as nobody who still receives unemployment benefits would have the dependent variable set equal to *exit into employment* in the same month. On the other hand, with the procedure used here, we do not have the information that unemployment benefits run out included in the *unemployment benefits* variable. As for most people benefits run out after twelve months, this information is implicit in the process time dummy variable, though. Thus, the effect of unemployment benefits is captured both in the *unemployment benefits* variable and the *process time* dummies.

#### General Observations

In some respects, the competing risks models yield expected results. Both men and women with a comparatively high level of education have better job prospects than people with lower educational attainments. Also, persons that became unemployed out of employment ($E_1 = 1$) have better employment chances than those who have not participated in the labour market just before becoming unemployed. In general, finding re-employment was easier *in or after 1994*. Although one may read off the tables that young persons find employment more quickly than older ones, it is important to note that school leavers, who have never been employed before, are included in *none, unknown* amongst the industrial categories. As the coefficient on *none, unknown* is far larger than the one on *age between 16 and 25*, but negative, young school leavers have extremely bad opportunities on the Polish labour market. This has also been documented in Puhani (1996) and Boeri and Steiner (1997) and is valid for both men and women.

Differences between men and women arise through the fact that young women are more likely to leave the labour force, most probably to take up family responsibilities. Whether those young women are discouraged from job search or whether they have only been on the register to draw unemployment benefits cannot be answered here. What is striking, though, is the comparatively high chance for women in big cities with *100,000 inhabitants or more* to leave the labour force. As access to labour offices is likely to be comparatively good in these places, this evidence is consistent with the view that some pure benefit take-up effects are at work here. Nevertheless, there is no proof for this hypothesis. It may also be that women in big cities are more likely to be both active and then discouraged on the Polish labour market.

A further difference between the genders is observed in the effect of being *single*. Being single lowers men's re-employment chances, but raises the ones for women. This is probably due to a preference for single rather than married women on the side of employers due to their lower risk of quitting for family responsibilities. The same argument applies to women who have already born their *children*, which has a positive coefficient on re-employment. Moreover, single women are less likely to leave the labour force, as they are more likely to be responsible for earning income than married women.

To our knowledge, this is the first study on Poland which estimates *ceteris paribus* re-employment chances for each voivodship. In the tables, we have indicated for significant coefficients on *exit into employment* the classification of the voivodship in terms of unemployment (high, middle, and low) and employment structure (modern, industrial, agricultural, and other). The classifications can be checked in Figure 2 and Figure 3 on page 16. Roughly speaking, the voivodships with significantly low re-employment chances are either *high unemployment / industrial* ones or *mid* to *low unemployment / agricultural* ones. This result is revealing. It shows the true nature of employment opportunities in the agricultural areas of Poland. The low unemployment rates there may be a result of fewer mass lay-offs, which have mainly occurred in industrial areas. However, there is a clear lack of new job opportunities in these regions. Much surplus labour is taken up in the agricultural sector so that the unemployment rate is low. However, those people who search for new jobs have difficulties finding them.

The coefficients on the voivodship dummies for *exit into non-participation* are all negative for both genders, which means that people registered as unemployed in Warsaw (the base category) are more likely to leave the labour force than people who are registered in other voivodships. As one might expect that the labour office infrastructure is comparatively good in the capital of Poland, it is probably more convenient to register as unemployed and visit the labour office regularly in Warsaw than in other areas of Poland. Although no proof can be given, the estimation results are consistent with the hypothesis that more people in Warsaw than in other voivodships register as unemployed to draw benefits without searching for a job or while working in the black economy.

The fact that unemployment benefits have a negative influence on the re-employment effects of the recipients is both documented in the *unemployment benefits* variable and the *process time* dummies. Although the *unemployment benefits* variable is only significant for women, the *process time* dummies have very high and positive coefficients between the 10th and 15th month in unemployment, which is the time when benefits usually run out. This has also been found by Boeri and Steiner (1997). For women, we also observe that the receipt of unemployment benefits increases the likelihood of leaving the labour force, which probably stems from the fact that *some* women join the dole queue mainly to draw benefits and less for job search purposes. In the following discussion of the effects of active labour market programmes, we will have to refer back to the (passive) unemployment benefit system and its interactions with the active programmes.

**Table 39:** Competing Risks Model for Men

| Variable | Exit into employment | | Exit into non-participation | |
|---|---|---|---|---|
| | Coeff. | t-value | Coeff. | t-value |
| Age between (35 and 45) | | | | |
| 16 and 25 | 0.488 | 4.89 | -0.013 | -0.08 |
| 26 and 35 | 0.234 | 2.82 | -0.169 | -1.25 |
| 46 and 55 | -0.425 | -3.77 | -0.270* | -1.76 |
| 56 and 65 | -1.801 | -4.23 | -0.367 | -1.19 |
| Education (basic vocational) | | | | |
| Higher | 0.732 | 2.80 | -0.126 | -0.28 |
| Post–secondary | 0.098 | 0.43 | -0.173 | -0.39 |
| Secondary vocational | 0.118 | 1.40 | 0.336 | 2.61 |
| Secondary general | 0.146 | 0.83 | -0.018 | -0.07 |
| Primary or less | -0.272 | -3.47 | -0.175 | -1.45 |
| Occupation (industrial worker) | | | | |
| Manager | 0.397* | 1.91 | 0.258 | 0.81 |
| Professional | 0.047 | 0.14 | -0.254 | -0.52 |
| Technician | 0.347 | 1.98 | -0.344 | -1.57 |
| White collar | 0.127 | 0.81 | -0.146 | -0.55 |
| Personal services | 0.242* | 1.95 | 0.104 | 0.53 |
| Farmer | -0.077 | -0.40 | -0.171 | -0.59 |
| Simple blue-collar | 0.335 | 3.74 | 0.036 | 0.25 |
| Other simple jobs | 0.075 | 0.89 | 0.064 | 0.50 |
| Single | -0.292 | -3.36 | 0.059 | 0.43 |
| Children | 0.148 | 1.41 | -0.083 | -0.50 |
| No information on children | -0.082 | -0.90 | -0.153 | -0.98 |
| Disabled | -0.819 | -4.04 | 0.765 | 4.27 |

**Table 39:** Competing Risks Model for Men (ctd.)

| Variable | Exit into employment | | Exit into non-participation | |
|---|---|---|---|---|
| | Coeff. | t-value | Coeff. | t-value |
| Industry (mining) | | | | |
| Agriculture, forestry, fishing | 0.356 | 0.79 | -0.153 | -0.30 |
| Manufacturing | 0.787* | 1.82 | 0.082 | 0.18 |
| Electricity, gas, water | 0.826* | 1.69 | -0.431 | -0.70 |
| Construction | 0.807* | 1.87 | 0.189 | 0.41 |
| Trade, repairs | 0.676 | 1.54 | 0.034 | 0.07 |
| Hotels, restaurants | 0.640 | 1.31 | 0.082 | 0.14 |
| Transport, communication | 0.693 | 1.58 | -0.097 | -0.20 |
| Financial intermediation | 0.786 | 1.45 | 0.476 | 0.67 |
| Real estates, renting | **0.959** | 2.02 | -0.251 | -0.45 |
| Administration | -0.063 | -0.14 | **-1.531** | -2.72 |
| Education | 0.556 | 1.12 | -0.045 | -0.08 |
| Health, social work | 0.554 | 1.16 | 0.537 | 0.95 |
| Other services | 0.613 | 1.34 | 0.268 | 0.54 |
| None, unknown | **-5.012** | -4.64 | -0.298 | -0.63 |
| Place of residence (countryside) | | | | |
| 100,000 inhabitants or more | **0.214** | 2.35 | 0.184 | 1.36 |
| 20,000 to 99,999 | **0.172** | 2.16 | 0.220* | 1.83 |
| 19,999 or less | 0.004 | 0.04 | 0.194 | 1.50 |
| Unemployment benefits | -0.116 | -1.55 | 0.012 | 0.11 |
| Employed 1 month before unemployment ($\varepsilon$) | **0.314** | 2.93 | -0.199 | -1.26 |
| Employed 3 months before unemployment ($\varepsilon$) | 0.043 | 0.30 | -0.348 | -1.59 |
| Employed 6 months before unemployment ($\varepsilon$) | **-0.285** | -2.87 | -0.019 | -0.12 |
| Previous months in unemployment | **0.019** | 3.48 | -0.003 | -0.24 |
| Training | **0.747** | 4.10 | 0.310 | 0.79 |
| Intervention works | **-0.651** | -5.04 | **-1.089** | -3.55 |
| Public works | -0.252 | -1.10 | -2.081* | -1.94 |

**Table 39:** Competing Risks Model for Men (ctd.)

| Variable | | Exit into employment | | Exit into non-participation | |
|---|---|---|---|---|---|
| | | Coeff. | t-value | Coeff. | t-value |
| Calendar time 1994 or after | | 0.369 | 5.04 | -0.168* | -1.70 |
| Voivodship (Warsaw) | | | | | |
| Bydgoskie | | -0.232 | -1.05 | -1.945 | -4.59 |
| Ciechanowskie | (mid U / agricultural) | -0.591* | -1.81 | -0.514 | -1.42 |
| Czestochowskie | | 0.365 | 1.57 | -0.675* | -1.93 |
| Elblaskie | | -0.102 | -0.41 | -1.088 | -2.63 |
| Gdanskie | | -0.155 | -0.69 | -0.686* | -1.93 |
| Jeleniogorskie | (high U / industrial) | -0.583 | -2.01 | -0.658* | -1.87 |
| Katowickie | (low U / industrial) | -0.379* | -1.66 | -0.328 | -1.17 |
| Kieleckie | (high U / industrial) | -0.573 | -2.57 | -0.497* | -1.67 |
| Koninskie | | -0.243 | -0.94 | -0.998 | -2.38 |
| Koszalinskie | (high U / modern) | -0.507 | -1.97 | -0.868 | -2.23 |
| Krosnienskie | (low U / agricultural) | -0.941 | -2.44 | -1.265 | -2.53 |
| Leszczynskie | | 0.184 | 0.67 | -0.953* | -1.96 |
| Lubelskie | | -0.372 | -1.53 | -1.024 | -2.92 |
| Lomzynskie | | -0.172 | -0.63 | -1.226 | -2.55 |
| Lodzkie | (high U / industrial) | -0.457 | -1.97 | -0.804 | -2.68 |
| Nowosadeckie | | -0.362 | -1.45 | -1.012 | -2.91 |
| Olsztynskie | (high U / other) | -0.556 | -2.49 | -1.218 | -3.40 |
| Opolskie | | -0.130 | -0.54 | -0.603* | -1.91 |
| Ostroleckie | | -0.355 | -0.90 | -1.148 | -2.09 |
| Piotrkowskie | | -0.418 | -1.56 | -1.166 | -3.41 |
| Plockie | | -0.021 | -0.07 | -1.746 | -3.56 |
| Przemyskie | | -0.365 | -1.23 | -1.234 | -2.86 |
| Radomskie | (mid U / agricultural) | -0.533 | -2.18 | -0.849 | -2.49 |
| Rzeszowskie | (mid U / industrial) | -0.607 | -2.40 | -0.815 | -2.36 |
| Siedleckie | | 0.191 | 0.72 | -0.934 | -2.27 |
| Suwalskie | (mid U / agricultural) | -0.908 | -3.24 | -0.917 | -2.54 |

**Table 39:** Competing Risks Model for Men (ctd.)

| Variable | | Exit into employment | | Exit into non-participation | |
|---|---|---|---|---|---|
| | | Coeff. | t-value | Coeff. | t-value |
| Tarnobrzeskie | (low U / agricultural) | -0.507* | -1.87 | **-1.450** | -3.22 |
| Torunskie | | -0.344 | -1.45 | **-1.554** | -3.49 |
| Walbrzyskie | (high U / industrial) | **-0.728** | -2.88 | -0.218 | -0.68 |
| Wloclawskie | | -0.247 | -0.96 | **-0.831** | -2.14 |
| Zamojskie | | -0.451 | -1.63 | **-1.307** | -3.43 |
| Seasonal Dummies (January-March) | | | | | |
| April-June | | **0.324** | 4.78 | **0.284** | 2.68 |
| June-September | | 0.080 | 1.12 | 0.112 | 1.00 |
| September-December | | -0.063 | -0.82 | **0.235** | 2.05 |
| Process time month (0-3) | | | | | |
| 4 – 6 | | **0.867** | 7.01 | **0.450** | 2.90 |
| 7 – 9 | | **0.792** | 5.48 | **0.763** | 4.62 |
| 10 – 12 | | **1.966** | 13.76 | **2.067** | 13.74 |
| 13 – 15 | | **2.004** | 11.93 | **2.234** | 11.82 |
| 16 – 18 | | **1.507** | 7.96 | **1.446** | 6.17 |
| 18 – 21 | | **1.360** | 6.64 | **0.857** | 2.76 |
| 22 – 24 | | **1.295** | 5.91 | **1.281** | 4.38 |
| 25 – 30 | | **0.937** | 4.21 | **1.218** | 4.39 |
| 31 – 36 | | **1.208** | 5.21 | 0.594 | 1.50 |
| 37 – 60 | | **1.063** | 4.30 | **0.862** | 2.45 |
| Constant | | **-5.135** | -10.27 | **-4.173** | -7.48 |

**Table 39:** Competing Risks Model for Men (ctd.)

| Variable | Exit into employment | Exit into non-participation |
|---|---|---|
| $\varepsilon^1$ (s.e.) | -0.288 (0.052) | |
| $\varepsilon^2$ (s.e.) | 4.679 (0.336) | |
| $\varepsilon^3$ (s.e.) | 1.613 (0.624) | |
| $\Pr(\varepsilon^1)$ (s.e.) | 0.876 (0.026) | |
| $\Pr(\varepsilon^2)$ (s.e.) | 0.017 (0.005) | |
| $\Pr(\varepsilon^3)$ (s.e.) | 0.107 (0.026) | |
| Number of persons | 3,439 | |
| Number of spells | 4,206 | |
| Number of observations | 51,442 | |
| *ln* likelihood | -11,273.95 | |

*Note:* shaded (asterisked) coefficients are significant at the 5 (10) percent level; the data is structured so that each month corresponds to one observation, as a consequence, the number of observations equals the number of spells times the average number of observed months in a spell; the total number of spells (4206) is smaller than the number of comparison spells plus the number of treatment spells in each programme in Table 31 (52 + 193 + 50 + 3,922 = 4,217), because 5 spells include both training and intervention works, and 6 spells include both intervention and public works (4,217 - 5 - 6 = 4,206);
the age dummies are time-varying;
$\varepsilon$ and $\Pr(\varepsilon)$ are the estimated mass points and probabilities of the non-parametrically-estimated distribution of the unobserved individual heterogeneity component; (s.e.): standard errors in parentheses;
the classifications of the voivodships according to U (unemployment), and *modern*, *industrial*, *agricultural*, and *other* employment structures, correspond to Figure 2 and Figure 3 on page 16; the estimated standard errors (and hence the t-values) are heteroskedasticity-consistent.

Source: *Polish Labour Force Survey; own calculations.*

**Table 40:** Competing Risks Model for Women

| Variable | Exit into employment | | Exit into non-participation | |
|---|---|---|---|---|
| | Coeff. | t-value | Coeff. | t-value |
| Age between (35 and 45) | | | | |
| 16 and 25 | 0.392 | 3.944 | 0.681 | 5.03 |
| 26 and 35 | 0.095 | 1.082 | 0.243 | 1.97 |
| 46 and 55 | -0.239* | -1.742 | -0.131 | -0.82 |
| 56 and 65 | -0.039 | -0.060 | 0.807 | 1.62 |
| Education (basic vocational) | | | | |
| Higher | 0.859 | 3.793 | 0.110 | 0.38 |
| Post–secondary | 0.621 | 4.676 | 0.128 | 0.69 |
| Secondary vocational | 0.257 | 3.286 | 0.103 | 0.94 |
| Secondary general | 0.114 | 1.037 | 0.280 | 2.10 |
| Primary or less | -0.252 | -2.592 | 0.171 | 1.39 |
| Occupation (industrial worker) | | | | |
| Manager | 0.010 | 0.040 | -0.323 | -0.80 |
| Professional | -0.707 | -2.985 | 0.016 | 0.06 |
| Technician | -0.177 | -1.232 | -0.111 | -0.66 |
| White collar | -0.570 | -3.697 | -0.256 | -1.36 |
| Personal services | -0.443 | -3.136 | -0.150 | -0.92 |
| Farmer | -0.635 | -2.317 | -0.188 | -0.66 |
| Simple blue-collar | -0.141 | -0.722 | -0.392 | -1.52 |
| Other simple jobs | -0.426 | -3.334 | -0.093 | -0.59 |
| Single | 0.271 | 3.592 | -0.422 | -4.15 |
| Children | 0.402 | 3.988 | 0.133 | 0.96 |
| No information on children | 0.182 | 2.037 | -0.095 | -0.86 |
| Disabled | -0.374* | -1.712 | 1.413 | 9.81 |

**Table 40:** Competing Risks Model for Women (ctd.)

| Variable | Exit into employment | | Exit into non-participation | |
|---|---|---|---|---|
| | Coeff. | t-value | Coeff. | t-value |
| Industry (mining) | | | | |
| Agriculture, forestry, fishing | 0.912 | 1.111 | -0.389 | -0.71 |
| Manufacturing | 0.750 | 0.947 | -0.149 | -0.30 |
| Electricity, gas, water | 1.052 | 1.099 | -0.742 | -0.80 |
| Construction | 0.703 | 0.857 | -0.864 | -1.31 |
| Trade, repairs | 1.058 | 1.339 | 0.044 | 0.09 |
| Hotels, restaurants | 1.003 | 1.255 | 0.114 | 0.22 |
| Transport, communication | 0.584 | 0.709 | -0.207 | -0.37 |
| Financial intermediation | 1.374* | 1.698 | -0.409 | -0.68 |
| Real estates, renting | 0.921 | 1.137 | -0.344 | -0.61 |
| Administration | 0.965 | 1.207 | -0.755 | -1.33 |
| Education | 1.307 | 1.629 | -0.158 | -0.29 |
| Health, social work | 1.010 | 1.273 | -0.142 | -0.28 |
| Other services | 0.993 | 1.249 | -0.146 | -0.28 |
| None, unknown | **-3.526** | -3.733 | -0.263 | -0.52 |
| Place of residence (countryside) | | | | |
| 100,000 inhabitants or more | -0.035 | -0.381 | **0.458** | 4.11 |
| 20,000 to 99,999 | -0.071 | -0.850 | 0.118 | 1.14 |
| 19,999 or less | 0.114 | 1.287 | -0.126 | -0.99 |
| Unemployment benefits | **-0.307** | -4.124 | **0.295** | 3.14 |
| Employed 1 month before unemployment ($\varepsilon$) | **0.478** | 4.628 | -0.249* | -1.75 |
| Employed 3 months before unemployment ($\varepsilon$) | -0.086 | -0.619 | -0.106 | -0.54 |
| Employed 6 months before unemployment ($\varepsilon$) | -0.199* | -1.831 | -0.174 | -1.18 |
| Previous months in unemployment | 0.007 | 1.161 | 0.016 | 1.58 |
| Training | **0.416** | 2.168 | -0.024 | -0.09 |
| Intervention works | **-0.327** | -2.037 | -0.057 | -0.26 |
| Public works | 0.101 | 0.178 | -0.739 | -0.60 |

**Table 40:** Competing Risks Model for Women (ctd.)

| Variable | | Exit into employment | | Exit into non-participation | |
|---|---|---|---|---|---|
| | | Coeff. | t-value | Coeff. | t-value |
| Calendar time 1994 or after | | 0.355 | 4.637 | -0.018 | -0.19 |
| Voivodship (Warsaw) | | | | | |
| Bialostockie | | -0.329 | -1.137 | -0.953 | -2.77 |
| Bielskie | | -0.281 | -1.164 | -0.483* | -1.70 |
| Bydgoskie | (high U / industrial) | -0.441* | -1.786 | -0.994 | -3.56 |
| Chelmskie | (high U / agricultural) | -1.125 | -2.868 | -1.204 | -2.59 |
| Ciechanowskie | | -0.353 | -1.279 | -1.028 | -3.17 |
| Czestochowskie | (low U / industrial) | -0.599 | -2.209 | -0.414 | -1.46 |
| Elblaskie | | -0.232 | -0.801 | -0.607 | -2.05 |
| Gdanskie | | -0.224 | -0.958 | -1.462 | -4.79 |
| Gorzowskie | | -0.207 | -0.695 | -1.283 | -2.90 |
| Jeleniogorskie | (high U / industrial) | -0.541* | -1.870 | -0.694 | -2.05 |
| Kaliskie | | -0.248 | -0.994 | -1.321 | -3.78 |
| Katowickie | (high U / industrial) | -0.556 | -2.385 | -0.772 | -3.25 |
| Kieleckie | (low U / industrial) | -0.633 | -2.625 | -1.333 | -4.32 |
| Koninskie | (mid U / agricultural) | -0.554 | -2.040 | -1.183 | -3.25 |
| Koszalinskie | | -0.237 | -0.955 | -1.517 | -3.72 |
| Krosnienskie | | -0.250 | -0.789 | -0.783 | -2.01 |
| Legnickie | (mid U / industrial) | -0.605* | -1.821 | -0.661 | -2.28 |
| Leszczynskie | | -0.363 | -1.001 | -0.693* | -1.95 |
| Lubelskie | (high U / industrial) | -0.716 | -2.542 | -1.050 | -3.08 |
| Lomzynskie | | -0.445 | -1.236 | -0.960* | -1.88 |
| Lodzkie | | -0.272 | -1.108 | -1.301 | -4.42 |
| Nowosadeckie | (low U / agricultural) | -0.597 | -2.073 | -1.159 | -3.16 |
| Olsztynskie | (high U / other) | -0.473* | -1.781 | -1.057 | -3.75 |
| Opolskie | | -0.172 | -0.645 | -1.035 | -3.14 |
| Ostroleckie | | -0.525 | -1.547 | -1.501 | -3.32 |

**Table 40:** Competing Risks Model for Women (ctd.)

| Variable | | Exit into employment | | Exit into non-participation | |
|---|---|---|---|---|---|
| | | Coeff. | t-value | Coeff. | t-value |
| Pilskie | (mid U / other) | **-0.949** | -2.949 | **-0.779** | -2.28 |
| Piotrkowskie | | -0.423 | -1.470 | **-0.755** | -2.11 |
| Plockie | (mid U / agricultural) | -0.701* | -1.892 | **-1.795** | -3.53 |
| Poznanskie | | 0.233 | 0.931 | -0.620* | -1.87 |
| Przemyskie | | -0.498 | -1.255 | -0.792* | -1.95 |
| Radomskie | (mid U / agricultural) | **-0.646** | -2.386 | **-0.713** | -2.53 |
| Rzeszowskie | (mid U / industrial) | -0.460* | -1.752 | **-1.178** | -3.06 |
| Siedleckie | (low U / agricultural) | **-0.911** | -2.906 | -0.631* | -1.80 |
| Sieradzkie | (mid U / agricultural) | **-0.995** | -2.946 | **-0.856** | -2.59 |
| Slupskie | | -0.300 | -1.028 | **-0.828** | -2.55 |
| Suwalskie | | -0.287 | -0.942 | -0.734* | -1.93 |
| Szczecinskie | | -0.379 | -1.498 | **-0.805** | -2.68 |
| Tarnobrzeskie | (low U / agricultural) | **-0.906** | -2.930 | **-1.548** | -3.60 |
| Tarnowskie | | -0.153 | -0.550 | **-1.288** | -3.12 |
| Torunskie | (high U / industrial) | -0.497* | -1.674 | **-0.884** | -2.64 |
| Walbrzyskie | (high U / industrial) | **-1.116** | -2.972 | **-0.990** | -2.85 |
| Wloclawskie | (mid U / agricultural) | **-0.789** | -2.327 | **-1.241** | -3.27 |
| Wroclawskie | | -0.419 | -1.622 | **-0.886** | -3.15 |
| Zamojskie | (low U / agricultural) | **-0.592** | -2.029 | **-0.946** | -2.40 |
| Zielonogorskie | | -0.060 | -0.200 | -0.595* | -1.85 |
| Seasonal Dummies (January-March) | | | | | |
| April-June | | **0.288** | 3.704 | **0.392** | 3.97 |
| June-September | | **0.171** | 2.160 | 0.100 | 0.96 |
| September-December | | 0.167* | 1.947 | 0.165 | 1.47 |

**Table 40**: Competing Risks Model for Women (ctd.)

| | | | | |
|---|---|---|---|---|
| Process time month (0-3) | | | | |
| 4 – 6 | 0.253 | 2.052 | -0.245 | -1.56 |
| 7 – 9 | 0.111 | 0.865 | -0.266 | -1.54 |
| 10 – 12 | 1.338 | 12.387 | 1.486 | 12.16 |
| 13 – 15 | 1.179 | 9.220 | 1.853 | 13.75 |
| 16 – 18 | 0.644 | 4.329 | 1.062 | 6.08 |
| 18 – 21 | 0.549 | 3.335 | 0.681 | 3.08 |
| 22 – 24 | 0.537 | 3.090 | 0.584 | 2.51 |
| 25 – 30 | 0.114 | 0.653 | 0.346 | 1.53 |
| 31 – 36 | 0.172 | 0.868 | 0.484* | 1.87 |
| 37 – 60 | 0.426 | 2.326 | 0.653 | 2.60 |
| Constant | -5.053 | -6.038 | -4.261 | -7.37 |
| $\varepsilon^1$ (s.e.) | -0.041 (0.014) | | | |
| $\varepsilon^2$ (s.e.) | 4.871 (2.145) | | | |
| $\Pr(\varepsilon^1)$ (s.e.) | 0.992 (0.004) | | | |
| $\Pr(\varepsilon^2)$ (s.e.) | 0.008 (0.004) | | | |
| Number of persons | 3,671 | | | |
| Number of spells | 4,260 | | | |
| Number of observations | 61,223 | | | |
| *ln* likelihood | -10,739.48 | | | |

*Notes:* shaded (asterisked) coefficients are significant at the 5 (10) percent level; the data is structured so that each month corresponds to one observation, as a consequence, the number of observations equals the number of spells times the average number of observed months in a spell; the total number of spells (4,260) is smaller than the number of comparison spells plus the number of treatment spells in each programme in Table 31 (88 + 155 + 14 + 4,010 = 4,267), because 5 spells include both training and intervention works, and 2 spells include both intervention and public works (4,267 - 5 - 2 = 4,260);
the age dummies are time-varying;
$\varepsilon$ and $\Pr(\varepsilon)$ are the estimated mass points and probabilities of the non-parametrically-estimated distribution of the unobserved individual heterogeneity component; (s.e.): standard errors in parentheses;
the classifications of the voivodships according to U (unemployment), and *modern*, *industrial*, *agricultural*, and *other* employment structures, correspond to Figure 2 and Figure 3 on page 16; the estimated standard errors (and hence the t-values) are heteroskedasticity-consistent.

Source: *Polish Labour Force Survey; own calculations.*

**Estimated Effects of Active Labour Market Programmes**

The estimation results in Table 39 and Table 40 on *training* are consistent with the ones obtained from the matching approach in Section 5.2.3 above. Both the coefficients for transition into employment are positive and significant for both genders. The analysis based on matched samples has also found positive effects for men and women. However, the effect was not significant for women there.

Participation in *intervention works* seems to exert both a negative effect on re-employment (for men and women) and on the probability to leave the labour force (for men). As concerns *public works*, the coefficient for *exit into non-participation* is significant at the 10 percent level only in the model for men. Otherwise, there either seem to be no effects, or the number of completed spells with public works participation is too small to make any statistically safe statements (*cf.* Table 31 on page 148). The results from the econometric analysis on works programmes are thus also broadly consistent with those obtained from the matched sample approach. From the duration models we also get the impression that intervention works (and maybe also public works) have negative effects on re-employment. This may be either through stigma effects or for institutional reasons concerning the unemployment benefit system. As mentioned in Section 2.4, the participants in intervention and public works programmes regained their full unemployment benefit entitlement period after the programmes under the regulations valid until the 1$^{st}$ of January 1997. Thus there were institutional incentives to stay on the unemployment register and draw benefits after a works programme. The evidence on intervention works is consistent with the view that the programme participants reacted to these incentives.

To obtain a clearer picture on the magnitude of the estimated effects of the ALMP programmes, we plot simulated survivor functions for men and women in Figure 24. The survivor curves can be interpreted in the following way. Take a point on the *process time* axis, say 12 months. Then read off the estimated value of the survivor function of a curve, say the one for men in training. In this case, the survivor function roughly takes on the value 0.5, which means that 12 months after the beginning of their unemployment spell with training, 50 percent of the (former) training participants have left unemployment already. Alternatively, one can say that it takes 12 months until 50 percent of the unemployed people who received training drop off the register (either because they find a job or leave the labour force). 12 months is then the *median unemployment duration* for this group.

**Figure 24:** Simulated Survivor Functions for ALMP Participants and Non-Participants

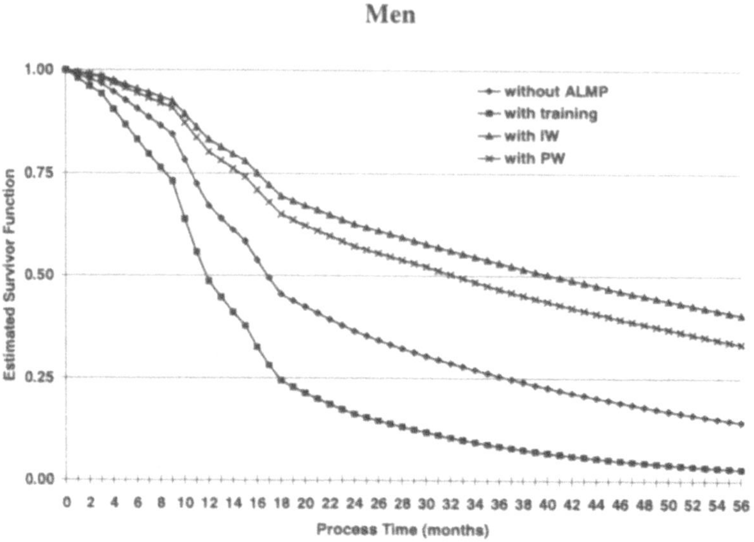


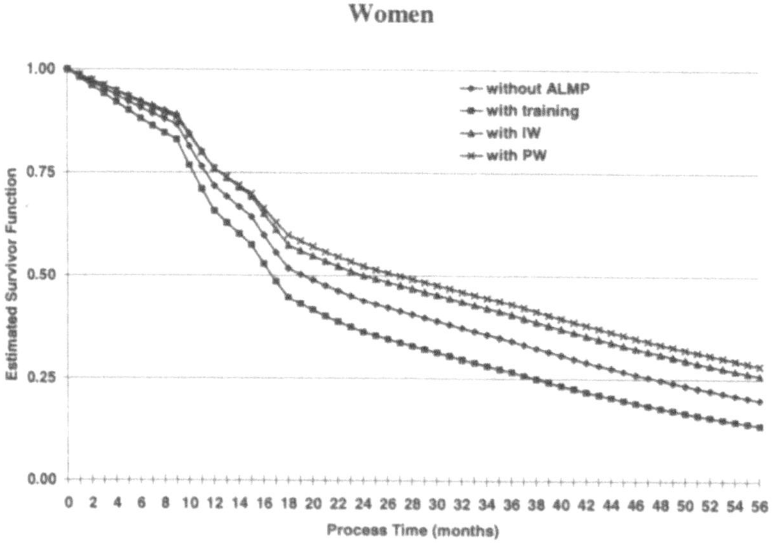


*Notes*: for all curves, the *unemployment benefit* dummy is set equal to *one*; for the curves with ALMP participation, the ALMP dummy variable is constantly set to *one*; IW: intervention works; PW: public works; for men $\varepsilon$=-0.288; for women $\varepsilon$=-0.041 in all simulations; these are the $\varepsilon$-values with the highest probabilities (*cf.* Table 39 and Table 40); all other variables are set to their mean at the end of the spells.

Source: *Polish Labour Force Survey; own calculations.*

We display the simulated median unemployment durations in Table 41. Note that because we have unobserved individual heterogeneity, the median unemployment durations differ even for a given set of exogenous variables depending on the value of $\varepsilon$. Table 41 shows that, when unemployment benefits are received and all other variables (except ALMP programme participation) are set to their means, the estimated median unemployment duration is 16 months for men and 19 months for women. Many studies that estimate duration models do not interpret their coefficients in terms of their effects on unemployment duration. The only study which has done this for Poland is to our knowledge Puhani (1996). There we have estimated a median duration of 18 and 23 months for men and women, respectively. The somewhat higher estimate in that paper probably stems from the fact that data on the time span 1990 to 1994 have been used, whereas our observation period here is 1992 to 1996. As we know, there has been a revival on the Polish labour market from 1994 onwards. In spite of these long median unemployment durations, we see from Table 41 that there are also groups who have very short unemployment spells (between 1 and 6 months). These are mostly people for whom unemployment is only a short intermittent period between two jobs. The reason that our observed variables are not able to explain these short spells gives credence to the view that unobservable factors such as motivation or flexibility play an important role on the labour market. Nevertheless, the fact that the estimated share of unemployed people with very short durations is below 10 percent for men and below one percent for women substantiates the view of the stagnant Polish unemployment pool (Boeri, 1994a; 1994b).

Table 41 indicates the order of magnitude of the ALMP programme effects to show whether the programmes make an economically significant difference. It is seen that the impacts are larger for men than for women. Training programmes reduce the unemployment duration of men by about 5 months, whereas the simulated effect for women is only around 2 months. As for intervention works, the increase in unemployment duration is economically significant for both genders. The simulated effects are over 20(!) months for men and 5 months for women. The order of magnitude of the unemployment prolongation through intervention works for men roughly corresponds to the time in intervention works (6-12 months) plus another full unemployment benefit entitlement period (12 months).

Although the effects for public works are not statistically significant at the 5 percent level, the point estimates - just like for intervention works - suggest that public works programmes prolong unemployment duration for more than half a year (women) or more than one year (men).

**Table 41:** Estimated Labour Market Policy Impacts on the Duration in Unemployment

| Model | | Simulated median unemployment duration | | | |
|---|---|---|---|---|---|
| | | Without ALMP but with UB | With training and UB | With IW and UB | With PW and UB |
| | | *Men* | | | |
| $\varepsilon$=-0.215 | Pr($\varepsilon$)=0.907 | 17 | 12 | 40 | 32 |
| $\varepsilon$=-1.637 | Pr($\varepsilon$)=0.079 | 6 | 4 | 10 | 9 |
| $\varepsilon$=-4.515 | Pr($\varepsilon$)=0.015 | 1 | 1 | 1 | 1 |
| Weighted average | | 16 | 11 | 37 | 30 |
| | | *Women* | | | |
| $\varepsilon$=-0.041 | Pr($\varepsilon$)=0.992 | 19 | 17 | 24 | 27 |
| $\varepsilon$=4.871 | Pr($\varepsilon$)=0.008 | 1 | 1 | 1 | 1 |
| Weighted average | | 19 | 17 | 24 | 27 |

*Notes:* UB: unemployment benefits, IW: intervention works, and PW: public works; estimated ALMP effects include the time spent in the ALMP programmes; $\varepsilon$ and Pr($\varepsilon$) are the estimated mass points and probabilities of the non-parametrically estimated distribution of the unobserved individual heterogeneity component (*cf.* Table 39 and Table 40).

Source: *Polish Labour Force Survey; own calculations.*

As mentioned at the end of Section 5.2.3, the positive impact of training programmes has not been established before in microeconometric analyses for Poland. In previous studies (Puhani and Steiner, 1996; 1997; Puhani, 1996) training turned out to be insignificant for both men and women. However, Puhani and Steiner (1996; 1997) have also found negative employment effects of works programmes. We summarise the conclusions from both the statistical matching and the duration model analysis in the following section.

## 5.4 Conclusions from the Microeconometric Analysis

Generally speaking, we have found similar results from our two microeconometric methods of inference: the statistical matching approach and the duration model approach. According to our estimates, training programmes improve the employment opportunities of unemployed men and maybe also of women, whereas intervention (and perhaps public) works lower the re-employment chances of their participants. From the statistical matching approach, we conclude that the unemployment rate for former trainees is around 10 percentage points lower than the one of non-trainees in the first 20 months after the beginning of training. As to intervention and public works, the unemployment rate of former male participants is estimated to be around 30 percentage points higher than the one of non-participants. For women, the unemployment rates of intervention and public works participants were only 10 percentage points higher than the ones of non-participants, although the effects of public works for women could not be reasonably estimated with the few number of observations at hand.

The estimates of the duration models not only suggest the same qualitative effects of the programmes, but also accord with the matching results in that the effects of ALMPs are more pronounced for men than for women. For training, our simulations display a 5-month reduction in the median unemployment duration for men, and a 2-month reduction for women. On the other hand, intervention works seem to prolong the median unemployment duration by around 20 months for men and 5 months for women. The effects of public works are only marginally significant, but also suggest a 14-month prolongation of unemployment for men. The public works effect for women is insignificant, which is most likely due to the small number of observations in this group. The programmes of subsidised jobs (intervention works) and direct job creation (public works) coupled with renewed rights to unemployment benefits thus seem to shoot off in the wrong direction. The warnings by Schwanse (1996) as well as Góra, Lehmann, Socha, and Sztanderska (1996) that the incentive interactions between active and passive policies (renewed unemployment benefit entitlement after works programmes) have to be carefully considered, seem to be warranted by our findings. However, we cannot test here whether incentive interactions between the active and passive systems are responsible for the negative effects of intervention or public works or whether there are stigmas attached to these programmes.

The robustness of the estimation results with respect to the statistical approach gives credence to the evidence presented here. Although the outcome variables slightly differ in definition between the non-parametric analyses on matched samples (unemployment rate) and duration models (duration of unemployment spell), the conclusions on the relative effectiveness of the main Polish ALMP programmes do not. The author of this study nevertheless has a personal preference for the results of the statistical matching approach. The reasons are both methodological and practical. From a methodological point of view, we argue that the explicit selection of comparison persons which are similar to the treatment persons is less liable to misspecifications than the building of an econometric model for a large sample which also includes comparison persons who are very different to the treatment group. On the practical side, we believe that non-parametric comparisons of the unemployment rates after ALMP participation provide more convincing evidence than simulation results which are based on both the model's assumptions and on the assumptions of the author who simulates the model. By graphing both pre- and post-treatment outcomes one can test for the adequacy of the matched comparison group and the causal effect at one sight. What is more, in trying to emulate the experimental situation, matching on non-experimental data comes closest to an evaluation based on experimental data both conceptually and in terms of ease of interpretation and communication of the results.

# 6 Conclusions

The effectiveness of the current active labour market programmes (ALMPs) in Poland has been the subject of inquiry in this study. The main focus has lain on training programmes, subsidised employment (intervention works), and direct job creation (public works). As the main purpose of these programmes is to re-integrate the unemployed into the labour market, we have investigated the effects of ALMPs in terms of re-employment chances. A variety of approaches have been applied which are known from the empirical evaluation literature. These include both macro- and microeconometric models.

Our macroeconometric study is based on the recently established concept of the augmented matching function and has been presented in Chapter 3. Due to the structure of the data at hand, only training programmes could be evaluated in terms of their effects on outflows from unemployment at the regional (voivodship) level. The microeconometric part of this study builds the core of our evaluation. It is presented in Chapters 4 and 5. The programmes analysed are training, intervention, and public works, which are the most important Polish ALMPs in terms of participants. We have applied the two most commonly used statistical approaches in the microeconometric evaluation literature. These are comparisons of ALMP participants and non-participants based on matched samples on the one hand, and analysis based on econometric modelling (duration models) on the other. As demonstrated in Section 2.4, active labour market programmes swallow up enormous sums of taxpayers' money. This money could be used otherwise, and hence it is important to discuss the policy conclusions that may follow from the findings of this work.

We conclude that *training* programmes have positive effects on the re-employment chances of the trainees. In the macroeconometric analysis, we have found positive effects of training on the outflows from unemployment for *industrialised* and maybe *agricultural* voivodships using data from the labour office registers (*cf.* Figure 3 on page 16 for classification of the voivodships). Although there are no significant effects for *modern* voivodships (and when using data from the Polish Labour Force Survey), there is evidence that Polish training programmes are able to reduce unemployment both at the macro- and the microeconomic level. Indeed, the average costs to increase the outflow from unemployment by one person have been estimated to lie between € 200 and € 500, which is below previous estimates for the Czech and Slovak Republics (between € 1,000 and € 3,000). The microeconometric results suggest that the unemployment rate of trainees in the first 20 months after the beginning of training lies around 10 percentage points below those of non-trainee unemployed people.

Our microeconometric results on *intervention works* programmes are alarming. We find that the re-employment chances of unemployed people worsen through participation in these schemes. This result is robust across all specifications. The estimates from the matched samples suggest that the unemployment rate of former male and female intervention works participants is 30 and 10 percentage points higher than the ones of non-participants, respectively. That works programmes can have a negative impact on employability has already been found in previous work on Poland by Puhani and Steiner (1996; 1997). Also, the evaluation results on programmes similar to intervention works in Hungary by O'Leary (1997b) and in eastern Germany by Hübler (1997) as well as Kraus, Puhani, and Steiner (1998) suggest that these types of programmes can have negative impacts on the job opportunities of the unemployed.

On the one hand, participation in these programmes may carry stigma effects. Employers who know that somebody has participated in an intervention works scheme might consider this information as a signal for low productivity and loose labour market attachment. A potential remedy for this problem could be wage supplements instead of subsidies (O'Leary, 1997b). Whereas wage subsidies are paid out to the employer, wage supplements are given to the unemployed worker in case he manages to find an employer. As the worker searching for a job does not have to reveal to his or her potential employer that he or she receives a wage supplement, stigma effects can be avoided. The other side of the coin, though, is that collective agreements on wages may prevent unemployed workers from being able to work for low enough wages to induce the employer to take them on.

On the other hand, there is a completely different explanation for the prolonged unemployment duration through intervention works. Schwanse (1996, p.18) notes that

> *'In several OECD countries the role of ALMPs has [...] been downgraded [...] to serve as a means to prevent benefit exhaustion: participation in ALMPs re-establishes entitlements to unemployment insurance benefits. This has led for a considerable number of the long-term unemployed to a 'carousel effect' and made benefit duration virtually indefinite.'*

Such 'carousel effects', as Schwanse (1996) calls them, may also be at work in Poland. Indeed, the estimation results in our duration models show that intervention works participants have both a lower probability to leave unemployment for a job and a lower probability to leave the labour force than non-participants. This is consistent with the view that the renewed eligibility to the full entitlement period to receive unemployment benefits after an intervention works programme gives incentives to stay in the labour force just to draw benefits. Hence, intervention works instead of shortening unemployment spells seem to intervene in the opposite direction. Unfortunately, one cannot test whether many of those people, who register themselves as unemployed again after an intervention works programme, actually hold jobs in the allegedly large black economy in Poland.

The same can also be said on *public works*. For men, public works have about the same negative effect on the re-employment probability as intervention works. For women, no significant effects have been found. Unfortunately, the number of observations on public works is very low for women so that it was difficult to obtain any reasonable estimates. However, the evidence from both the matched sample and the duration model on women suggests negative effects on re-employment in the order of the effects of intervention works on female participants.

Whether the effectiveness of works programmes has been improved by the new regulation on the renewal of the unemployment benefit entitlement period which took effect on the 1st of January 1997, will have to be seen when data on ALMPs for the years 1997 and after are available. Under the new regulation, one has to be employed (where works programmes count as employment) for 12 months in the last 18 months to be eligible for unemployment benefits. Hence, works programmes do not automatically renew the entitlement period as under the old regulation, where 6 months of employment during the last 12 months was sufficient. Clearly, the new regulation weakens the interactions between ALMPs and the unemployment benefit system. On the other hand, we do not believe that the negative effects of works programmes can be *entirely* traced back to these interactions. There are probably other factors, such as stigma effects or failures in the implementation of these programmes, which can play a role. One crucial problem with works programmes may be the fact that – unlike in training – the participants do not improve their qualifications, but only carry out unskilled tasks. Wilson and Fretwell (1996) point out in an international comparison of works programmes that the lack of skills lies at the heart of the long-term unemployment problem in both western and transition countries. Training thus seems conceptually a more suitable means to improve the employability of the unemployed than temporarily subsidised employment in low skilled jobs.

A radical interpretation of our results would be that Polish works programmes between 1992 and 1996 were a waste of money. Especially in the context of transition, one can expect that many people still dwell in the perception of the state as the provider of job opportunities. Works programmes may perpetuate this perception and prevent adjustment to the new situation. Whilst we believe that it is possible to draw the just outlined conclusions from our results, we nevertheless would consider them as extreme, because they put little or no weight on alternative channels through which works programmes may provide utility to the participants or even the general political climate in Poland. There might be important psychological and social effects of programme participation. The fact that everybody is responsible for him- or herself has come as a shock to many people in the formerly planned economies. Active labour market policies can be a means to make that shock more bearable. This way, ALMPs can also contribute to the political stability of a country and make voters accept the changes that are hard but necessary. As Sachs (1993) notes, political stability and the acceptance of the economic reforms cannot be taken for granted. Hence, economic policy makers naturally have to take these factors into account, too, when making fundamental decisions.

In spite of these *caveats*, it remains the task of social scientists to put an objective but critical eye on the claims that are made on the potential of active labour market programmes. If we focus our attention on the capabilities of ALMPs to provide a 'step towards regular employment' as has been hoped by the OECD (1990) and many policy makers and officials (Buttler, 1992), we can now say that works unlike training programmes have not been an appropriate tool to contain the unemployment problem in Poland. With respect to the quote of the OECD (1990) made in the introduction, we argue that intervention and public works programmes should be sold to the electorate as a social policy measure, not as a magic wand which provides a step towards regular employment. However, the evidence on training calls for optimism.

# List of Figures

# List of Tables

# List of Abbreviations

| | |
|---|---|
| ABM | *Arbeitsbeschaffungsmaß-nahmen*; German for: public works and subsidised employment programmes |
| ADF | Augmented Dickey-Fuller Test |
| ALMP | Active Labour Market Policy |
| AR | Autoregressive Model |
| CES | Constant Elasticity of Substitution |
| CPS-SSA | (United States) Current Population Survey - Social Security Administration File |
| DF | Dickey-Fuller Test |
| ECM | Error Correction Model |
| € | Euro / European Currency Unit |
| FuU | *Fortbildungs- und Umschu-lungsmaßnahmen*; German for: training and retraining measures |
| GLS | Generalised Least Squares estimator |
| GSOEP | German Socio-Economic Panel |
| GUS | Glówny Urzad Statystyczny; Polish for: Central Statistical Office (of Poland) |
| HUF | Hungarian Forint |
| ILO | International Labour Office |
| IV | Instrumental Variable Estimator |

| | |
|---|---|
| IW | Intervention Works (Subsidised Job Schemes in Poland) |
| JTPA | Job Training Partnership Act |
| LMM | (German) Labour Market Monitor |
| NSW | (United States) Nation Supported Work Demonstration Programme |
| OECD | Organisation for Economic Co-operation and Development |
| OLS | Ordinary Least Squares Estimator |
| PES | Public Employment Service |
| PLFS | Polish Labour Force Survey |
| PLZ | Polish Zloty |
| PSID | (United States) Panel Study of Income Dynamics |
| PUJ | Publicly Useful Jobs (in the Czech and Slovak Republics) |
| PW | Public Works |
| SDA | Service Delivery Area (of JTPA) |
| SPJ | Socially Purposeful Jobs (in the Czech and Slovak Republics) |
| SUTVA | Stable Unit-Treatment Value Assumption |
| TSU | Territorial Statistical Unit (of Poland) |
| UB | Unemployment Benefits |
| WWII | Second World War |

# References


Ahn, S.C. and P. Schmidt (1995): Efficient Estimation of Models for Dynamic Panel Data, *Journal of Econometrics* 68: 5-27.

Angrist, J.D. and G.W. Imbens (1995): Two-Stage Least Squares Estimation of Average Causal Effects in Models with Variable Treatment Intensity, *Journal of the American Statistical Association* 90: 431-442.

Angrist, J.D., G.W. Imbens and D.B. Rubin (1996): Identification of Causal Effects Using Instrumental Variables, *Journal of the American Statistical Association* 91: 444-472.

Angrist, J.D. and A.B. Krueger (1991): Does Compulsory School Attendance Affect Schooling and Earnings? *The Quarterly Journal of Economics* 106: 979-1014.

Angrist, J.D. and A.B. Krueger (1995): Split-Sample Instrumental Variables Estimates of the Return to Schooling, *Journal of Business & Economic Statistics* 13: 225-235.

Ashenfelter, O. and D. Card (1985): Using the Longitudinal Structure of Earnings to Estimate the Effect of Training Programs, *Review of Economics and Statistics* 66: 648-660.

Balcerowicz, L. (1994): Transition to the Market Economy: Poland, 1989-93 in Comparative Perspective, *Economic Policy* 19S: 72-97.

Baltagi, B.H. (1995): *Econometric Analysis of Panel Data*, Chichester: John Wiley & Sons.

Baltagi, B.H. and Q. Li (1990): A Lagrange Multiplier Test for the Error Components Model with Incomplete Panels, *Econometric Reviews* 9: 103-107.

Banerjee, A., J. Doladao, J.W. Galbraith and D.F. Hendry (1993): *Co-Integration, Error-Correction, and the Econometric Analysis of Non-Stationary Data*, Oxford: Oxford University Press.

Björklund, A. (1989): *Evaluations of Training Programs: Experiences and Proposals for Future Research*, Wissenschaftszentrum Berlin für Sozialforschung, Discussion Paper FS I 89-13, Berlin.

Blanchard, O.J. and P. Diamond (1989): The Beveridge Curve, *Brookings Papers on Economic Activity* 1: 1-60.

Blanchard O.J., and P. Diamond (1990): The Aggregate Matching Function, in: Diamond, P. (ed.): *Growth, Productivity, Unemployment, Essays to Celebrate Bob Solow's Birthday*, 159-201, Cambridge MA: MIT Press.

Blossfeld, H.P. and G. Rohwer (1995): *Techniques of Event History Modelling, New Approaches to Causal Analysis*, Mahwah (New Jersey): Lawrence Erlbaum.

Boeri, T. (1994a): Transitional Unemployment, *Economics of Transition* 2: 1-26.

Boeri, T. (1994b): Labour Market Flows and the Persistence of Unemployment in Central and Eastern Europe, in: OECD (ed.): *Unemployment in Transition Countries: Transient or Persistent?*, 13-56, Paris: OECD.

Boeri, T. (1996): Unemployment Outflows and the Scope of Labour Market Policies in Central and Eastern Europe, in: OECD (ed.): *Lessons from Labour Market Policies in Transition Countries*, 41-70, Paris: OECD.

Boeri, T. and M.C. Burda (1996): Active Labor Market Policies, Job Matching and the Czech Miracle, *European Economic Review* 40: 805-817.

Boeri, T. and S. Scarpetta (1995): Emerging Regional Labour Market Dynamics in Central and Eastern Europe, in: OECD (ed.): *The Regional Dimension of Unemployment in Transition Economies, A Challenge for Labour Market and Social Policies*, 75-87, Paris: OECD.

Boeri, T. and V. Steiner (1997): *'Wait Unemployment' in Economies in Transition: The Case of Poland*, ZEW, Mannheim, mimeo.

Breitung, J. (1997): *Testing for Unit Roots in Panel Data Using a GMM Approach*, Institut für Statistik und Ökonometrie, Humboldt University Berlin, mimeo.

Breitung, J. and W. Meyer (1994): Testing for Unit Roots in Panel Data: Are Wages on Different Bargaining Levels Cointegrated? *Applied Economics* 26: 353-361.

Breusch, T.S. and A.R. Pagan (1980): The Lagrange Multiplier Test and its Applications to Model Specification in Econometrics, *Review of Economic Studies* 47: 239-253.

Bundesanstalt für Arbeit (1993): *Amtliche Nachrichten der Bundesanstalt für Arbeit, Arbeitsstatistik 1992 – Jahreszahlen*, 41 (Sondernummer), Nuremberg.

Burda, M. (1993): Labour Markets in Eastern Europe. *Economic Policy* 16: 101-137.

Burda, M. (1994): Modelling Exits from Unemployment in Eastern Germany: A Matching Function Approach, in: König, H. and V. Steiner (eds.): *Arbeitsmarktdynamik und Unternehmensentwicklung in Ostdeutschland*, Schriftenreihe des ZEW Nr.1, 97-122, Baden-Baden : Nomos.

Burda, M. and M. Lubyova (1995): The Impact of Active Labour Market Policies: A Closer Look at the Czech and Slovak Republics, in: Newberry, D. (ed.): *Tax and Benefit Reform in Central and Eastern Europe*, 173-205, London: CEPR, also: CEPR Discussion paper No.1102, London.

Burda, M. and S. Profit (1996): Matching Across Space: Evidence on Mobility in the Czech Republic, *Labour Economics* 3: 255-278.

Burda, M. and C. Wyplosz (1994): Gross Worker and Job Flows in Europe, *European Economic Review* 38: 1287-1315.

Burtless, G. (1993): The Case for Social Experiments, in: Ministry of Labour, Denmark (ed.): *Measuring Labour Market Measures - Evaluating the Effects of Active Labour Market Policy Initiatives*, 15-34, Copenhagen.

Burtless, G. (1995): The Case for Randomized Field Trials in Economic and Policy Research. *Journal of Economic Perspectives* 9: 63-84.

Burtless, G. and L.L. Orr (1986): Are Classical Experiments Needed for Manpower Policy? *The Journal of Human Resources* 21: 606-640.

Buttler, F. (1992): Wie weit reicht die Brückenfunktion der Arbeitsmarktpolitik in Ostdeutschland?, *WSI Mitteilungen* 11/1992: 721-727.

Chapman, P.G. (1993): *The Economics of Training*, LSE Handbooks in Economics, New York: Harvester Wheatsheaf.

Coopers & Lybrand (1991): *Poland: Gender Issues in the Transition to a Market Economy*, U.S. Agency for International Development, report.

Cox, D.R. (1972): Regression Models and Life-Tables, *Journal of the Royal Statistical Society* 2: 187-218.

Cox, D.R. (1975): Partial Likelihood, *Biometrica* 62: 269-276.

Davidson, J., and J. MacKinnon (1993): *Estimation and Inference in Econometrics*, New York: Oxford University Press.

Dehejia, R.H. and S. Wahba (1995a): *A Matching Approach for Estimating Causal Effects in Non-Experimental Studies*, Department of Economics, Harvard University, Cambridge, MA, mimeo.

Dehejia, R.H. and S. Wahba (1995b): *Causal Effects in Non-Experimental Studies*, Department of Economics, Harvard University, Cambridge, MA, mimeo.

Deutsche Bundesbank (1992): *Statistische Beihefte zu den Monatsberichten der Deutschen Bundesbank* 1992(4), Reihe 5: Die Währungen der Welt, Frankfurt / Main.

Deutsche Bundesbank (1995): *Monatsbericht*, August 1995.

Dickey, D.A. and W.A. Fuller (1979): Distribution of the Estimators for Autoregressive Time Series with a Unit Root, *Journal of the American Statistical Association* 74: 427-431.

Disney, R. *et al.* (1992): *Helping the Unemployed, Active Labour Market Policies in Britain and Germany*, Worcester: Billing & Sons.

Engle; R.F. and B.S. Yoo (1987): Forecasting and Testing in Co-Integrated Systems, *Journal of Econometrics* 35: 143-159.

Entorf, H. (1995): Mismatch-Arbeitslosigkeit in Deutschland: Eine Kritik bestehender Meßkonzepte und neue Evidenz, in: Steiner, V. and L. Bellman (eds.): *Mikroökonomik des Arbeitsmarktes*, Beiträge zur Arbeitsmarkt und Berufsforschung, Nuremberg.

Entorf, H. (1997): *Random Walks With Drifts: Nonsense Regressions and Spurious Fixed-Effect Estimation*, Department of Economics, University of Mannheim, mimeo.

European Commission (1995): *Employment Observatory, Central and Eastern Europe, Employment Trends and Developments*, No.8, Brussels.

Fitzenberger, B. and H. Prey (1995): *Assessing the Impact of Training on Employment, The Case of East Germany*, Center for International Labor Economics (CILE), Discussion Paper 23-1995, University of Konstanz.

Fitzenberger, B. and H. Prey (1996): *Training in East Germany. An Evaluation of the Effects on Employment and Wages*, Center for International Labor Economics (CILE), Discussion Paper 36-1996, University of Konstanz.

Fitzenberger, B. and H. Prey (1997): Assessing the Impact of Training on Employment, The Case of East Germany, *ifo Studien* 43: 71-116.

Fitzenberger, B. and H. Prey (1998): Beschäftigungs- und Verdienstwirkungen von Weiterbildungsmaßnahmen im ostdeutschen Transformationsprozeß: Eine Methodenkritik, to be published in: Pfeiffer, F. and W. Pohlmeier (eds.): *Qualifikation, Weiterbildung und Arbeitsmarkterfolg*, ZEW Schriftenreihe, Baden-Baden: Nomos.

Franz, W. (1995): *Central and East European Labour Markets in Transition: Developments, Causes, and Cures*, CEPR Discussion Paper No.1132, London.

Franz, W. (1996): *Arbeitsmarktökonomik*, 3rd edition, Berlin: Springer.

Fuller, W.A. (1976): *Introduction to Statistical Time Series*, New York: John Wiley.

Góra, M. (1994): Labour Market in Poland, in: OECD (ed.): *Unemployment in Transition Countries: Transient or Persistent?*, 201-245, Paris : OECD.

Góra, M. and H. Lehmann (1995): *Labour Market Policies in Poland, An Assessment*, paper presented at a OECD–ifo–IHS workshop at the Vienna Institute for Advanced Studies, mimeo.

Góra, M., H. Lehmann, M. Socha and U. Sztanderska (1996): Labour Market Policies in Poland, in: OECD (ed.): *Lessons from Labour Market Policies in Transition Countries*, 151-176, Paris: OECD.

Góra, M. and C. Schmidt (1997): *Long-term Unemployment, Unemployment Benefits and Social Assistance: The Polish Experience*, Discussion Paper No.249, Faculty of Economics, University of Heidelberg.

Gourieroux, C. and A. Monfort (1989): *Statistique et Modèles Econometriques*, Vol.2, Paris: Economica.

Granger, C.W.J. and P. Newbold (1974): Spurious Regressions in Econometrics, *Journal of Econometrics* 2: 111-120.

Greene, W.H. (1997): *Econometric Analysis*, 3rd edition, New York: Macmillan.

Gritz, R.M. (1993): The Impact of Training on the Frequency and Duration of Employment, *Journal of Econometrics* 57: 21-51.

GUS (1994): *Bezrobocie Rejestrowane w Polsce (Registered Unemployment in Poland)*, 1st Quarter 1994, Warsaw.

GUS (1995): *Bezrobocie Rejestrowane w Polsce (Registered Unemployment in Poland)*, 1st-2nd Quarter 1995, Warsaw.

GUS (1996): *Bezrobocie Rejestrowane w Polsce (Registered Unemployment in Poland)*, 1st-2nd Quarter 1996, Warsaw.

GUS (1997): *Poland, Quarterly Statistics* 5(5), Warsaw.

Ham, J.C. and R. LaLonde (1996): The Effect of Sample Selection and Initial Conditions in Duration Models: Evidence from Experimental Data on Training, *Econometrica* 64: 175-205.

Ham, J.C. and S.A. Rea *Jr.* (1987): Unemployment Insurance and Male Unemployment Duration in Canada, *Journal of Labour Economics* 5: 325-353.

Ham, J.C., J. Svejnar and K. Terrell (1996): *Unemployment, the Social Safety Net, and Efficiency During the Transition to a Market Economy: Evidence from Micro Data on Czech and Slovak Men*, Department of Economics, University of Pittsburgh, mimeo.

Hamerle, A. (1991): On the Treatment of Interrupted Spells and Initial Conditions in Event History Analysis, *Sociological Methods and Research* 19: 388-414.

Hamerle, A. and G. Tutz, (1989): *Diskrete Modelle zur Analyse von Verweildauer und Lebenszeiten*, Frankfurt: Campus.

Han, A. and J.A. Hausman (1990): Flexible Parametric Estimation of Duration and Competing Risk Models, *Journal of Applied Econometrics* 5: 1-28.

Haskel, J. and R. Jackman (1988): Long-Term Unemployment in Britain and the Effects of the Community Programme, *Oxford Bulletin of Economics and Statistics* 50: 379-408.

Hausman, J.A. (1978): Specification Tests in Econometrics, *Econometrica* 46: 1251-1271.

Heckman, J.J. (1976): The Common Structure of Statistical Models of Truncation, Sample Selection and Limited Dependent Variables and a Simple Estimator for Such Models, *Annals of Economic Social Measurement* 5: 475–492.

Heckman, J.J. (1978): Dummy Endogenous Variables in a Simultaneous Equitation System, *Econometrica* 46: 931-959.

Heckman, J.J. (1979): Sample Selection Bias as a Specification Error, *Econometrica* 47: 153–161.

Heckman, J.J. (1995): *Randomization as an Instrumental Variable*, National Bureau of Economic Research (NBER), Technical Working Paper No.184, Cambridge, MA.

Heckman, J.J. (1997): Instrumental Variables, A Study of Implicit Behavioral Assumptions Used In Making Program Evaluations, *The Journal of Human Resources* 32: 441-462.

Heckman, J.J. and V.J. Hotz (1989): Choosing Among Alternative Nonexperimental Methods for Estimating the Impact of Social Programs: The Case of Manpower Training, *Journal of the American Statistical Association* 84: 862-880.

Heckman, J.J., H. Ichimura and P. Todd (1997): Matching As An Econometric Evaluation Estimator: Evidence from Evaluating a Job Training Programme, *Review of Economic Studies* 64: 605-654.

Heckman, J.J. and R. Robb *Jr.* (1985): Alternative Methods for Evaluating the Impact of Interventions, in: Heckman, J.J. and B. Singer (eds.): *Longitudinal Analysis of Labor Market Data*, 256-245, Cambridge: Cambridge University Press.

Heckman, J.J. and B. Singer (1984): Econometric Duration Analysis, *Journal of Econometrics* 24: 63-132.

Heckman, J.J. and J. Smith (1993): Assessing the Case for Randomized Evaluation of Social Programs, in: Ministry of Labour, Denmark (ed.): *Measuring Labour Market Measures - Evaluating the Effects of Active Labour Market Policy Initiatives*, 35-95, Copenhagen.

Heckman, J.J. and J. Smith (1996): Experimental and Nonexperimental Evaluation, in: Schmid, G., J. O'Reilly and K. Schömann (eds.): *International Handbook of Labour Market Policy and Evaluation*, 37-88, Cheltenham: Edward Elgar.

Hotz, V.J. (1992): Designing an Evaluation of the Job Training Partnership Act, in: Manski, C.F. and I. Garfinkel (eds.): *Evaluating Welfare and Training Programs*, 76-114, London: Harvard University Press.

Hübler, O. (1997): Evaluation beschäftigungspolitischer Maßnahmen in Ostdeutschland, *Jahrbücher für Nationalökonomie und Statistik* 216: 21-44.

Hujer, R., K.-O. Maurer and M. Wellner (1997a): *Estimating the Effect of Training on Unemployment Duration in West Germany, A Discrete Hazard-Rate Model with Instrumental Variables*, Faculty of Economics, University of Frankfurt, Discussion Paper No.73.

Hujer, R., K.-O. Maurer and M. Wellner (1997b): *The Impact of Training on Unemployment Duration in West Germany, Combining a Discrete Hazard Rate Model with Matching Techniques*, Faculty of Economics, University of Frankfurt, Discussion Paper No.74.

Hunt, J. (1995): The Effect of Unemployment, *Journal of Labour Economics* 13: 88-120.

Kalaska, M. and J. Witkowski (1997): *Labour Market in Poland in 1996: Continuation of Positive Trends. Statistical Studies and Trends*, Central Statistical Office, Department of Labour Statistics, Warsaw.

Kaplan, E.L. and P. Meier (1958): Nonparametric Estimation from Incomplete Observations, *Journal of the American Statistical Association* 53: 457–481.

Katz, L.F. and B.D. Meyer (1990): The Impact of the Potential Duration of Unemployment Benefits on the Duration of Unemployment, *Journal of Public Economics* 41: 45-72.

Keynes, J.M. and H.D. Henderson (1929): Can Lloyd George Do It? in: Keynes, J.M. (1972): *Essays in Persuasion*, The Collected Writings of John Maynard Keynes, Vol.9., 86-125, London: Macmillan.

Kiviet, J.F. (1995): On bias, inconsistency, and efficiency of various estimators in dynamic panel data models, *Journal of Econometrics* 68: 53-78.

Kotowska, I. (1992): *Changes in Women's Position in the Labour Market after Two Years of Transition Process in Poland*, paper prepared for the EALE Conference, Warwick, 3.–6. September 1992, mimeo.

Kraus, F., P.A. Puhani and V. Steiner (1997): *Employment Effects of Publicly Financed Training Programmes: The East German Experience*, ZEW Discussion Paper No.97–33, Mannheim.

Kraus, F., P.A. Puhani and V. Steiner (1998): *Do Public Works Programmes Work? Some Unpleasant Results from the East German Experience*, ZEW Discussion Paper No.98–07, Mannheim.

Kwiatkowski, E. (1995a): *Remarks on the Role of Active Labour Market Policies in Poland*, Institute of Economics, University of Lodz, mimeo.

Kwiatkowski, E. (1995b): *The System of Unemployment Benefits in Poland*, Institute of Economics, University of Lodz, mimeo.

Kwiatkowski, E. and B. Gawronska (1995): *Variation of Regional Unemployment and Regional Employment Structure in Poland*, Institute of Economics, University of Lodz, mimeo.

Kwiatkowski, E., P. Kubiak and L. Kucharski (1997): *Targeting Efficiency of the Active Labour Market Policies in Poland*, Institute of Economics, University of Lodz, mimeo.

Kwiatkowski, E. and L. Kucharski (1995): *The Private Sector in the Polish Labour Market in Transition*, Institute of Economics, University of Lodz, mimeo.

Kwiatkowski, E. and T. Tokarski (1997): *Active Labour Market Policies in Poland, An Augmented Matching Function Approach*, Institute of Economics, University of Lodz, mimeo.

LaLonde, R.J. (1986): Evaluating the Econometric Evaluations of Training Programs with Experimental Data, *The American Economic Review* 76: 604-620.

Lancaster, T. (1979): Econometric Methods for the Duration of Unemployment, *Econometrica* 47: 939-956.

Lancaster, T. (1985): Simultaneous Equations Models in Applied Search Theory, *Journal of Econometrics* 28: 113-126.

Lancaster, T. (1990): *The Econometric Analysis of Transition Data*, Cambridge: Cambridge University Press.

Layard, R., S. Nickell and R. Jackman (1991): *Unemployment: Macroeconomic Performance and the Labour Market*, Oxford: Alden Press.

Lechner, M. (1995): *Effects of Continuous Off–the–Job Training in East Germany after Unification*, ZEW Discussion Paper No.95–27, Mannheim.

Lechner, M. (1996a): *Earnings and Employment Effects of Continuous Off-the-Job Training in East Germany After Unification*, Faculty of Economics, University of Mannheim, Discussion Paper No.539-96.

Lechner, M. (1996b): *The Effects of Enterprise-related Continuous Vocational Training in East Germany on Individual Employment and Earnings*, Faculty of Economics, University of Mannheim, Discussion Paper No.542-96.

Lehmann, H. (1995): *Active Labor Market Policies in the OECD and in Selected Transition Economies*, World Bank Policy Research Working Paper No.1502, Washington D.C.

Leigh, D.E. (1995): *Assisting Workers Displaced by Structural Change*, W.E. Upjohn Institute for Employment Research, Kalamazoo, Michigan.

Leiprecht, I. (1997): *Who leaves the agriculture sector? Uncovering Hidden Flows in Agricultural Employment in the Process of Transition in Poland,* ifo Discussion Paper No. 37, Munich.

Lenkova, C. (1997): *Persistently High Unemployment throughout the Transition – What is the Reason? (The Bulgarian Case)*, CERGE and IHS, Prague and Vienna, mimeo.

Leung, S.F. and S. Yu (1996): On the Choice Between Sample Selection and Two–Part Models, *Journal of Econometrics* 72: 197–229.

Levin, A. and C.F. Lin (1992): *Unit Root Tests in Panel Data: Asymptotic and Finite-Sample Properties*, Department of Economics, University of California, Discussion Paper 92-23, San Diego.

Levin, A. and C.F. Lin (1993): *Unit Root Tests in Panel Data, Asymptotic and Finite-Sample Properties*, Department of Economics, University of California, San Diego, mimeo.

Lippman, S.A. and J.J. McCall (1976): The Economics of Job Search: A Survey, *Economic Inquiry* 14: 155–189 and 347–369.

Lipton, D. and J. Sachs (1990): Creating a Market Economy in Eastern Europe: The Case of Poland, *Brookings Papers on Economic Activity* 1: 75-133.

Lucas, R.E. *Jr.* (1976): Econometric Policy Evaluation: A Critique, in: Brunner, K. and A.H. Meltzer (eds.): *The Phillips Curve and Labor Markets*, Amsterdam: North-Holland.

Maddala, G.S. (1983): *Limited Dependent and Qualitative Variables in Econometrics*, Cambridge: Cambridge University Press.

Maddala, G.S. (1992): *Introduction to Econometrics*, 2nd edition, New York: Macmillan.

McCloskey, D. N. and S.T. Ziliak (1996): The Standard Error of Regressions, *Journal of Economic Literature* 34: 97-114.

McKenna, C.J. (1985): *Uncertainty and the Labour Market: Recent Developments in Job-Search Theory*, Brighton: Harvester.

Meyer B.D. (1990): Unemployment Insurance and Unemployment Spells, *Econometrica* 58: 757-782.

Micklewright, J. and G. Nagy (1997): *Living Standards and Incentives in Transition: The Implications of UI Exhaustion in Hungary*, European University Institute, Robert Schumann Centre and European Forum, Florence, mimeo.

Moffitt, R. (1985): Unemployment Insurance and the Distribution of Unemployment Spells, *Journal of Econometrics* 28: 85-101.

Moffitt, R. (1991): Program Evaluation with Nonexperimental Data, *Evaluation Review* 15: 291-314.

Mortensen, D.T. (1986): Job Search and Labor Market Analysis, in: Ashenfelder, O. and R. Layard (eds.): *Handbook of Labor Economics*, Vol. II, 849-919, Amsterdam: North-Holland.

Mühleisen, M. and K.F. Zimmermann (1994): New Patterns of Labour Mobility. A panel analysis of job changes and unemployment, *European Economic Review* 38: 793-801.

Narendranathan, W., S. Nickell and J. Stern (1985): Unemployment Benefits Revisited, *Economic Journal* 95: 307-329.

Narendranathan, W. and M.B. Stewart (1993): How does the Benefit Effect Vary as Unemployment Spells Lengthen? *Journal of Applied Econometrics* 8: 361-381.

Nawata, K. (1993): A Note on the Estimation of Models with Sample–Selection Biases, *Economics Letters* 42: 15–24.

Nawata, K. (1994): Estimation of Sample Selection Bias Models by the Maximum Likelihood Estimator and Heckman's Two–Step Estimator, *Economics Letters* 45, 33–40.

Nickell, S.J. (1979): Estimating the Probability of Leaving Unemployment, *Econometrica* 47: 1249-1266.

O'Leary, C.J. (1997a): *Employment Policy for Transition in Hungary and Poland*, paper presented at the PHARE-ACE Workshop on Labour Market Policies, Income Support, and Work Incentives in Transition Economies Ljubljana, Slovenia, 21st February 1997, mimeo.

O'Leary, C.J. (1997b): An Impact Analysis of Labor Market Programs in Hungary, *Economics of Transition* 5: 271-287.

OECD (1990): *Labour Market Policies for the 1990s*, Paris: OECD.

OECD (1992): *Regional Development Problems and Policies in Poland*, Paris: OECD.

OECD (1993a): *The Labour Market in Poland*, Paris: OECD.

OECD (1993b): *Employment Outlook*, Paris: OECD.

OECD (1996): *Poland 1996-1997*, OECD Economic Surveys, Paris: OECD.

Pannenberg, M. (1995): *Weiterbildungsaktivitäten und Erwerbsbiographie. Eine empirische Analyse für Deutschland*, Studien zur Arbeitmarktforschung, Band 8, Frankfurt: Campus.

Pannenberg, M. (1996): *Zur Evaluation Staatlicher Qualifizierungsmaßnahmen in Ostdeutschland: Das Instrument Fortbildung und Umschulung (FuU)*, Institut für Wirtschaftsforschung, Discussion Paper No.38, Halle.

Pesaran, M.H. and B. Pesaran (1991): *Microfit 3.0*, User Manual, Oxford: Oxford University Press.

Petersen, T. (1986a): Estimating Fully Parametric Hazard Rate Models with Time-Dependent Covariates, Use of Maximum-Likelihood, *Sociological Methods & Research* 14: 219-246.

Petersen, T. (1986b): Fitting Parametric Survival Models With Time-Dependent Covariates, *Applied Statistics* 35 Series C: 281-288.

Pissarides, C.A. (1986): Unemployment and Vacancies in Britain, *Economic Policy* 3: 500-559.

Pissarides, C.A. (1990): *Equilibrium Unemployment Theory*, Cambridge, MA: Basil Blackwell.

Puhani, P.A. (1995): *Labour Supply of Married Women in Poland, A Microeconometric Study Based on the Polish Labour Force Survey*, ZEW Discussion Paper No. 95–12, Mannheim.

Puhani, P.A. (1996): *Poland on the Dole - Unemployment Benefits, Training, and Long-Term Unemployment during Transition*, ZEW Discussion Paper No. 96–30, Mannheim, forthcoming 1999/2000 in: *Journal of Population Economics.*

Puhani, P.A. (1997a): *All Quiet on the Wage Front? Gender, Public-Private Sector Issues, and Rigidities in the Polish Wage Structure*, ZEW Discussion Paper No. 97-03, Mannheim.

Puhani, P.A. (1997b): *Foul or Fair? The Heckman Correction for Sample Selection and Its Critique - A Short Survey*, ZEW Discussion Paper No. 97-07, Mannheim, forthcoming 1999/2000 in: *Journal of Economic Surveys.*

Puhani, P.A. and V. Steiner (1996): *Public Works for Poland? Active Labour Market Policies During Transition*, ZEW Discussion Paper No. 96–01, Mannheim.

Puhani, P.A. and V. Steiner (1997): The Effectiveness and Efficiency of Active Labour Market Programmes in Poland, *Empirica* 24: 209-231.

Riddell, C. (1991): Evaluation of Manpower and Training Programmes: The North American Experience, in: OECD (ed.): *Evaluating Labour Market and Social Programmes, The State of a Complex Art*, 43-72, Paris: OECD.

Rosenbaum, P.R. and D.B. Rubin. (1983): The Central Role of the Propensity Score in Observational Studies for Causal Effects, *Biometrica* 70: 41-50.

Rubin, D.B. (1974): Estimating Causal Effects of Treatments in Randomized and Nonrandomized Studies, *Journal of Educational Psychology* 66: 688-701.

Rubin, D.B. (1977): Assignment to Treatment Group on the Basis of a Covariate, *Journal of Educational Statistics* 2: 1-26.

Rubin, D.B. (1980): Comment on Basu, D.: Randomization Analysis of Experimental Data: The Fisher Randomization Test, *Journal of the American Statistical Association* 75: 591-593.

Rutkowski, J.J. (1996a): High Skills Pay Off: The Changing Wage Structure during Economic Transition in Poland, *Economics of Transition* 4: 89–112.

Rutkowski, J.J. (1996b): *Changes in the Wage Structure during Economic Transition in Central and Eastern Europe*, World Bank Technical Paper No. 340, Social Challenges of Transition Series, The World Bank, Washington D.C.

Sachs, J. (1993): *Poland's Jump to the Market Economy*, London: MIT Press.

Scarpetta, S. and P. Huber (1995): Regional Economic Structures and Unemployment in Central and Eastern Europe: An Attempt to Identify Common Patterns, in: OECD (ed.): *The Regional Dimension of Unemployment in Transition Economies, A Challenge for Labour Market and Social Policies*, 206-233, Paris: OECD.

Scarpetta, S. and A. Reutersward (1994): Unemployment Benefit Systems and Active Labour Market Policies in Central and Eastern Europe: An Overview; in: OECD (ed.): *Unemployment in Transition Countries: Transient or Persistent?*, 255-307, Paris: OECD.

Schmidt, C.M. and R. Winkelmann (1993): Reservation Wages, Wage Offer Distribution and Accepted Wages, in: Bunzel, H., P. Jensen and N. Westergard-Nielsen (eds.): *Panel Data and Labour Market Dynamics*, Elsevier Science Publishers B.V..

Schwanse, P. (1996): The Effectiveness of Active Labour Market Policies: Some Lessons of the Experience of OECD Countries, in: OECD (ed.): *Lessons from Labour Market Policies in Transition Countries*, 17-36, Paris: OECD.

Staat, M. (1997): *Empirische Evaluation von Fortbildung und Umschulung*, Schriftenreihe des ZEW, Band 21, Baden-Baden: Nomos.

Stata Corp. (1995): *Stata Statistical Software Manual: Release 4.0*, Stata Corporation, College Station, Texas.

Statistisches Bundesamt (1994): *Statistisches Jahrbuch für die Bundesrepublik Deutschland 1994*, Wiesbaden.

Statistisches Bundesamt (1997): *Statistisches Jahrbuch für die Bundesrepublik Deutschland 1997*, Wiesbaden.

Steiner, V. (1987): *Ereignisanalyse, Ein Instrument zur Analyse dynamischer Arbeitsmarktprozesse – dargestellt am Beispiel des Abgangs aus der Arbeitslosigkeit*, Forschungsschwerpunkt S44 Discussion Paper No. 15, University of Linz.

Steiner, V. (1990): Long-Term Unemployment, Heterogeneity, and State Dependence. New Microeconometric Evidence on Unemployment Persistence, *Empirica* 17: 41-60.

Steiner, V. (1993): *Long-Term Unemployment During the Transition to a Market Economy - East Germany after the Unification*, ZEW Discussion Paper No. 93-14, Mannheim.

Steiner, V. (1994): *Labour Market Transitions and the Persistence of Unemployment - West Germany 1983-1992*, ZEW Discussion Paper No. 94-20, Mannheim.

Steiner, V. (1997): *Extended Entitlement Periods and the Duration of Unemployment in West Germany*, ZEW Discussion Paper No. 97-14, Mannheim.

Steiner, V. and F. Kraus (1995): Haben Teilnehmer an Arbeitsbeschaffungsmaßnahmen in Ostdeutschland bessere Wiederbeschäftigungschancen als Arbeitslose?; in: Steiner, V. and L. Bellmann (eds.): *Mikroökonomik des Arbeitsmarktes, Beiträge aus der Arbeitsmarkt- und Berufsforschung*, Band 192, Nuremberg.

Steiner, V. and E. Kwiatkowski (1995): *The Polish Labour Market in Transition*, ZEW Discussion Paper No. 95-03, Mannheim.

Steiner, V., P.A. Puhani and E. Kwiatkowski (1995): *A Proposal for a New Supplementary Labour Force Survey on the Evaluation of Labour Market Policies*, ZEW, Mannheim, mimeo, presented to the Central Statistical Office (GUS) of Poland.

Steiner, V. *et al.* (1998): *Strukturanalyse der Arbeitsmarktentwicklung in den neuen Bundesländern, Endbericht für das Bundesministerium für Wirtschaft*, Zentrum für Europäische Wirtschaftsforschung and Rheinisch-Westfälisches Institut für Wirtschaftsforschung, Mannheim and Essen.

Svejnar, J., K. Terrell and D. Münich (1995): Unemployment in the Czech and Slovak Republics, in: Svejnar, J. (ed.): *The Czech Republic and Economic Transition in Eastern Europe*, 285-316, San Diego, CA: Academic Press.

Szarkowski, A. and J. Witkowski (1994): The Polish Labour Force Survey, Statistics in Transition, *Journal of the Polish Statistical Association* 1: 467–483.

Torp, H., O. Raaum, E. Hernaes and H. Goldstein (1993): The First Norwegian Experiment, in: Ministry of Labour, Denmark (ed.): *Measuring Labour Market Measures - Evaluating the Effects of Active Labour Market Policy Initiatives*, 97-140, Copenhagen.

Tschernig, R. and K.F. Zimmermann (1992): Illusive Persistence in German Unemployment, *Recherches Economiques de Louvain* 58: 441-454.

Veall, M.R. and K.F. Zimmermann (1996): Pseudo-$R^2$ Measures for some Common Limited Dependent Variable Models, *Journal of Economic Surveys* 10: 241-259.

Vodopivec, M. (1995): *Unemployment Insurance and Duration of Unemployment: Evidence from Slovenia's Transition*, The World Bank, mimeo.

Wilson, S. and D. Fretwell (1996): *Public Service Employment, A Review of Programmes in Selected OECD Countries and Transition Economies*, OECD, Paris, mimeo.

Winter-Ebmer, R. (1996): *Benefit Duration and Unemployment Entry: Quasi Experimental Evidence for Austria*, Institute of Economics, University of Linz, Discussion Paper No. 9615.

Witkowski, J. (1995): *The Labour Market in Poland in 1994, New Trends, Old Problems*, Central Statistical Office, Department of Labour Statistics, Warsaw.

Wolff, J. (1996): *Unemployment Duration in East Germany: An Analysis using Non- and Semi-Parametric Hazard Rate Models*, Department of Economics, European University Institute, Florence, mimeo.

World Bank (1993): *Poland: Income Support and the Social Safety Net during the Transition*, Washington D.C.

World Bank (1994): *Poverty in Poland*, Vol. II, Washington D.C.

Wurzel, E. (1993): *An Econometric Analysis of Individual Unemployment Duration in West Germany*, Heidelberg: Physica.

Zimmermann, K.F. (1993): Labour Responses to Taxes and Benefits in Germany, in: Atkinson, A.B. and G.V. Mogensen (eds.): *Welfare and Work Incentives, A North European Perspective*, 192-240, Oxford: Clarendon Press.

GPSR Compliance

*The European Union's (EU) General Product Safety Regulation (GPSR) is a set of rules that requires consumer products to be safe and our obligations to ensure this.*

*If you have any concerns about our products, you can contact us on ProductSafety@springernature.com*

In case Publisher is established outside the EU, the EU authorized representative is:

Springer Nature Customer Service Center GmbH
Europaplatz 3
69115 Heidelberg, Germany

**Batch number: 10725973**

Printed by Printforce, the Netherlands